MW01064959

1st 1/2 of 1800s

THE

DOCTRINE OF THE TRINITY,

FOUNDED NEITHER ON

SCRIPTURE,

NOR ON

REASON AND COMMON SENSE,

BUT ON

TRADITION AND THE INFALLIBLE CHURCH:

AN ESSAY OCCASIONED BY A LATE CONTROVERSY BETWEEN THE
REV. RICHARD T. P. POPE, AND THE REV. THOMAS MAGUIRE.

By WILLIAM HAMILTON DRUMMOND, D.D.

" There is ONE God ; and there is none other but he."—MARK xii. 32.

" The doctrine of the Trinity appears to me so obviously unscriptural, that I am
pretty sure, from my own experience and that of others, that no one possessed of
merely common sense, will fail to find its unscripturality after a methodical study of
the Old and New Testaments, unless previously impressed in the early part of his
life with creeds and forms of speech preparing the way to that doctrine." *Rammohun
Roy's Final Appeal*, p. 354.

THIRD EDITION, WITH CONSIDERABLE ADDITIONS.

R. HUNTER, LONDON;

HODGES AND SMITH, DUBLIN ; KING AND RIDINGS, CORK ;
ARCHER, BELFAST.

M.DCCC.XXXI.

M. GOODWIN, PRINTER,
29, Denmark-street, Dublin.

Publishing Statement:

This important reprint was made from an old and scarce book.

Therefore, it may have defects such as missing pages, erroneous pagination, blurred pages, missing text, poor pictures, markings, marginalia and other issues beyond our control.

Because this is such an important and rare work, we believe it is best to reproduce this book regardless of its original condition.

Thank you for your understanding and enjoy this unique book!

TO

RAMMOHUN ROY,

THE LEARNED CHRISTIAN BRAHMIN,

WHOSE WRITINGS,

DISTINGUISHED AS THEY ARE BY MILDNESS AND STRENGTH,
BY A CRITICAL KNOWLEDGE

OF THE

ORIENTAL LANGUAGES AND OF THE SACRED SCRIPTURES,

ABLY DEFEND AND CONVINCINGLY DEMONSTRATE

THE

GREAT DOCTRINE OF THE BIBLE,

𝕿𝖍𝖆𝖙 𝕲𝖔𝖉 𝖎𝖘 𝕺𝖓𝖊;

AND TO

W. E. CHANNING, D.D.

THE ZEALOUS ADVOCATE OF PRIMITIVE CHRISTIANITY
IN AMERICA;

DIVINE, IN WHOSE WRITINGS ARE BLENDED

THE GENTLENESS OF PERSUASION

WITH THE

ENERGIES OF TRUTH;

JUDGMENT WITH TASTE;

AND SPLENDID ELOQUENCE OF REASON

WITH THE HOLY FERVOURS

OF

CHRISTIAN PIETY AND LOVE;

THIS TRACT

IS, WITH GREAT RESPECT,

INSCRIBED BY THE

AUTHOR.

"As to personality in God—a trinity of persons, I think it the most absurd of all absurdities; and, in my opinion, a man who hath brought himself to believe the popular doctrine of the Trinity, *hath done all his work ;* for after that there can be nothing hard—nothing inevident ; the more unintelligible, the more credible; and as this serves the purpose of producing implicit faith in pretended guides, priests will always try to keep it in credit."

R. ROBINSON.

PREFACE

TO THE FIRST EDITION.

THE writer of the following Essay divides all Christians into two denominations, Unitarians and Trinitarians. With their various subdivisions he does not interfere, deeming it enough, at present, to contend for the Supreme Deity of God alone, and believing that every departure from that doctrine, leads to a perversion of the Scriptures, and the adoption of opinions hostile to the religion of the Gospel. He is no follower either of Arius or Socinus, of Price or Priestley; but taking the Scriptures, with REASON and COMMON SENSE, as his guides, he adopts whatever doctrine he judges to be true, and rejects whatever he can prove to be false, no matter in what region it is found, nor by what names it is sanctioned. There are learned and pious men in all the great Christian denominations. He is glad to profit, where he can, by the labours of them all; and would rejoice to collect into one focus whatever scattered rays of light may render Gospel truths more clear, whether they emanate from Boston or Calcutta; from Geneva or Rome.

The more simple the creed of Christians, the more chance of harmony. In proportion as the chords of a musical instrument are multiplied, the difficulty of preserving concord is increased. A belief in the One only living and true God, and that he is a rich rewarder of those who diligently seek him, and in Jesus Christ his well-beloved Son, that he is the Author of eternal salvation to all who obey him; commingled with that Charity, which the inspired Apostle declares to be superior to Faith and Hope, and without which there is no Christianity; should be a sufficient bond of fraternity and affection, among all who would be followers of Christ, not in name only, but in deed and in truth. Unitarian Christians of other countries, are wisely acting on this conviction. Let their brethren in Ireland follow their example, and quit their disputations about obscure questions, concerning which they cannot come to a perfect agreement; and which, therefore, should be deemed of very inferior importance. All who do not embrace the doctrine of the Trinity, are ranked by their opponents in one class; and whether they be Arians or nick-named Socinians, are all alike said to be infected with leprosy and heresy: for, that theological phantom known by the name of Orthodoxy, that heterogeneous compound of errors and contradictions, like Popery, deems itself infallible; and makes no distinction among those who separate from its communion. It brands them all with the name of Socinians, though, in truth, there is no Socinianism in Ireland, nor any approximation to it, except among those who declaim against it most loudly. But the word " Socinian" has become an uncharitable term of reproach, and is to the disciples of Calvin and of the Pope, what the term Nazarene was to the Pharisees of old. The same spirit which prompted the words, " Can any good thing come out of Nazareth ?" and "Look and see, for out of Galilee ariseth no prophet," has lost no particle of its malignity in the lapse of eighteen hundred years.

It is not without the most painful reluctance, that the Author has entered into the stormy region of controversy, for he greatly prefers quiet and the shade. But there are times and occasions when silence would be criminal ; and being considered as denoting either a want of confidence in the truth, or of ability to defend it, might seem to give sanction and currency to error. Of all denominations of Christians in this country, none, except the *Society of Friends,* is less prone to give offence, than that to which he belongs. Their love of peace has often exposed them to the charge of indifference. Notwithstanding this, they are not indifferent. Their zeal, indeed, is seldom displayed in thunder, and lightning, and brimstone-hail; it burns with a calm and steady heat; and may, perhaps, if much excited, be kindled into a blaze. When their tenets are stigmatized as leprosies and soul-destroying heresies, by those who see them only with a "mind diseased," and "a jaundiced eye," and through the distorting and discolouring medium of human creeds, they think it their duty to shew that, to the sound vision of reason, and in the clear light of the Gospel, they appear to be the purest and healthiest out-flowings of evangelical truth. They have provoked no quarrel, unless their repose be a provocation : and even when wantonly assailed, they war not with men, but with false opinions. For Mr. Pope and Mr. Maguire, the Author entertains no sentiments but those of kindness. He admires the zeal and talents of both, and only laments, that they have not been employed in what he would esteem a better cause.—But their controversy has not been unprofitable. In the collision of their arguments, the sparks of divine truth have leaped forth, and formed a bright and radiant glory round the brow of Unitarian Christianity. Though regarded by the one as a leper, and by the other as a heretic, he wishes them health and happiness; and hopes to be recognized at a higher tribunal than theirs, as a worshipper of the true God, and a sincere, though humble follower of Christ. Truth is his object as well as theirs. Let the candid decide, which of them is farthest from the mark.

In a land of liberty all have an equal right to defend their religious opinions ; and it is imperative on the advocate of Truth, when her interests call him forth, to assert his right, and wing a shaft against error, wherever it is discovered, whether perched upon a mitre, or nestling in the triple crown.

PREFACE

TO THE SECOND EDITION.

THE Author, though anxious to please his Athanasian and Calvinistic readers, finds it to be a task of extreme difficulty. They are dissatisfied with what he has written, because it sets before them some great and important truths, which they have seldom, if ever, heard discussed; and they are dissatisfied because he is silent on some mysterious points of doctrine, of which he is ignorant, and of which he can find nothing revealed in the Word of God. Hard fate!—to offend both by his speech and his silence.

*   *   *   *   *   *

As to the arguments hitherto arrayed against the chief doctrine of the Essay, they are thin and vapoury, and of no consistence. When touched by a single spark of truth, like the chymist's bubbles of gas, they explode and disappear.

One of the Author's chief misdemeanours is the construction of a creed, so simple and so Scriptural, that all can understand it. Would that every creed had been so constructed! then, instead of being involved in contentions and animosities, which destroy all the kind affections, the Christian world would be at rest, and the religion of the Gospel would be producing its genuine fruits— " Glory to God in the Highest—on the earth peace, good will to men."

Another offence is the attempt to revive some good old doctrines, which, in this corner of the world, seem to have been almost forgotten. The Dublin " Christian Examiner" says, that the Author " has not even the meagre satisfaction of being original in his statements." Most true. He lays no claim to originality or invention ; and therefore his readers may enjoy, with him, not the meagre, but the plump, round, and full satisfaction of knowing, that the doctrines contained in these pages, are not the discoveries of a new adventurer in the field of theological inquiry. They are of much older date than those of Calvin, Athanasius, or Pope Nicholas the First. They are founded on the ROCK OF AGES, and are coeval with the Bible.

The Author is farther charged with having taken an argument, *without acknowledgment*, from Dr. Samuel Clarke, viz. that though Christ were proved by one text of Scripture to be God over all, it would not follow that the Son is consubstantial, and coeternal, and possessed of equal power with the Father. For the same

Apostle who has written this, tells us elsewhere, (1 *Cor.* xv. 27,) that when he says "all things are put under him, it is manifest that HE is excepted which *did put* all things under him." The argument is so extremely obvious that it can scarcely not occur to every mind capable of reasoning on the subject. It has been stated at least a thousand and one times. But the Examiner, throughout, betrays an impatient solicitude to fix a stigma of dishonesty on the Author's character. Here, however, he will find the usual well-known stratagems of his school of no avail. The Author, so far from having a wish to repel the charge, that he has borrowed it, rejoices that it is now presented to the reader, armed with the sanction of so learned and distinguished a divine as Dr. Samuel Clarke. He writes for a nobler object than literary renown, and cares not if every line in the Essay be traced to a higher and more creditable authority than his own. Let the Examiner quit his personalities and answer the argument. His attempt, so far, is miserably abortive. It is plain to the common sense of a child, that HE who *did put* all things under Christ, must be superior to Christ ;—even the Examiner's understanding, it is presumed, would revolt from the idea of Christ putting all things under the Father. If what is predicated of the one, cannot be predicated of the other, there is no equality. But even though their equality were established, it would not prove them to be coeternal and consubstantial, for equality and identity are not the same. The Apostle, however, does not leave the question to be thus decided ; but, as if to guard his readers from being imposed on by the sophistry of such writers as the Christian Examiner, adds, "when all things shall be subdued unto him, (τοτε και) even then shall the *Son also himself be subject unto him that put* all things under him, that God may be all in all." 1 *Cor.* xv. 28. Let the Examiner quit his sophisms, and answer the argument.

. The Examiner and his Athanasian and Calvinistic friends are indignant at our assuming the name of Unitarian Christians, and affirm that they believe in the divine unity as well as we. Be it so. Paul informs us, that in his days "some preached Christ even of envy and strife—of contention and not sincerely. What then (says he)—notwithstanding, every way, whether in pretence or in truth, Christ is preached; and I therein do rejoice, yea, and I will rejoice." *Phil.* i. 15, 18. So do we, Unitarians, rejoice that the divine unity is acknowledged in any sense.* But let not the disciples of Athanasius, and the Pope, be under any apprehension that we shall identify their three persons with our one God. There is an essential difference between us. Our idea of unity has no resemblance to theirs. Ours is a monad—theirs a triad ; ours a mathematical point, theirs a triangle ; ours a monarchy, theirs an aristocracy ; ours a clear simple idea, theirs a

---

* Est quoddam prodire tenus, si non detur ultra.

dark complexity; or, to give back to the Athanasians a word which they have flung at Unitarians, an "Artifice." Their unity resembles the harmony produced by an old monk's treble note, my nurse's lullaby, and my grandmother's recitative; ours is the voice of nature from her thousand and ten thousand realms, blended with the halleluiahs of Revelation, and ascending in one mighty volume of sound to the throne of the Eternal.

The title of Unitarian Christian, therefore, is one to which we have the first and most indisputable claim. We hope to see it more extensively embraced, and that those who have received the name of Arians or Socinians, will lay aside such appellations, and assume that of Unitarians, or Bible Christians; and not circumscribe themselves within a circle drawn by any uninspired mortal whatever, since one is our master, even Christ. Let us stand on a space so broad, that it will include all who believe in the strict unity of Jehovah, and in his only Son, Jesus Christ our Lord.

When the Author referred to Priestley, he might have known that he was giving an occasion to the orthodox, for repeating the illiberal reflections with which they still continue to assail that great and injured name. Priestley may have fallen into errors, (who has not?) by trusting more to the fidelity of others, than to his own patient investigation. *He was in none as to the fact for which he was quoted.* When he did err, his error was that of an HONEST MAN. A mitre would not have tempted him to deviate a hair's breadth from what he regarded as the strict line of truth. With him there was no shuffling nor tampering, nor special pleading against the dictates of his own conscience. He entered the field of controversy, not as a prize-fighter, determined to overcome his antagonist whether by force or guile. He fought not in "a coat of darkness," with the poisoned weapons of insinuation and personality. The arrows of malevolence were never lodged in *his* quiver. He disdained to assail the character of his antagonist, when he should be combating his argument; and he would have scorned the victory that was not fairly won, for he was an *honest man.*

"Let Dr. Priestley be confuted where he is mistaken; let him be exposed where he is superficial; let him be repressed where he is dogmatical; let him be rebuked where he is censorious; but let not his attainments be depreciated, because they are numerous almost without a parallel;—let not his talents be ridiculed, because they are superlatively great; let not his morals be vilified, because they are correct without austerity, and exemplary without ostentation."—*Dr. Parr.*

"From him," says the Rev. Robert Hall, "the poisoned arrow will fall pointless." Will it not sometimes recoil, and wound the hand from which it flew?

In Hutton's Phil. and Math. Dictionary, 2nd Ed. is inserted, "The following faithful portrait of a man, whose character has been grossly misrepresented by interested enemies, and misconceived by a deluded public.

b

The "Christian Examiner," who has declared Priestley to be of no authority in Ecclesiastical History, joins with an "Eclectic Reviewer" in lauding Bishop Bull, as affording unanswerable proofs against Lindsey, Belsham, and all who affirm with Priestley, that the majority of Christians were Unitarians, prior to the Council of Nice. Has either of the learned gentlemen, who speak thus confidently of Bull, as their champion, ever read his works? If he has, he will meet some quotations, in the following Essay, which he will recognize to be genuine; and which will shew that those who have his works before them, need not travel far for a confirmation of the opinion expressed by Priestley.*

He was a patient, indefatigable disputant in theology, a sincere and zealous Christian, a serious and rational preacher of the practical morality of religion, without the least pretension to, or affectation of, oratorical ornaments. His mind embraced the whole extent of knowledge and literature in his closet; but in the affairs of the world, he was a plain, uninformed, unaccomplished, honest man. What he believed to be true, he thought it his duty to propagate, without any regard to his own interest, or the prejudices of mankind; but being overpowered by calumny and oppression, he was compelled to seek a residence among strangers, and leave his principles and character to the impartial judgment of posterity."

The Rev. J. Kentish, of Birmingham, in the notes to his excellent Sermon on the Death of Belsham, justly observes, that "the name of Priestley is now gathering, although it has not yet gathered all its fame."

> "At ultimi nepotes,
> Et cordatior ætas,
> Judicia rebus æquiora forsitan,
> Adhibebit, integro sinu;
> Tum, livore sepulto,
> Si quid meremur, sana posteritas sciet."

To this apt quotation, we may add another almost as appropriate,

> Crescit, occulto velut arbor ævo,
> Fama Priestlæi.

* Those who read Bull, ought also to read "Ante-Nicenismus, sive Testimonia Patrum qui scripserunt ante Concilium Nicenum, &c. Cosmopoli, Anno 1694." Disquisitiones Modestæ in Clarissimi Bulli Defensionem Fidei Nicenæ. Authore Daniele WHITBY, D.D. Lond. 1718. and Wakefield's Enquiry into opinions concerning the person of Christ.

No writer is more easily refuted than Bull. He refutes and contradicts himself; a common practice with the disciples of Athanasius. The views of Bull are justly characterised in the following extracts from a valuable work on the divinity of Christ, by Robert Perceval, M.D. a physician of Dublin, of great learning, and piety, and of long-established and well-merited professional celebrity.

"However successful Bull's efforts may be considered, in clearing the Fathers of the three first centuries of the charge of Arianism, (in the sense of a doctrine, which teaches the created nature and limited existence of Christ,) yet be himself continually represents, as *their undoubted and unanimous sentiment*, that self-existence belongs to God the Father exclusively, and subscribes to their opinion." This is made evident by extracts from his works too long for present quotation—See the Summary of Cap. 1, Sect. iv. p. 251. Def. Fid. Nic. *De subordinatione filii ad Patrem, ut ad sui originem et principium.*—See Thesis II. p. 258.

Though the Author has had the misfortune to offend some
readers, by the plain Scriptural truths expressed in this Essay,
he has the satisfaction of knowing, that he has pleased others,
whose judgment he values, and of whose esteem he is proud;
and he hopes to see their numbers greatly increased. The film,
which long obstructed the mental vision of many, is now beginning to dissolve away, and a few more rays emitted from the
Word of God, will dispel their darkness, and enable them to see
Unitarian Christianity in all its beauty and in all its loveliness.
Then will they begin to have a true perception of the super-
excellence of that religion which came from heaven to be our
guide to happiness and salvation. Let the friends of Unitarian,
or Bible Christianity, unite, co-operate, and act with energy and
zeal; and their cause, being the cause of REASON AND COMMON
SENSE, of NATURE AND REVELATION, of the SAVIOUR and of
GOD, must eventually triumph.

SOME readers may be disposed to ask, why the Author has
been so long in reviewing Mr. Carlile's Book, on what is called
"The Deity of Christ." More, perhaps, will inquire, why it
has been thought worth while to notice it at all. The fact is,
when it first came before the public, a friend who read it, informed
the Author, that it gave up the chief point at issue, and admitted
that the doctrine of the Trinity is a doctrine of *inference,* and not
of explicit revelation. Satisfied with this admission, the Author
suffered two years to elapse before he sat down to its perusal;
when being about to prepare a new edition of his Essay, he
thought it a fit occasion to examine Mr. C.'s doctrines, and to
animadvert on such of them as he should deem erroneous.
Though there be little good in disturbing the ashes of the dead,
as the principles of Mr. C.'s Book are still advocated, the Author
thought it a duty which he owed to the cause of truth, to protest
against them, as being, in his judgment, a reproach to the age,
and in direct hostility to the plainest declarations, both of reason
and revelation.

"To do justice to the nicety of our author's distinctions, stated in Thesis II,
requires much metaphysical acuteness; a common understanding would
conceive, that self-existence and supreme authority, compared with a *derived*
existence and Deity, are *essential* perfections. Pearson (p. 34,) asserts, that
the Father has communicated his entire essence to the Son: now, if to be
unoriginated, which Pearson most explicitly admits, be part of the essence of
the Father, and of him exclusively, how can he be said to communicate his
entire essence to a divine being, whose origination is admitted?"

"Bull seems substantially to grant all that can be desired, and the point at
issue appears to be a logical, and not a theological distinction; yet that is of
more importance than might be imagined, for once grant the metaphysical
use of the το ἀπαυρεύσιον, and it is employed as a charm to raise such a cloud
of unscriptural intricacies, as quite obscures the region of common sense, and
intercepts all prospects of a termination of the controversy."

CONTENTS.

DOCTRINE OF THE TRINITY

NOT

FOUNDED ON SCRIPTURE.

SECTION FIRST.

*Origin of the present Controversy—Unitarian Christian's
Belief—Proofs from Scripture of the Divine Unity.*

A CONTROVERSY, attractive of much public attention has for
some time been carried on between the Rev. Mr. Maguire and
the Rev. Mr. Pope; the former an able advocate of the Roman
Catholic Church, the latter an eloquent supporter of some of the
tenets of the Church established by law, in this country.

In the course of the controversy, Mr. Maguire has affirmed
that there are certain doctrines of religion embraced by a considerable number of the Protestant denomination, which cannot
be successfully maintained without the aid and authority of an
Infallible Church. He grounds his opinion on the doctrine of
the Trinity, and challenges Mr. Pope to prove against the Socinian, that that doctrine rests on a Scriptural foundation. " The
Socinian's objections," he says, " are solid and stubborn. He
has REASON and COMMON SENSE on his side. He will quote
text against text, enjoying, as he does, the latitude of private
judgment, till not a single shred of argument remains."

In these sentiments of Mr. Maguire, Unitarians (which name
is here preferred to that of Socinians, for reasons to be afterwards
shewn) most cordially concur. They have long felt that they
have reason and common sense, as well as Scripture on their
side; and they rejoice that this is acknowledged by a gentleman
of Mr. Maguire's studies and profession. They duly appreciate
his admissions as a valuable offering at the shrine of truth: and
they pay no empty compliment to Mr. Maguire's polemic skill,
when they allege that he has entrenched himself in a position
from which it will require a more powerful tactician than even
Mr. Pope to dislodge him. If the doctrine of the Trinity has

A

any foundation at all, it is not in reason, in common sense, nor in Scripture; but in tradition and the authority of an Infallible Church.*

A brief review of THE UNITARIANS' CREED may help the reader to ascertain how far it accords with the principles on which they affirm it to be founded. With respect to the being and perfections of God, their belief is this:—That there is ONE only living and true God—*one* in the strict and absolute sense of unity—a spirit, simple, uncompounded, indivisible, without parallel or equal—self-existent—immutable—eternal—almighty—omniscient—omnipresent—possessed of wisdom, truth, holiness, goodness, justice, with all other perfections, in their highest possible excellence. They believe that this great being created the heavens and the earth, and all things visible and invisible—that he continually presides over every part of the vast universe—that he is good to all, and that his tender mercies are over all his works. They believe that he is a God, not of inextinguishable wrath, but of infinite placability and mercy—that he requires no bloody sacrifice, for, according to Scripture, "the sacrifices of God are a broken spirit—a broken and a contrite heart, O God, thou wilt not despise:" Psalm li. 17—that he is the sole object of divine worship, and that prayer should be addressed to him alone. The character in which Unitarians delight most to contemplate God is that in which he was contemplated, and in which we are instructed to address him in prayer, by our Blessed Saviour,—that of a FATHER. This contemplation, always hostile to bigotry, and favourable to that universal love which Jesus taught, naturally leads them to regard all mankind as their brethren, whatever be their name, country, complexion, or creed. They believe that God placed man on earth, in a state of probation and trial—endowed him with many noble faculties and powers, of which HE requires a proper use and improvement—that HE is a righteous moral governor, and will reward the virtuous and punish the wicked. They believe that God presides over his intelligent offspring, as the wisest and kindest of parents over a numerous family; that he employs various means, according to

---

* Mr. Maguire does not stand alone; nor is he the first who has held the strong post which he now occupies. About one hundred and fifty years ago, some of the most learned Trinitarians confessed, that the doctrine of the Trinity was not founded on the Scriptures, but on *the tradition of the Church.* The Unitarians were then obliged to maintain, as a previous step to the establishment of their opinions, that "the Scriptures are the only infallible rule whereby to determine religious controversies." *Yates's Answer to Wardlaw,* p. 17.

"Mr. Chillingworth, in the preface to his book, quotes Hosius, Gordonius, Huntlæus, Gretserus, Tannerus, Vega, Possevin, Wickus, and others, as so many witnesses to shew, that in the opinion of the Papists, the modern doctrine of the Trinity cannot be proved either from the Scripture, or the ancients." *Ben Mordecai. Note,* p. 187. vol. 1.

their different tastes and dispositions, to bless them and to do them good—that the sufferings and deprivations which they have, sometimes to endure, are sent, or permitted, in mercy, to correct, to reform, to discipline the soul to virtue—that HE educes good from evil, and causes all things to co-operate for the everlasting felicity of the righteous.

Unitarian Christians believe in the revealed Word of God. They receive the Scriptures of the Old and New Testament as the sole rule of their faith and practice; and hold them in such reverence that they never virtually deny their sufficiency by the substitution of creeds and articles of human contrivance. All the articles of their faith they can express in the very words of inspiration; nor are they ever obliged by the adoption of unscriptural tenets to employ an unscriptural phraseology. They believe that "all Scripture given by inspiration of God, is profitable for doctrine, for reproof, for correction, for instruction in righteousness; that the man of God may be perfect, thoroughly furnished unto all good works."—2 Tim. iii. 16. Deeming the pure light from heaven sufficient to guide them to all truth, they require no guidance from the dark lantern of tradition, or the erratic wisp-fires of an earth-born theology. They learn from the sacred volume, and they own it with gratitude and joy, that God is love, and that he so loved the world that he gave his only begotten Son to be our instructor, our example, our guide, and "the author of eternal salvation to all who obey him."—Heb. v. 9, They believe in the divinity of the Son of God, that his character, his mission, his doctrine, his power, his authority, were all divine, In a word, they believe whatsoever is written of him in the inspired volume,—with Paul, that he was the brightness of the Father's glory, and the express image of his person—with Peter, that he was the Christ, the Son of the living God—the Messiah, or Spiritual Deliverer of the Jews, foretold by the prophets; and, as he declared of himself, that he was "the light of the world, the way, the truth, and the life," that to him the spirit was given without measure, and that "in him dwelt all the fulness of the godhead* bodily;"—Col. ii. 9. or, in other words, that

---

* Godhead, a Scholastic term for Deity; "to be rejected," says Lindsey, "because to common readers it countenances the strange notion of a God consisting of three persons." Bodily in the original σωματικως is opposed according to Pierce and Le Clerc, to στοιχεια rudiments or shadows, in the preceding verse. The apostle, speaking of the ceremonal institutions of the Jews, in the subsequent (17th) verse, says, "they are a shadow of the things to come; but the body is of Christ."

Col. ii. 9. is a favourite text with the supporters of the doctrine of an Incarnate Deity; though affording it no foundation. The candid reader is requested to ask himself what is meant by the abstract term fulness, and not to confound it with essence, to which it has no reference. The apostle prays for the Ephesians, c. iii. 17, 19. "That Christ may dwell in their

he was richly and substantially replenished with all spiritual graces, and with a full communication of his heavenly Father's will; "that in all things he might have the pre-eminence—for it pleased the Father, that in him should all *fulness* dwell."— Col. i. 18, 19.—"And of his fulness have we all received."— John i. 16. They believe that his morality far surpassed that of every other moral teacher, in purity, in motive, and in extent— that his discourses are heavenly, and that he practised what he taught—that he came to redeem us from all iniquity—to purify unto himself a peculiar people, zealous of good works—to turn us from darkness to light, and from the power of Satan unto God; that in the prosecution of this design, and in obedience to his heavenly Father's will, he submitted to a life of suffering and deprivation, and at length died upon the cross, to seal by his blood the truth of his doctrine, and by his subsequent resurrec-tion from the grave, and his manifest ascension into heaven, bring life and immortality to light—that having deprived death of his sting, and the grave of its victory, God exalted him to be a Prince and a Saviour, to give repentance and forgiveness of sins, and ordained him to be the judge of all, when God "will render unto every man according to his deeds: to them who, by patient continuance in well-doing, seek for glory, and honour, and im-mortality, eternal life; but unto them that are contentious, and do not obey the truth, but obey unrighteousness, indignation and wrath."—Rom. ii. 6, 8.

Farther—Unitarians believe that "without *faith* it is impos-sible to please God,"—but "as the body without spirit is dead, so faith without works is dead also:" that of the Christian graces "faith, hope, and charity, these three, the greatest is charity"— that "love is the fulfilling of the law," and "charity the bond of perfectness"—and that the true disciple of Christ is to be known not by exclamations of Lord! Lord! but by earnest continued endeavours *to do the will* of his Father who is in heaven.

Such are some of the doctrines which Unitarian Christians generally believe. But they admit no formula of human com-position as their creed. They yield their "assent and consent" to the truth of no volume but the Bible—for "*the Bible, the Bible alone is the religion of Protestants:*" neither do they call any man "*master* upon earth; for one is our master, even Christ." In numerous points they agree with their Christian brethren of other denominations;—in some they differ, not only from them, but, with reciprocal good will, from one another; and herein is the truly Christian philanthropic tendency of their

---

hearts, by faith, and that they may be *filled* with all the *fulness of God.*" What! know ye not that your body is the temple of the Holy Spirit *which is* in you."—1 Cor. vi. 19. "Whosoever shall confess that Jesus is the Son of God, God dwelleth in him, and he in God."—1 John iv. 15.

5

principles conspicuous. They pronounce no anathema on those who seek the kingdom of God, by a path diverging from that which they choose for themselves; they only desire that every man may be "fully persuaded in his own mind, for to his own master he standeth or falleth," and "God alone is Lord of the conscience." They are aware that uniformity of belief in speculative questions is, by the very constitution of the human mind, impossible—and though it were possible, not to be desired. Therefore, they "endeavour to keep the unity of the spirit in the bond of peace:" knowing that "there are diversities of gifts, but the same spirit: and there are differences of administrations, but the same Lord: and there are diversities of operations, but it is the same God which worketh all in all."—1 Cor. xii. 4, 6. Instead of shackling the mind and controuling its exercise by the imposition of damnatory creeds, articles and confessions of faith, those impious devices of ecclesiastical tyranny to guard an unrighteous domination, to rob man of his birth-right and defraud the Christian of that holy charter of liberty which was sealed by the Saviour's blood, they would send it forth free as it was created, in all the might and in all the energy of its powers, illumined by Divine knowledge, and stimulated by immortal love, puissant and indomitable as a spirit of light, ardently and fearlessly to pursue the truth to her profoundest depths and loftiest elevations.

Unitarian Christians hold as their distinguishing tenet, to which the reader's attention is now particularly solicited, a belief in the divine unity. This belief they derive not, as has been asserted, "from a priori speculations on the incomprehensible nature of the Deity," but from a clear interpretation of the two great volumes of the Almighty, Nature, and Revelation. The one corroborates the language of the other. What nature teaches, revelation does not contradict but confirm. The visible frame of the universe has been well denominated the "elder scripture," and it is a work to which the book of Inspiration does not disdain to refer. The eternal power and Deity of the one supreme intelligence are clearly seen in the things that are made. "The earth is full of the goodness of the Lord, the heavens declare his glory, and the firmament sheweth forth the work of his hand;" so that they are without excuse who do not read the volume of nature, and learn from the unity of design apparent in the creation, the unity of the great first cause. Still more inexcusable are they who do not read it in the plain declarations of Scripture.

Moses, speaking by the immediate inspiration of heaven, asserts not only the absolute unity, but the sole unrivalled supremacy, and the exclusive Deity of Jehovah.

His *unity*, in the solemn annunciation to the people of Israel—

"Hear, O Israel, the Lord our God is one Lord—or—Jehovah, our God, is one Jehovah."—Deut. vi. 4.

His sole unrivalled *supremacy*—

"Jehovah he is God in heaven above, and upon the earth beneath; there is none (*i. e.* no one) else."—Deut. iv. 39.

His exclusive *Deity*—

"That thou mightest know that Jehovah, he is God; there is none else besides him."—Deut. iv. 35.

"*I* am the first, and *I* am the last, besides me there is no God. Is there a God besides me? Yea, there, is no God; I know not any."—Isaiah, xliv. 6, 8.

"I am the the Lord thy God, the Holy One of Israel. Before me there was no God formed, neither shall there be after me. *I*, even *I*, am the Lord, and besides me there is no Saviour."—Is xliii. 3, 10, 11.

The prophets teach the same doctrine—

"Jehovah shall be King over all the earth, and in that day Jehovah shall be *one*, and his name *one*."—Zech. xiv. 9.

"Have we not all ONE Father? Hath not ONE God created us?"—Mal. ii. 10.

Christ and his apostles confirmed the doctrine of Moses, and the prophets. When Jesus was asked by a Scribe, "which is the first commandment of all?" He replied, "the first of all the commandments is—

"Hear, O Israel; The Lord our God is one Lord."—Mark xii. 29.

The Scribe approved of the answer, and said,

"Well, Master, thou hast said the truth,; for there is one God; and there is none other but he."—Mark xii. 32.

Our Lord in a solemn prayer attests the divine unity, and makes a clear distinction between God and himself.

"This is life eternal, that they might know thee the ONLY TRUE GOD, and Jesus Christ, *whom thou hast sent.*"—John xvii. 3.

The Apostle Paul observes the same distinction.

"We know ** that there is none other God but ONE *** to us there is but ONE GOD, the Father—and One Lord Jesus Christ."—1 Cor. viii. 4, 6.

"To God *only wise*, be glory through Jesus Christ for ever."—Rom. xvi. 27.

"There is one Lord, one faith, one baptism, ONE GOD and Father of all, who is above all, and through all, and in you all."—Eph. iv. 5, 6.

"There is ONE GOD and One Mediator between God and men, the man Christ Jesus."—1 Tim. ii. 5.

The absolute Oneness of the Deity is asserted, with the clearness and force of demonstration, in these passages of the sacred volume, and in a multitude of others which it would be superfluous to quote. Suffice it to say, that this is the grand and fundamental principle of all religion. It corresponds with the conclusions of the most sublime philosophy, and the plainest dictates of inspiration. It was taught, as has been demonstrated, by Moses and the prophets—by Christ and his apostles. It has been adopted by many of the wisest and best of our species—by men who devoted their lives to the study of the Scriptures; and whose early prejudices, education, profession, and worldly interest were all arrayed against its reception—by men who have honoured it by the most heroic sacrifices of fortune and ambition—by the greatest philanthropists, philosophers, poets, and metaphysicians—by Newton, Milton, and Locke : yet, Mr. Pope and the Theologians of his school, have no scruple to class those who profess Unitarianism with Deists and Infidels, (why not with Atheists?) and to brand their faith with the name of leprosy, and soul-destroying heresy !

How simple and how grand is the Unitarian's faith compared with the Trinitarian's ! When we turn from the one to the other, it is like turning from the contemplation of a beautiful world, when the sun is in the firmament, " rejoicing in his strength," to the view of a sterile and deformed waste, "a land of brimstone, and salt, and burning,—of blood, fire, and vapour of smoke."

SECTION SECOND.

What is Trinitarianism?

WHAT IS TRINITARIANISM ? The Scriptures are silent. They never present God under any aspect but that of unity. Of a plurality of persons in the Godhead they know nothing. We must therefore turn for information to the " Infallible Church," and to those other churches which, having thrown off her yoke, still adhere to her creeds—from the assembly of the disciples at Jerusalem to the councils of fathers ; from Paul, the inspired apostle, to Athanasius, the factious and turbulent ecclesiastic.

The doctrine of the Trinity then, informs us that the Godhead consists of " three persons, of one substance, power, and eternity;" "God the Father, God the Son, and God the Holy Ghost." Now, any man, under the influence of such vulgar principles as " reason and common sense," would conclude that three persons must mean three distinct beings, and consequently that there are three Gods. This, Dr. Sherlock candidly admits, and says " it is plain the persons are perfectly distinct. A person is an intelligent being, and to say there are three divine persons and not three distinct infinite minds, is both heresy and nonsense." Here then is palpable polytheism, from which thus fairly exhibited, even orthodoxy recoils astounded. Doctor South, scandalized by such an admission, from a Doctor of his own church, showers down upon him a torrent of theological vituperation; and alleges that there is only " one infinite mind, with three modes, attributes, or offices, manifested under the different states or relations of father, son, and spirit." Thus the meaning of the word person is explained away ; and after the most painful struggles against the conviction of their own minds, that God is one, the most eminent divines are reduced to the necessity of maintaining that the three persons of their imaginary Trinity are not persons, but something else. Tillotson calls them " three differences,"—Burnet " three liversities,"—Secker "three subsistencies,"—others "three postures!"—Le Clerc thought them to be "three distinct cogitations;"—and that the subject might be explained by the philosophy of Des Cartes. Some are for a specific, some for a numerical unity, and others for both united, though involving a monstrous contradiction. Waterland speaks of a "three-fold generation of the son, two antemundane and one in the flesh. The substance of the one person," he says " is not the substance of either of the others, but different, however of the same kind or united." Barrow speaks of "the mutual inexistence of one in all, and all in one." "They are joined together," says another, " by a perichoresis—and this perichoresis, circumincession or mutual inexistence is made very possible and intelligible by a mutual conscious sensation." Some divines understand the words person and personality in a philosophical sense, others in a political, and a third class in a theological sense. The doctrine of three persons, according to Watts, must be true, "at least in a political sense, yet cannot amount to so much as a philosophical personality, unless we allow a plurality of Gods." We sometimes find the same Trinitarian Divine confuting himself, for error is always inconsistent, and maintaining in one part of his writings, propositions subversive of those which he has maintained in another. Thus Bishop Bull, against the Arians, asserts the consubstantiality and coeternity of Christ with the Father: but against the Tritheists and Sabellians, "he argueth the necessity of believing the father to be the fountain, original and principle of the son, and that the son is hence *subordinate* to the father!"* What is this but Unitarianism?—We are told of a Ciceronian, a Platonic, an Aristotelian, and a Swedenborgian Trinity, and finally "the Trinity of the *Mobile*, or common people and lazy divines, who content themselves by calling it an inconceivable mystery."†

Now, what is this but darkening of counsel by words without knowledge? Which of these contradictory schemes is to be embraced by the man who is determined to depart from the simple truth, that God is one? "What is there" asks the author of an excellent letter‡ on this subject, "to guide me through the dark and dreary labyrinth? Not one solitary ray of light glimmers to direct my path. All is darkness and confusion: the more I read, the more I am confounded. I cannot advance a step, and I end as I began, without being able to find two men or two creeds agreeing in a similar answer to my inquiry: What is the Trinity?"

---

* Nelson's Life of Bull, p. 303.
† Ben Mordecai.
‡ The Doctrine of the Trinity Indefensible, by Edward Taylor, Esq.

9

Perhaps the light of an Infallible Church might be of use to this importunate inquirer.

If we turn to the popular creeds we shall find that they only render confusion worse confounded, and add a deeper shade to Egyptian darkness. The Athanasian creed, the most accredited standard of the orthodox faith, teaches that "the Father is made of none, neither created nor begotten; the Son is of the Father *alone*, not made, nor created, but *begotten*; the Holy Ghost is of the Father and of the Son, neither made, nor created, nor begotten, but *proceeding*." "In this Trinity none is afore or after other." But that which is *begotten*, if language has any meaning, must be posterior to that which *begets* it; and that which *proceeds* must be subsequent to the source from which it issues. As the very terms *begotten* and *proceeding* cannot be in any way applicable to the Father, they demonstrate an essential difference between Him and every being to whom they can be applied. There is also an essential difference between the Son and the Holy Ghost, for the one is *begotten*, and the other *proceeds*; so that each has a peculiar and distinguishing characteristic. Moreover, both the Athanasian and Nicene creeds contradict the Apostle's creed, which so far from affirming that the Holy Ghost proceeds from the Son, says that the Son was "conceived by the Holy Ghost:" whereas the Athanasian creed says that "the Son is of the Father alone!"

Such are the inconsistencies and contradictions of the creeds and articles which we are told we must believe or "perish everlastingly!" They not only contradict the Scriptures but themselves and one another. It would seem that their fabricators, by some signal act of providence, laboured under an insuperable disability of giving them coherence, and that every scheme tending to subvert a belief in the Divine unity, should contain in itself the elements of its own destruction.

Horsley, notwithstanding his being regarded as a chief pillar of orthodoxy, took the liberty of differing from the creeds which he subscribed, and supposed that the second person in the Trinity was "*an effect*" produced by the first person contemplating his own perfections! No wonder that Priestley on reading such *ægri somnia*, sick man's dreams, could "hardly help fancying that he had got back into the very darkest of the dark ages, or at least that he was reading Peter Lombard, Thomas Aquinas, or Duns Scotus.*"

The three persons of the Trinity, after all that is said by the bishops and archbishops, about diversities and subsistences,

* Horsley in his controversy with Priestley, says, it is a *contradiction* that "a part is equal to the whole, or that the same thing, in the same respect, is at the same time, one and many." This he admits that nothing can prove. "No testimony that a contradiction *is*, should be allowed to overpower the intuitive conviction that it *cannot be*."

B

modes and relations, perichoresis and circumincession, can be contemplated only as "three distinct infinite minds." The advocates of the doctrine speak of them as such, and assign to each his different province. The father commands, the son obeys, the holy spirit sanctifies. But though they are one God, the first and second persons do not appear to be always influenced by the same principles. It might be expected when such enormous sacrifices as "reason and common sense" are made in support of the doctrine, that it would be consistent in itself—that the three persons being one God, they would act together with perfect harmony. The Unitarian maintains that God and Christ are one—one in the sense declared by the Saviour himself—*one in affection and design*. He never can admit the idea that any difference of mind subsisted between the father and the son on any subject whatsoever. The father speaks by or through the son, and hence the Unitarian receives the precepts and doctrines of Christ as those of God himself. Now for this unity which is rational and scriptural, and most beneficially influential on the conduct of men, Trinitarianism sets up another of its own, which is chimerical and full of conflicting imaginations. It represents the father and son as actuated by different principles, and on the most important of all subjects, moral virtue—the one as rigorous and inflexibly just, the other as merciful and compassionate. Here their unity is abolished. An act of disobedience is committed by the first of God's intelligent creatures placed upon this earth; and he who "knoweth our frame and remembereth that we are but dust," filled with ineffable fury, sentences man, and, in him, all his innocent and unconscious posterity, to everlasting perdition! Then had man been irrecoverably lost—but God the Son interferes; and since nothing less than a ransom of infinite price should atone for the smallest offence against an infinite being, (as theologians tell us—though

---

"Now," asks Dr. Priestley, "Wherein does the Athanasian doctrine of the Trinity differ from a contradiction as you have defined it? It asserts, in effect, that nothing is wanting to either the Father, the Son, or the Spirit, to constitute each of them truly and properly God; each being equal in eternity and all divine perfections; and yet that these three are not *three Gods*, but only *one God*. They are therefore, both one and many in the same respect, viz: in each being *perfect God*. This is certainly as much a contradiction as to say that Peter, James, and John having each of them every thing that is requisite to constitute a complete man, are yet, all together, not *three men*, but only *one man*. For the ideas annexed to the words *God man*, cannot make any difference in the nature of the two propositions. After the council of Nice, there are instances of the doctrine of the Trinity being explained in this very manner. The fathers of that age being particularly intent on preserving the full *equality* of the three persons, they entirely lost sight of their proper *unity*. And explain this doctrine as you will, one of these things must ever be sacrificed to the other."—Priestley's Letters to Horsley, p. 78. Lond. 1815.

they have forgotten to shew how a finite creature can merit the
inflictions of infinite and eternal wrath,) he offers to pay the
price required—to assume a human form and die the death of
the cross, that the curse may be annulled.

Accordingly the proposal is accepted, and the Father Almighty suffers his son, who is equal to himself in majesty and
power, to assume the form of an embryo in the virgin's womb—
to be born—to encrease in stature like an ordinary mortal—to
appear in the humble condition of a carpenter's son—to undergo
the most cruel sufferings, bodily and mental; and after a life
of poverty and pain, and all the bitter feelings of degradation,
of which the highest celestial spirit exiled from heaven and tabernacled in flesh, may be supposed susceptible—to be accused
of blasphemy and sedition, to be mocked, spat on, scourged,
nailed to a cross as a malefactor, and raised up before an aston-
ished universe—the sacrifice of a son to a father—of a God of
superlative benevolence, to the inexorable wrath of an offended
Deity*—and all for a single act of disobedience in a frail child
of the dust! What an awful and tremendous idea of the father
of all, does this doctrine convey! Is this the God whom we
are instructed to love with all our hearts? What lesson do we
read like this in the heavenly discourses of him who said
"What man is there of you, of whom if his son ask bread, will
he give him a stone—or if he ask a fish, will he give him a ser-
pent?"—of him who has so beautifully depicted the Creator as
the kindest and most affectionate of parents; whom even the
extravagant guilt of his prodigal son could not alienate from his
affections—but who "when he was yet *a great way off*, saw
him, and had compassion, and ran and fell on his neck and
kissed him."

Our blessed Saviour delighted to appeal to the natural feelings of the human heart, to enable us to form just notions of
the mercy and beneficence of the universal parent. But priests
and theologians, in support of their unscriptural systems, outrage
every sentiment of justice and mercy; and hesitate not to ascribe
to God such conduct as would horrify them in a mortal like
themselves.† "Shall mortal man be more just than God? Shall
a man be more pure than his maker?"

---

* See Channing's admirable Sermon, entitled "The superior tendency of
Unitarianism to form an elevated religious character." It is stated in the
larger Catechism joined to the Westminster Confession of Faith, that Christ
"felt and bore the weight of God's wrath." Q. 49,—"and it was requisite the mediator should be *God*, that he might sustain and keep the human
nature from sinking under the *infinite wrath of God!*" Q. 38.

† The doctrine that God could not be appeased without an infinite satisfaction, and a bloody sacrifice, is such an atrocious libel on the character
of the beneficent Father of all, that even orthodoxy is beginning to be
ashamed to avow it—and to explain it away. It robs God of his glorious

Christ, according to covenant, having paid the infinite ransom, it might be concluded that the salvation of all men would be secured. But this, as we are told by the disciples of Calvin, would be an egregious mistake, for though the uttermost farthing has been paid, a large majority of mankind are predestinated to hell-fire, by an omnipotent decree which not even the bloody sacrifice of the Eternal Son of God could avert or annul! So that, after all, the benefits of Christ's death are extended to only a chosen few—the elect—" The rest of mankind," as the Westminster Confession of Faith *charitably* informs us, (c. iii. 7.) " God was pleased to pass by and ordain them to dishonour and wrath for their sin, to the praise of his glorious justice."

Now it is evident from this scheme, that God the Father and God the Son entertained totally contradictory views of man's first offence. Though consubstantial they are dissentient, for if they are one in mind, why did not the Son join in the curse, and demand an infinite ransom as well as the Father? Again, by whom was the ransom paid? By God the Son, or by the man Jesus? If by the former, then one person of the Godhead suffered and died to make atonement to another person, and yet both persons are the same God!—This is truly marvellous. On the other hand, if only the human nature of Christ suffered, how was the infinite debt discharged? Moreover—why is God the Holy Ghost passive or neutral in this transaction? Why did not the Third person of the Trinity demand satisfaction as well as the First? Were his ideas of justice less rigorous, his majesty less offended, or his spirit less vindictive?

These, no doubt, are audacious questions, but those who advocate the free use of Scripture, and the right of private

---

attributes of justice, mercy, forgiveness. It represents him as surpassing in cruelty the legislator whose laws were written in blood. If the natural sentiments of right and wrong in the breast of a heathen poet, rose indignant at the dogmas of the Stoics, that all faults are equal, and should be punished with equal rigour, how would he have shrunk with horror from this monstrous Calvinistic heresy !

——————— adsit
Regula, peccatis quæ pœnas irroget æquas."
                                        Hor.

" —— let the punishment be fairly weighed
Against the crime."
                                        Francis.

This is the language of nature, and it is confirmed by revelation, which tells us that God is an equitable judge; that he is merciful and gracious, long-suffering, and abundant in goodness and truth." Exod. xxxiv. 6. IT says, " Let the wicked forsake his ways, and the unrighteous man his thoughts, and let him return unto the Lord, and he will have mercy upon him ; and unto our God, for he will abundantly pardon."—Isaiah, lv. 7.

judgment, will excuse them. The only mode of preventing their repetition, as Mr. Maguire will candidly admit, is quiet submission to the authority of an Infallible Church.

SECTION THIRD.

The Doctrine of the Trinity not taught in the Scriptures.

Revelation was given to man, by the mercy of an ever blessed God, to lead to virtue, happiness, and immortality; not to perplex and confound with such questions as that under discussion. Being intended for universal benefit, for the Barbarian as well as the Greek, for the Gentile as well as the Jew, it teaches all that is necessary to be known as instrumental to salvation, in perspicuous language, and leaves no doctrine of vital importance in obscurity. It has been well observed that " the gospel is full in telling us what is to be done, sparing of what we are to believe." Its articles of belief are few, and these few intelligible to the rude and ignorant. Its radical truth is, that *God is one*— This truth which is so simple, and so easily comprehended, it repeats again and again, and fences it round with such barriers as exclude every imagination that would vitiate its simplicity. It utters not a syllable of three persons, one in substance, equal in power and glory. " God the Son," and " God the Holy Ghost," are phrases no where to be found in the sacred writings—nor the Incarnate God—nor the Tri-une God—nor the God-man. Such epithets and barbarous compounds, applied to the Deity, are redolent of heathen superstition. They have no affinity to the pure and simple language of Inspiration. They were never used by the Apostles in all their preaching, either to Jew or Gentile, though now so frequently resounded from many a popular pulpit, falsely reputed orthodox. Had such a doctrine as the Trinity constituted any part of the Christian Religion, we must believe, on every principle of reason and common sense, that it would have been revealed as clearly, and as much to the satisfaction of every inquirer, as the being of God himself. Nay, it required stronger evidence, and more ample illustration. We can acquire some knowledge of God by the light of nature, and therefore it was less necessary to insist on that subject; but we derive from nature no intimation whatever of a Trinity, and therefore it must be presumed that a revelation from God would have dwelt with force, and at considerable length, in inculcating and explaining a doctrine so novel: and we are justified in holding this opinion by our certainty that the gospel does insist, with copiousness and perspicuity, on every necessary topic of belief, and most of all on such doctrines as are of most utility. For instance, as nature affords but a glimpse of a future state, and as a belief in this doctrine, has an almost unbounded influence on the conduct and happiness of man, the gospel, in every page, brings it before us with all the evidence of its reality, and all the power of its fears, its hopes and consolations. But of the Trinity it says nothing, though a doctrine so stupendous and so utterly destitute of foundation in nature and reason, demanded, for its reception, the whole weight of inspired authority. It is inconsistent with every just view of Divine revelation to suppose that it would dwell on topics of minor interest, and pass by those of the greatest unnoticed. Nay, more, as the doctrine of the Trinity is not only unsupported by nature, but subversive of the first great truth of the Jewish religion, it demanded ten-fold weight of evidence to set the old doctrine aside, and make room for the introduction of the new. The new doctrine, therefore, would have been proclaimed in a style suited to its dignity—preached in the streets, and shouted from the house tops—argued in the school, and thundered forth in the synagogue, established by miracles for the satisfaction of the multitude, and demonstrated with power for the conviction of the learned. An object so weighty would not have been based on an epithet or exclamation, nor left to pendulate by the spider-thread of an inference. The use of the Greek article, or Hebrew plural, the precise meaning of an obscure word, or ambiguous phrase, or the admission or rejection of a text stamped with the brand of interpolation, would have had little influence in a question of such magnitude. That which was intended to illuminate the world, would not, in contradiction to a declaration of the Saviour, have been hid "under a bushel," but presented to us in a volume of light, and made to shine upon us like the sun in his brightness, that all might see and understand. In a word, had the Doctrine of the Trinity been a revelation from heaven, it is but reasonable to suppose that it would have formed the leading and most prominent article of revealed religion, run parallel to the first commandment, and told us that besides the great Jehovah, whom the Israelites believed to be one being, or person, two other persons were to be admitted into the Godhead, equally claiming our adoration; and that it would be "a leprosy and a soul-destroying heresy" to deny it. But our Blessed Saviour taught a different lesson. "This is life eternal," said he, "that they might know thee the ONLY True God, and Jesus Christ whom thou hast sent."—John xvii. 3.

If Christ were really Almighty God, it is inconceivable why he did not avow it distinctly; and that it was not as distinctly taught by the Apostles. Strange, that his own family and disciples never once suspected him to be the God of Israel! So far from admitting a thought that would have paralysed them, and falsified what they were taught in their law, "that no man could see the face of God and live."—Exod. xxxiii. 20,—they lived with him on terms of the most friendly and familiar intercourse. On one occasion, Peter rebuked him.—Mat. xvi. 22.

It may be alleged by Mr. Pope, that the disciples, apostles, and all who had the best opportunities of contemplating our Lord, entertained erroneous opinions of him, (yet Peter was in no error when he said, "thou art the Christ the Son of the Living God,") and that it was not till after his resurrection, ascension, and the effusion of the Holy Spirit, that their minds were enlarged to form a true conception of his character. Well, what was their opinion then? Did they suppose him to be the Eternal God? Never. When they were busily occupied in laying the foundation of the Christian Church among both Jews and Gentiles, they declared that Christ was the chief corner stone in the edifice; but that the Almighty was the supreme architect. In all their preaching, as recorded in their "Acts," they never made the Deity of Christ the theme of a single discourse. They spoke of him as he had spoken of himself—as deputed by the Father to rescue man from the bondage of sin and death. But they never spoke of the Son's consubstantiality with the Father—nor of three persons in one God. The Jews vanquished as their prejudices were, by arguments deduced from their own Scriptures, and corroborated by miracles, would not have endured such language. Nor can it be contended that the Apostles, from fear of the Jews,* suppressed any truth which it was their duty to reveal, much less a truth of such paramount importance. The Jews did not require to be instructed in the nature of the Deity—they had learned from the writings of Moses and the prophets, that he is one, all powerful, wise, and good; and it was never so much as hinted to them by the Saviour, that their notions of God were erroneous. The points, therefore, on which the Apostles insisted to them, were the Messiah-ship of Christ, obedience to his precepts, faith in his doctrines, the resurrection and judgment. The Gentiles who were universally corrupted by Polytheism, did require to be taught a pure theology; and in Paul's discourse to the Athenians we have a most edifying specimen of the mode in which they were addressed. Having seen an altar dedicated to the unknown God, the Apostle takes occasion to expatiate on the being and character of the God who is made known by revelation—and his discourse throughout is most decidedly Unitarian. He speaks of the great Creator of the World, the Lord of Heaven and Earth—of his having made of one blood all nations of men, who, according to the saying of one of their own poets, are "*his offspring;*" that he is not to be represented by images of gold, silver, or stone, for as he is a

---

* The author has somewhere read that Athanasius imputes it to the Apostles' fears of the Jews, that they did not preach the Deity of Christ. The true reason was, that they knew no such fiction. To allege that men, who were prepared at all times, to die for the truth, dared not to advocate any doctrine essential to salvation, even before their most infuriated enemies, is to slander their character.

spirit, he must be contemplated by the spiritual part of man;
that being infinitely beneficient, he connived at their past ignorance, but now commanded them to repent, to depart from their
idolatry, to worship and obey the great Jehovah alone. To give
efficacy to his admonition, he then speaks of the great topics
never neglected by the Apostles, resurrection, and judgment—
declaring unto them that God had appointed a day in which he
would "judge the world, in righteousness, by that MAN whom
he had ordained," and that he had given the most incontestible
proof of this truth, by having already raised him from the dead.*
—Acts, xvii.

All this discourse was highly beautiful and instructive. It contained nothing but what " reason and common sense" could
approve and adopt. The only circumstance about which his
hearers felt distrust, was the resurrection. But what would have
been their thoughts, had the Apostle, after having revealed to them
the true God—brought them down from the elevation to which he
had raised them, and alleged that the Almighty Creator, of whom
he had just declared that " he dwelleth not in temples made
with hands"—that he whom " the heaven and the heaven of
heavens cannot contain," was cradled in a manger, and after a
life of suffering, was put to death upon a cross? Would they

---

* It is argued by Burgh who wrote, against Lindsey's Apology, a book
which he was pleased to entitle a " Scriptural Confutation," that because
Paul preached Jesus to the Athenians, they said, he seemed to be a setter-
forth of *strange Gods*, Acts, xvii. 18. Here, upon a call to explain himself and answer the charge of setting forth *strange Gods*, in having preached
Jesus, he avows that he whom he had preached was that God whom they
knew not, (the unknown God) but worshipped ignorantly : but he had
preached Jesus ; therefore Jesus Christ was that God hitherto unknown to
them, and one with the Father."

Such is a specimen of the miserable and contemptible sophistry of a man
who thought he could confute Lindsey ! He makes *strange Gods* (or foreign demons) and *unknown God*, relate to the same person, ignorant or
forgetful that the word rendered *Gods* is δαιμονων which, in general, if
not in every other instance, in the common version of the Scriptures, is rendered *Devils*. The Athenians were so much addicted to the fear and worship of
these Devils or Demons, that Paul charged them with being δεισιδαιμονεστερους
too superstitious—more literally, too fearful of Demons. The foreign Demons of which "he seemed to be a setter-forth," were Jesus and *Anastasis*,
i. e. Resurrection, and it would be as consistent to assert of *Anastasis* as of
Jesus, that *she* was the unknown God. What analogy there is, either grammatical or physical, between "foreign Demons" plural, and the " unknown
God" singular, such writers as Burgh may determine. This confuter of
Lindsey says, " I thank God and my pious parents for it, that with my
nurse's milk I did imbibe the doctrine (of the Trinity) which I now maintain ; and at the same time, I imbibed a belief, that grass was green, that
fire was hot, that snow was cold, and that two and two make four." Prodigious ! What pity that he did not add to these liberal scientific attainments, the belief that one is one, and that three are three !

not have supposed the Apostle to be amusing them with some idle tale for which they had a parallel in their fables of the birth and sepulchre of Cretan Jove?

It is clearly demonstrable then from the records extant of the preaching of the Apostles, that they did not teach the doctrine of the Trinity to the Jews. It is equally demonstrable that they taught Unitarianism to the Gentiles—that faith which the eloquent reformers of the nineteenth century stigmatize as a "leprosy, and a soul-destroying heresy."

In the writings as well as the preaching of the Apostles, we find many passages strongly expressive of their belief in the divine unity—not one in which the holders of that doctrine are censured, as they must inevitably have been, if their doctrine were erroneous. The Apostle John combats the errors of the Gnostics and condemns the Churches of Asia, for various lapses and defections from the truth. But no where is any condemnation either direct or implied attached to Unitarianism. How should it? The inspired writers were all Unitarians, and knew no more of the tritheistic hypothesis than of the Pope's infallibility. The Apostle Paul spoke not only his own sentiments but those of his Brethren, when he affirmed that the "head of Christ is God." But of all the sacred authors John is the most copious in attesting the Supreme Deity of God, and shewing the derived existence. and derived miraculous powers of Christ. If one Apostle might claim pre-eminence above the rest, as the advocate of the divine unity, John would have a fair claim to be entitled *the Apostle of Unitarianism.**

As the doctrine of the Trinity is no where taught in the Scriptures, it is *inferred* by Trinitarians; and some of its ablest advocates admit that it is altogether *a doctrine of inference.* They cannot find it in Matthew—nor in Mark—nor in Luke—nor in John—nor in Paul—nor in Peter—nor in James—nor in Jude—but they give us to understand that there are certain hints and expressions in the one and in the other, from a judicious combination of which it may be extracted, by a little knowledge of the dialectics of theology. The Scriptures, we suppose, contain its elements as the alphabet contains the elements of the mysterious *tetragrammaton!* The picture is in the colours of the painter's pallet, and requires only to be transferred to the canvas! The statue which may "enchant the world," and claim its idolatry, lies in the marble block,

---

* See this most satisfactorily proved by the Rev. W. J. Fox, in his letter to the Rev. Dr. Blomfield, now Bishop of London, entitled "The Apostle John a Unitarian." The Bishop is to be commended for his *prudence* in not attempting an answer to so powerful and eloquent an antagonist. His silence may be deemed a sufficient concession, though it would be more magnanimous to declare himself vanquished.—See also "the Apostle Paul a Unitarian," by the Rev. B. Mardon.

C

and asks but the chisel of some Phidias or Praxiteles to rescue it from concealment! The golden calf of Aaron had its component parts, its *membra disjecta*, in the ear-rings of the wives and of the sons and daughters of Israel. It required but the blast of the furnace, and the graving tool of the artist to fashion them into a four-footed idol. Thus, from a skilful amalgamation of heathenish inventions and traditions, with certain garbled extracts from Scripture, do the advocates of Athanasianism form a triplicate object of worship, and with their predecessors in the wilderness of old, exclaim, "These be thy Gods, O Israel!"

But why a triplicate object? Ah! there is a great mystery in the number *three*, and, as heathen mythology will teach us, it has many an ancient hereditary claim to respect. But on what particular passages of Scripture the doctrine of the Athanasian Trinity is founded, the reader who has nothing but revelation for his guide, cannot easily discover; for though it often speaks of the *Holy One*, and the *Blessed One*, it never speaks of *the holy three*, nor *the blessed three*. The advocates of the doctrine refer us to the Saviour's command, to baptize in the name of the Father, the Son, and the Holy Spirit,* and after informing us that to baptize in the name of a person, is to ascribe Supreme Deity to that person, a statement which at once makes Moses the Supreme Deity,† they ask in a tone of conscious triumph, "Is not the Father one—is not the Son one—and is not the Holy Ghost one—and are not three ones—three?" We answer—unquestionably. And ask in return—three what?—Gods?—No. That would be polytheism. Names of the same God? No. That would confound the persons and plunge us in what Athanasians would call the "damnable heresy" of Sabellianism—Persons? Yes.—And the three persons are one God? Yes.—Then is each person but the third part of the one God. This divides the essence and robs God of his *simplicity*. Again, we are referred to 1 John, v. 7—a text universally rejected as an interpolation by learned and honest critics. But, admitting it as genuine, it could give no more support than the former text, to the doctrine of *three in one*. The connexion would lead us to conclude, that the three witnesses were one only in testimony. Of essence it says nothing—it insinuates nothing. The same principles of inference which deduce a Trinity from these verses might deduce an *Enneity*, or *nine in one*, from Rev. i. 4, 5—and we might ask, is not "he which was, and which is, and which is to come," *one?*—And are not the "seven spirits before the throne," *seven?*—and is not "Jesus Christ the faithful witness," *one?* $1 + 7 + 1 = 9$. This doctrine may be supported by 1 Tim. v. 21. "I charge thee before God, and the Lord Jesus Christ, and the Elect Angels." What angels? The

---

* Mat. xxviii. 19.　　† 1 Cor. x. 2.

seven spirits of John, forsooth. Thus is the doctrine of John confirmed by that of Paul. It has the high sanction also of Burgh, who says, that he " may possibly surprise Mr. Lindsey, by an assurance that these seven spirits are God." It is, no doubt, a very surprising assurance ! but, he continues, " this is a position very easily explained to the man who remembers that ' Noah found grace in the *eyes* of the Lord.' The seven spirits are the *eyes* of the Lamb—(they were God just now,) and the Lamb is Jesus Christ himself." But Christ is God—and therefore he which was, and is, and is to come,—the seven spirits and Jesus Christ are one God ! Thus is the doctrine of an *Enneity* proved by genuine orthodox inference. Let not the courteous reader object to the term *Enneity*, on account of its novelty. That of *Trinity* was as novel many years after the first dispensation of the gospel. The one word—the one doctrine, is as scriptural as the other ; and the *Enneity* wants nothing but a little aid from tradition, the Infallible Church, and the Synod of Ulster, to fix it on as stable and permanent a foundation as the Trinity.

SECTION FOURTH.

The inferiority of Christ to the Father proved by his own declarations.

Mr. Pope has quoted the long list of texts usually employed in this controversy, to shew that Christ possessed all the attributes of the Supreme Deity. A similar task has been repeatedly executed by men whose erudition and critical ingenuity were fully equal to those of Mr. Pope, but with a success similar to that of the architects of the tower of Babel. Many of the texts quoted, are irrelevant and misunderstood. It would be a labour more tedious than difficult, to shew that none of them, when rightly interpreted, yields any support to the doctrine of three persons in one God. Mr. Maguire's assertion could be amply verified, that every text in support of the doctrine, could be confronted by another, till not a shred of argument remained. The New Testament is redundant in passages proving the supremacy of the Father, and the subordination of the Son. The very ideas of Father and Son imply superiority in the one—inferiority in the other. The Nicene and Athanasian Creeds, in fact, admit this, though it is denied by the " Article," which affirms that the three persons are of one substance, power, and eternity. They admit that Christ was begotten of the Father, and thus contradict the coeternity and coequality which the article asserts. The words of the second article of the Church of England " begotten from everlasting of the Father," are nonsense, for they involve two ideas which destroy each other—

that which is begotten is not self-existent, therefore not eternal—that which is eternal is self-existent, therefore not begotten. So little consistency is there in the creeds and articles of man's invention. So difficult it is to put a total extinguisher on the truth, that God is one !

Again, as reason and common sense tell us that a father must exist before a son can be begotten, so must he who commands be greater than he who obeys; the bestower is superior to the receiver; the sender to him who is sent; and he who prescribes a task, to him by whom it is executed. Now Christ is represented in the Scriptures as in all things subordinate to the Father. He declares his own inferiority, and so strongly and so frequently disclaims the ascription to himself of the attributes that belong to Jehovah alone, that it is really a matter of astonishment how any one can entertain a doubt on the question.

He affirms the supremacy of the Father in terms the most explicit, undeniable, and unqualified.

" My Father is greater than all."—John, x. 29.

Consequently greater than the Son—and that there may be no doubt of this, he says again,

" My Father is greater than I."—John, xiv. 28.

He declares that the same great being who is our God and Father, is also his God and Father.

" I ascend unto my Father and your Father : and to my God and your God."—John, xx. 17.

He denies independant and underived existence when he says,

" I live by the Father."—John, vi. 57.

He denies that he is inherently and underivably possessed of any power whatsoever; and he does this with a solemn repeated asseveration.

" Verily, verily, I say unto you, the Son can do nothing of himself but what he seeth the Father do."—John, v. 19.

" To sit on my right-hand and on my left, is not mine to give, but it shall be given to them for whom it is prepared of my Father."—Mat.xx. 23.

He affirms that he is not omniscient—

" Of that day, and that hour, knoweth no man, no, not the angels which are in heaven; neither the Son, but the Father."—Mark, xiii. 32.*

---

* This is a most distressing text to Trinitarians. In vain have they tortured invention and falsified the meaning of the Greek text, to escape a conclusion which is fatal to their scheme. One informs us that the verb *οιδε* here signifies *maketh known*, though no instance of its having such a meaning occurs in the whole compass of Greek learning. Admit, it however, for a moment, and mark the consequence. " That day and that hour no man *maketh known*, no, not the angels which are in heaven, neither the Son, but the Father only *maketh known*." This is a direct contradiction of the Saviour's meaning, to avoid which, it is proposed by other expounders, to supply the words " in his official capacity," or " in his human nature,"

He refuses to be called good in the sense of infinitely benevolent.

"There is none good but ONE, that is God."—Mat. xix. 17.

He ascribes his mission and his works to his Father.

"The works which the Father hath given me to finish, the same works that I do, bear witness of me that the Father hath sent me."—John, v. 36.

He acknowledges that his power of exercising judgment is bestowed upon him by the Father.

"The Father judgeth no man, but hath *committed* all judgment to the Son."—John, v. 22.

He affirms that his doctrine did not originate with himself.

"My doctrine is not mine, but his that sent me. If any man will do his will, he shall know of the doctrine, whether it be of God, or whether I speak of myself."—John, vii. 16, 17.

He denies that he came of himself.

"Ye both know me, and ye know whence I am: and *I am not come of myself*, but he that sent me is true whom ye know not."—John vii. 28.

He denies that he came to do his own will.

"I seek not mine own will, but the will of the Father which hath sent me."—John, v. 30.

Or, that he sought his own glory.

"I seek not mine own glory—there is *one* (viz: God) that seeketh and judgeth."—John, viii. 50.

Or, that he is himself the ultimate end and object of our faith.

"He that believeth on me, believeth not on me, but on him that sent me."—John, xii. 44. *i. e.* not so much on me, as on him who sent me.

He makes it a less heinous offence to speak against himself than against the Holy Spirit, which is a clear acknowledgment of his inferiority.

"Whosoever speaketh a word against the Son of Man it shall be forgiven him; but whosoever speaketh against the Holy Ghost, it shall not be forgiven him."—Mat. xii. 32.

After his resurrection he says, that all his power is the gift of his Heavenly Father.

"All power is *given* unto me in heaven and in earth."—Mat. xxviii. 18.

The texts that speak a similar language are almost innumerable, and all so plain and intelligible, that their meaning is never disputed. How then avoid the conclusion to which they irresistibly compel? How maintain a doctrine by which that conclusion is utterly subverted? Certain creed-makers and In-

---

for which addition, even if it did not convert solemn truth into impious folly, they have no more authority, than for writing a new gospel. But this is not all. *Audi facinus majoris abollæ.* In order to parallel and neutralize the force of this vexatious text, they have actually quoted Hosea viii. 4. "They have made princes, and I (Jehovah) *knew it* not;" as if this was an expression of ignorance and not of disapproval—and in their anxiety to secure a point, have been contented to rob Jehovah of his Omniscience!

fallible Churches will inform us. They have inventions of their own which could never be found out by minds uninitiated in their mysteries. They inform us, though Scripture does not, that Christ had two natures, a human and a divine ; and that he speaks and acts sometimes in the one, and sometimes in the other nature. This, for a moment, being admitted, we naturally enquire, how is it to be ascertained when any of his discourses or actions are to be ascribed to him as God the Son, and when as the man Jesus? To a plain and unsophisticated reader this is a serious difficulty, *dignus vindice nodus*, a knot which can be untied only by the skill of the "Infallible Church."

By what rule Protestants are guided in this inquiry, or whether they have any rule, the writer must confess ignorance. The learned Rammohun Roy,* a name which there will be occasion often to mention in the sequel of this essay, has expressed a wish to be furnished with a list enumerating those expressions which are made in one and in the other capacity, with authorities for the distinction. What authorities should he expect but those of tradition and an Infallible Church? The list, perhaps, might be furnished, but it would scarcely yield the satisfaction which he seems to require—since one clause of the same text, as he has himself remarked and illustrated, would require to be spoken by the divine, and another by the human nature ; and even the same clause might have to be understood as spoken sometimes by the one and sometimes by the other, as it chanced so suit the argument of the polemic or expounder. A principle of conformity to the creed which they have brought from the nursery or college, is the only rule, as far as the Unitarian can discover, which Trinitarians employ in making the distinction. This is the touchstone by which every text must be proved.

* An Indian Brahmin, who from a diligent perusal of the Sacred Scriptures, has become a convert to Christianity, and whose intimate and most accurately critical knowledge of oriental customs and languages eminently qualifies him both to understand and explain the inspired volume. His work entitled " The precepts of Jesus, the guide to peace and happiness," with his first, second, and final appeal to the Christian public, in reply to Dr. Marshman of Serampore, should be in the hands of all lovers of truth. It might have been expected that such a convert would have been welcomed with delight by every disciple of Jesus ; but his love of truth preventing him from embracing certain "peculiar doctrines" which, with all his critical acumen, he could not find in the Bible ; he became as much an object of obloquy to the " Orthodox," in the East, as his Unitarian brethren are in the West. His editor, at length, refused to publish his works, and he was under the necessity of purchasing types and a printing press, to have them printed beneath his own immediate inspection. Happily for the cause of genuine Christianity, they have reached the shores of Great Britain, and the " Isle of Saints," and while paper, ink, and type, remain, they will not perish ; though some ardent proselyters decry them, and say their author is no Christian. Thus did their Jewish brethren of old declare of Christ, that he was a Samaritan and had a devil !

They cover the pure gold of gospel truth with the base alloy of human invention, stamp it with the image and superscription of Athanasius or Calvin, and circulate it as the true evangelical coin. When our blessed Saviour says, "I *live* by the Father,"—they exclaim, this is spoken in his human nature! When he says, "My Father and I are one," though it is clear as the sun, that he means one in the Unitarian sense; they immediately call out, here is a proof of the coexistence, coeternity, and consubstantiality of God and Christ! Mr. Pope adopts this mode of explanation, and alleges that "those passages which affirm the son's inferiority were not spoken of him *whole and entire,* but refer to his human nature, and mediatorial character; and that this view of the subject alone, harmonizes the seemingly contradictory descriptions which the Scriptures give of the Messiah."

Such vague and unfounded notions as this may content those who can "prostrate the understanding;" but reason and common sense must protest against them. Can it be imagined that a distinction of such importance to the right interpretation of Scripture, should be sought for in them in vain? By admitting it as necessary to explain certain fancied contradictions, we are involved in ten-fold difficulties, from which we cannot be extricated, even by the power of an Infallible Church. While it aims, on the one hand, to exalt the Saviour to Supreme Deity, it degrades him, on the other, beneath the level of an honest and true man. It grants the Unitarian more than he either asks or will accept. It strips part of our Lord's declarations of their sacred influence, by representing them as spoken of himself in the nature of a common uninspired mortal; whereas the Unitarian receives them all as coming from the inspiration of the Almighty. Nor is this all. It involves more awful consequences. We should have supposed from reading the Scriptures, "without note or comment." that the Saviour's character presented to us one symmetrical and consistent whole. But this invention affirms that he was not one but two persons; and since he did not always speak and act as a *whole and entire,* he must sometimes have spoken and acted as a part and a fraction. What he was ignorant of as a man, he knew as God. Each character had its peculiar language and mode of acting; and that which was utterly false, as coming from the one, was demonstratively true as coming from the other. He is, and he is not, omnipotent, and omniscient. He tells a female petitioner, that what she asks is not his to give—and notwithstanding, it is his to give! He cannot do what is requested of him, and yet it is perfectly in his power! What havoc does such a fancy make of the character of him who was full of grace and truth; who always acted with such perfect candour, and who branded hypocrites with his severest indignation? Let those who advocate the doctrine abide the consequence.

24

Such, it seems, is the only way to harmonize the discordancies, of a system which has neither reason nor Scripture for its support. Were Unitarians to have recourse to any such miserable expedients what a clamour would be raised? What epithets of abuse—what charges of blasphemy would be reverberated through the synods and convocations of orthodoxy! The dread sounds of *heretics—lepers—infidels—atheists—deniers of the God that bought them*, would be thundered in their ears: and all this for their adherence to the plain and unequivocal language of Scripture! We understand the Saviour's words in the sense which we believe they were intended to convey, and it would excite our special wonder, were we not accustomed to it, to witness the irreverence and disrespect with which they are treated by the upholders of Trinitarianism. These, seem to make it their uniform practise to contradict the plainest declarations of our Lord, as if they had taken part with the Scribes and Pharisees of old, and were determined to fix on him the very imputations which he repelled. When he says, "My Father is greater than I"—they virtually tell him that he utters a falsehood, for they know well that he is equal to the Father in all respects. When he denies that he knows when the day of judgment will arrive, they affirm that he knows it full well, and only imposes upon them by an equivocation. When he says, "It is not mine to give," they exclaim, this is only an ingenious mode of escaping from importunity, for though he cannot give in his assumed character, he can give all things in his real one! When he speaks of himself as of "a *man* who told the truth which he had heard of God," they say he is a man only in outward shew, but in reality the Omnipotent Jehovah! Thus, with the intention, as in charity we suppose, of exalting the Saviour, they heap upon him the greatest dishonour. They make him equivocate, dissemble, and falsify, and impute to him such a mode of speaking and acting, as they would be ashamed to impute to any man of common integrity.

These enormities Unitarians avoid, by adhering to the plain meaning of Scripture. They feel assured that the Saviour did not equivocate, nor practise any species of deception. They cannot find a single text which leads to such a horrible suspicion; neither are they able to discover any such contradictory views of his character and conduct as would lay them under the necessity of having recourse to Platonic inventions to reconcile them. They cannot "entangle him in his talk"—nor refuse to him the testimony which was given by his enemies, "Master, we know that thou art true, and teachest the way of God in truth; neither carest thou for any man, for thou regardest not the person of men."—Mat. xxii. 16. They contemplate our Lord not as a mysterious and ambiguous being, acting a double part, and paltering with language in a double sense, meaning one thing and expressing another—but as one being, sustaining one character, a beautiful, harmonious and consistent whole—without guile—of spotless purity, and unimpeachable rectitude, who spoke as inspired by the spirit of truth, and acted, in all respects, as became the Son of God, deputed with the high commission to instruct and reform the world; to leave us an example that we should follow his steps, and live and die for our salvation.

SECTION FIFTH.

The Titles and Epithets given to Christ in the Scriptures, no proof of his Deity.

Mr. Pope infers the Deity of Christ from certain titles and epithets given to him in the Scriptures: "the expression, Son of God," says he, "conveyed to the Jewish teachers and people the idea, that the person assuming the title asserted an equality with God." Where did Mr. Pope learn this? What is the proof? The appellation was too familiar, and too frequently ascribed to pious men to convey any such idea. Adam is denominated the Son of God.—Luke, iii. 38. Israel is the Son of God. Thus saith the Lord, "Israel is my Son, even my first born."—Exod. iv. 22. David is the Son of God. —Psalm, lxxxix, 26, 27. Solomon is the Son of God.— 2 Samuel, vii. 14. 1 Chron. xxii. 10. "As many as received him," says John, (i. 12, 13,) "to them gave he power to become the Sons of God, even to them that believe on his name; which were born, not of blood, nor of the will of the flesh, nor of the will of man, but of God."* "Do all things," says St. Paul, (Philip, ii. 14, 15,) "without murmurings and disputings; that ye may be blameless and harmless, the Sons of God, without rebuke." And again, "As many as are led by the Spirit of God, these are the Sons of God." All Christians are not only Sons but "Heirs of God, and joint-heirs with Christ."—Rom. viii. 14, 17.

That the title was pre-eminently due to the Blessed Saviour, is cheerfully admitted—but it was his own assumption of it, it seems, that caused the Jews to understand it in a peculiar sense. Entertaining, as they did, such exalted notions of the Supreme Jehovah, it is utterly incredible that they had annexed to the title "Son of God," any such idea as that he who claimed it, asserted an equality with him, in the unlimited sense contended for by Mr. Pope—nor will the account of the transaction on which he founds his opinion, yield it any valid support.—Let us examine. While Jesus was walking, in Solomon's porch, the

---

* "Can you produce a stronger or more explicit declaration of the divine generation of Christ than this is, taken literally, of the divine generation of believers? I am convinced you cannot, and yet they were not divine persons." *"The Apostle John an Unitarian."*

D

Jews came and asked him, to declare explicitly if he were the Christ? Our Lord answered, that he had told them before,—referred them, as he had referred the messengers from John the Baptist, to his miraculous works, accounted for their unbelief, and declared of his own sheep, that he will give them eternal life. "They shall never perish, neither shall any man pluck them out of my hand." Why? Because, "My Father which GAVE them me is greater than all, and no man is able to pluck them out of my Father's hand." God's omnipotence is the guarantee of my possession. "I and my Father are one;"— John x. 30. is one thing,* not one intelligent being; one, not in essence, for to this there is not the slightest allusion, but one as to the particular point mentioned; unanimous as to the security and salvation of the disciples.—When he had ended his discourse, the Jews took up stones to stone him, not merely for uttering the words, "I and my Father are one," for to the Jews they conveyed no idea of Christ's claiming substantial identity with God—nor had any man yet been so absurd as to draw from a declaration of unity of purpose, a declaration of unity of essence—but as they themselves affirmed for "blasphemy," generally; and specifically, because "thou being a man makest thyself God." (Elohim.†) By making himself God, they meant

---

* Newcome. Campbell. Cappe. _Une seule chose_—Le Clerc. _Une même chose._—Port Royal, Simon & Saci. See Slichtingius & Wolzogenius _in loc._ "They did not understand verse 30, of an essential union, or of any union implying equality, for if they had, it would have been a far more plausible foundation for the accusation than that which they selected."—Fox. · The meaning is fully developed in John c. xvii. v. 20, 23, "Neither pray I for these alone, but for them also who shall believe on me, through their word; that _they all_ may be ONE ἐν, as thou, Father, art in me, and I in thee, that they also may be _one_ in us: that the world may believe that thou hast sent me. And the glory which thou gavest me, I have given them, that _they_ may be _one, even as we are one_, I in them and thou in me; that they may be made perfect in _one_, and that the world may know that thou hast sent me, and hast loved THEM, as thou hast loved _me_. " I have planted," says Paul, 1 Cor. iii. 6, 8. " Apollos watered. Now he that planteth and he that watereth are _one_ "—" The _multitude_ of them that believed were of one heart and of one soul."—Acts, iv. 32. We being many are one bread and _one_ body; for we are all partakers of that one body."—1 Cor. x. 17. Admitting the much disputed text, 1 John v. 7. of the three heavenly witnesses to be genuine, it must be interpreted in a similar sense.

† The holy angels are styled Gods. "Thou hast made him a little lower _Me-elohim_ than the Gods."—Ps. viii. 5.

Also judges and rulers. "Thou shalt not revile the Gods,"—(or judges and rulers.)—Exod. xxii. 28. "God standeth in the Congregation of the Mighty, he judgeth among the Gods. I have said, ye are Gods; and all of you are children of the Most High."—Psalm, lxxxii. 1, 6. See also Exod. xxi. 6.

· The ambassadors and prophets of God were also called Gods. "And the Lord said unto Moses, see, I have made thee _Elohim_, a God to Pharaoh."—Exod. vii. 1. "Thou shalt be to him instead of God."—iv. 16.

that he had "assumed a divine authority without warrant"*—
not that he had pretended to be the infinite Jehovah. Even his
calumniators would have been ashamed of having such a meaning fixed on their expressions. But that their meaning was
what has been just stated, and that the Saviour understood them
in that sense, is clear as demonstration, from his reply. He
founds it on an argument taken from their own Scriptures, and
shews that if he had made himself God, or *Elohim*, in the sense
in which that term was applied to Moses, and the Jewish
prophets, judges, and legislators, he would have been perfectly
justifiable, for he spoke and acted by a warrant of divine authority as well as they. "Is it not written in your law," said he,
" Ye are Gods? *(Elohim.)* If he called them Gods (Elohim,)
to whom the word of God came, (and the Scriptures cannot
be broken,) say ye of him whom the Father hath sanctified and
SENT into the world, *thou blasphemest*, because I said, I am"—
What? not that I am God (Elohim) but "*the Son of God?*
Hence, it is apparent that it was on his assumption of this title
that they grounded their charge of blasphemy; and not on his
having made any pretensions to the name and character of Jehovah. He then proceeds to justify his claims to the title which
he did assume, and proposes an infallible test by which a judgment might be formed of their validity. "If I do not the works
of my Father believe me not. But if I do, though ye believe
not me, believe the works, that ye may know, and believe, that
the Father is in me, and I in him."†

As to the Jews confounding the Son with the Father, and
supposing that Christ's assumption of the former name, implied an assumption of the name and honours of Jehovah, and
an identity of essence, it is totally devoid of scriptural evidence.
In the passage which has just been under consideration, it appears that Christ, so far from adopting even the appellative
name of *Elohim*, much less that of Jehovah, designates himself
by the inferior title of Son; a title which no Jew could ever
be so preposterous as to identify with that of Father.

The Jews, on another occasion, understood Christ as making
himself equal with God. Let us consider this.

Our Lord had performed a miraculous cure on the sabbath-
day. This the Jews resented as a violation of the fourth commandment, and sought to slay him. Jesus seeing their intended
violence, justified what he had done, by pleading divine authority,
saying, "My Father worketh hitherto, and I work."—John, v. 17.
My Father conducts the beneficent operations of his providence on
the sabbath, as well as on other days, and I, by his special au-

---

* Cappe.

† "Compare John xiv. 10, 11; where this union is said to consist in speaking the words, and doing the works of the Father."—NEWCOME.

thority do those works of mercy which he has commissioned me to perform. This plea only incensed them the more; and they sought to kill him, because, as they affirmed, "he not only had broken the sabbath, but said also, that God was his Father, making himself equal with (like) God." Now, gentle reader, observe, this is not the sentiment of the Evangelist, but a calumny of the Jews—for Christ neither broke the Sabbath nor claimed equality with the Father.* It was only in their wicked imaginations that he had done either. The hypocrites who charged "the Lord of the sabbath," with breaking it, because he had healed an infirm man, had no scruple to take their ox, or their ass, to watering, on that day; nor had they any objection to exalt themselves above God, by "teaching for doctrines the commandments of men." Notwithstanding their perversity, however, our Lord condescended to answer and repel their calumny. He commenced a long address, by a solemn declaration, equivalent to a direct positive contradiction of their assertions. "Verily, verily, I say unto you, the Son can do nothing of himself, but what he seeth the Father do." The Son originates nothing—so far from claiming equality with the Father, he only follows his example. This be repeats again in the 30th verse, "I can of mine own self do nothing." Then he speaks of the Father as in every respect his superior. It is the Father who sheweth him all things—that commits all judgment to the Son—that sends him—gives him to have life in himself—gives him authority to execute judgment—assigns to him the task which he has to perform. So far from affording the least ground for the charge that he pretended to be equal with God, he thrice declares, in the same reply, that he was sent by the Father; and that he sought not his own will, but the will of him by whom he was deputed. The Jews, in defiance of their prejudice and malevolence, appear to have been overcome by the force of truth, and tacitly to have admitted that their charge was untenable; for they made no reply, but suffered him to depart unmolested.

Let us now, for the sake of argument, admit that the words "making himself equal with God," contain the sentiment of the Evangelist, as well as of the Jews. What, let us enquire, was the nature, or extent of the equality which, in this case, they may have supposed the Saviour to claim? Was it unlimited, and unqualified? Did it imply that the Son was consubstantial and coeternal with the everlasting Father? Nothing like it. No Jew ever maintained so preposterous an idea, nor is there

* "Hæc Joannes per mimesin, et ex illorum, non ex sua sententia loquitur. Nam reipsa nec sabbatum solvit, nec seipsum Deo æqualem fecit." Slichtingius, in loc.
Calumniam capitalem ei struebant.—Grotius.

even the shadow of an argument for it in all the sacred volume. They were exasperated at the Saviour for claiming a peculiar relationship to God, by stiling him *was his own* Father, as if he had excluded them, or deemed them unworthy of being reckoned in the same degree of affinity—and also for assuming a privilege to do works of mercy on the sabbath-day, equally as if he had been its institutor. This was the only point of equality or similitude which even they could charge the Saviour with assuming. As for metaphysical ideas about consubstantiality and coeternity, the Jews knew nothing about them—and if they had, our Lord, in the very first sentence of his reply, would have exposed their folly. "Verily, verily, I say unto you, the Son can do nothing of himself but what he seeth the Father do."*

The Jews, with all their malevolent and persecuting spirit, never thought that Christ assumed equality with God, in the sense alleged by Trinitarianism. Even when they brought him before Caiaphas, and made the strongest accusation they could, was it that he had pretended to be in all respects equal to the omnipotent Jehovah? No such thing. They accused him of saying, " I am able to destroy the temple of God, and to build it in three days;" a figurative way in which he had spoken of his resurrection. Then the high priest adjured him by the living God, to declare whether he were the Son of God? Can any one imagine that in this solemn adjuration, which preserves the distinction between the living God and the Son, so remarkably, the high priest had any idea that Christ had either assumed, or would assume the character of the Supreme Deity? His object was to ascertain whether he had named himself the Christ or the Messiah; and our Lord, as became him, replied in the affirmative. His declaring himself to be the Messiah was deemed blasphemy; not his assumption of the character of Deity, for this he never did assume—nor did the Jews when they brought him before Pilate, urge against him any such accusation. They said, " we have a law, by which law he ought to die, because he made himself the Son of God." Observe—this charge was made before a heathen, whose Polytheistic religion would have led him to consider this as no great offence, and the Jews could not be ignorant of a fact so notorious. Many among the Romans, were denominated Sons of Gods, by the flattery of poets, and the gratitude of their friends and admirers. Why then did the Jews prefer a charge which had no criminality in the eyes of a Roman, if they could, with any plausibility, bring forward the more grievous accusation of his assuming the character of Supreme Deity? It is not contended, indeed, that even this would have made any very unfavourable impression on Pilate; but it

* " Comparatio est sumpta a discipulo qui magistrum sibi præcuntem diligenter intuetur, ut imitari possit."—Grotius.

would have exasperated the multitude still more; and it is contrary to all experience, to suppose they would omit the greater and insist on the less offence. Their law to which they appealed, was directed against blasphemy in general. "He that blasphemeth the name of the Lord shall surely be put to death; and all the congregation shall certainly stone him."—Lev. xxiv. 16. They had also a law, (Deut. xviii. 20.) for putting a false prophet to death; much more, for executing the same sentence on any one making a false claim to the character and office of their Messiah. But they had no law against the specific crime of pretending to be the Almighty Jehovah. They never contemplated the possibility of such an extravagance. But they thought the assumption of any authority from heaven was blasphemy, and for this they accused him. This accusation failing, they charged him with a political crime, and succeeded.

It is lamentable that any man of Mr. Pope's talents and learning should hazard such an assertion as the following: "If the Redeemer were not God, then did he suffer himself to remain under a charge of blasphemy—then did he, by his words, both incur the guilt of wilfully contributing towards his own crucifixion, and justify his murderers in putting him to death as a blasphemer."

Whether the Redeemer was God, or not, he did not repel their last charge of blasphemy. He was consistent throughout, in maintaining that he was the character which he was persecuted for assuming. But he was not God; for this he most clearly and decidedly denied. He was the Son of God; for this he as decidedly asserted, before the people, before Caiaphas, and before Pilate. The assumption of this title, as claiming a peculiar interest with heaven, and the honour of being the Messiah, was deemed blasphemy by the Jews; and this charge he never refuted. Even so, he did not die the death of a blasphemer, which the law of Moses decreed to be by stoning, but the death of a political malefactor, by crucifixion, on a false charge of sedition, and by the sentence of a Roman governor.

Even when he hung on the cross, and his enemies gave vent to the full torrent of their reproaches, and upbraided him with all the offences, of which, in justification of their own cruelty, they wished to make him appear guilty, that of having assumed the name and character of Jehovah was not among them.

Mr. Pope thinks that the name EMMANUEL, which signifies *God with us*, proves the Supreme Deity of Christ.

The passage in Mat. i. 23, is this:—" Behold a virgin shall be with child, and shall bring forth a son, and they shall call his name Emmanuel, which being interpreted, is, God with us." Bishop Lowth says, that these words did not primarily apply to Christ; and Rammohun Roy has clearly shewn that they were applied by Isaiah, vii. 14,—" to Hezekiah, son of Ahaz, figuratively designated as the son of *The Virgin*; the daughter of Zion, to wit,

Jerusalem, foretold by the prophet, as the deliverer of the city
from the hands of its enemies, though its utter destruction was
then threatened by the kings of Syria and Israel. Orthodox
writers, in the interpretation of the text in Isaiah," observes the
same learned author, "have entirely disregarded the original Scripture, the context, and the historical facts." It should be rendered not "a virgin," but THE virgin, viz: " The virgin daughter
of Zion, the city of Jerusalem, is pregnant, and is bearing a Son,
and shall call his name Emmanuel." In accordance with this
version, it is translated by Bishop Lowth, with the definite
article, and in the present tense, thus, "Behold, THE Virgin
conceiveth and beareth a Son." The prophets, in their figurative language, often call Jerusalem, the Daughter of Zion,
and the Virgin*—thus, Isaiah, xxxvii. 22:—" The virgin, the
Daughter of Zion, hath despised thee, and laughed thee to
scorn ; the Daughter of Jerusalem hath shaken her head at
thee."—Thus, Jeremiah, xiv. 17. "Let mine eyes run down
with tears night and day, and let them not cease ; for the
virgin daughter of my people is broken with a great breach."
And again, xviii. 13. " Thus saith Jehovah, * * The virgin of
Israel hath done a very horrible thing."—Amos, v. 2. " The
virgin of Israel is fallen. She shall no more rise ; she is forsaken upon her land ; there is none to raise her up." The
original word virgin, in the passage under consideration, has
before it the emphatic or definite particle ה, ha, which incon-
testibly fixes its meaning : and it can be shewn by numerous instances, that the word הרה, harah, rendered in our translation
shall conceive, should be is with child. " Tamar hath played
the harlot, and she is (harah) with child."—Gen. xxxviii. 24.
"And the angel of the Lord said unto her, (Hagar) behold,
thou art (harah) with child."—Gen. xvi. 11. "If men strive
and hurt a woman with child," (harah) Exod. xxi. 22. The
Evangelist Matthew, quotes Isaiah, not from the original Hebrew, but from the Septuagint translation, which is here incorrect.
But it answers his purpose, which is merely to apply it by way
of accommodation† to Christ—"the son of Ahaz and the Saviour resembling each other, in each being the means, at differ-

* It is also called "barren."—Isaiah, liv. 1. "a captive Daughter,"—
lii. 2—and a "Harlot,"—Ezek. xvi. 35.
† " Accommodations are passages of the Old Testament which are adapted
by writers of the New Testament, to an occurrence that happened in their
time, on account of correspondence and similitude. These are not prophecies, though they are sometimes said to be fulfilled ; for any thing may
be said to be fulfilled when it can be pertinently applied. This method of
explaining Scripture by accommodation, will enable us to solve some of the
greatest difficulties relating to the prophecies."—Horne's Introduction to
the critical study of the Scriptures. Vol. 11. p. 438.

ent periods, though in different senses, of establishing the throne
of the house of David."*

All this, indeed, must appear most evident to any one who will
take the trouble of turning to the seventh chapter of Isaiah, and
examining the subject with candour. Ahaz, king of Judah, being thrown into consternation by the confederated arms of Rezin,
king of Syria, and Pekah, king of Israel; the prophet comes to
promise him safety, and desires him to ask a sign of his ap-
proaching deliverance. Ahaz declines this, saying, " I will not
ask, neither will I tempt the Lord." Then the prophet replies,
the Lord himself shall give you a sign: and repeats the words already quoted, with this addition: " Butter and honey shall he
eat that he may know to refuse the evil and choose the good.
For before the child shall know to refuse the evil and choose
the good, the land that thou abhorrest, shall be forsaken of both
her kings." The prophecy as applied to Hezekiah,† the Immanuel meant by the prophet, is clear and satisfactory. But it
is badly rendered in our common translation. There is no meaning in saying, " butter and honey shall he eat, that he may know
to refuse the evil and choose the good," as if knowledge were
to be the consequence of such food. *That he may know*, should
be *when he shall know*.‡ At this age he shall eat butter and
honey, the emblems of peace and plenty; for, even before he
shall arrive at years of discretion, the land shall be freed of her
oppressors. Here was a sign that could be seen and understood.
But what "sign," or consolation would it have been to Ahaz,
terrified as he was by the approach of a powerful enemy, and
the anticipated loss of his throne and life, to be told that a

---

* Because Rammohun Roy had the honesty to give the above explanation,
which is the only one that has sense, and can stand the test of fair criticism,
he was accused by the Rev. Editor who opposed him, of having *blasphemed*
the word of God. He says, with great innocence, that he did not expect
such an accusation from the editor ! and to acquit himself of the charge refers to the translation of the four Gospels, by Dr. Campbell, a celebrated
Trinitarian writer, in whose notes that learned divine says, " Thus, Mat.
ii. 15, a declaration from the prophet Hosea, xi. 1, which God made in
relation to the people of Israel whom he had long before called from Egypt,
is applied by the historian *allusively* to Jesus Christ, where all that is meant
is, that with equal truth, or rather with much greater energy of signification,
God might now say, *I have recalled my Son out of Egypt*. Indeed the import
of the Greek phrase (that it might be fulfilled) as commonly used by the
sacred writers, is no more, as Le Clerc has justly observed, than that such
words of any of the prophets may be applied with truth to such an event."

† Marshman says, the child could not be Hezekiah. But he founds his
observation on a mis-translation of the Hebrew, and is triumphantly confuted by Rammohun Roy, who understands Hebrew indeed. It did apply
to Hezekiah, not as a child that had yet to be conceived, but as a child
with which the virgin city was actually pregnant.

‡ Lowth.

Virgin, viz: Mary would conceive and bear a Son, above seven
hundred years after he should be gathered to his fathers?

A similar sign was given to the prophet himself, as we read
in the next chapter. The prophetess bare a son. "Then said
the Lord to me, call his name Maher-shalal-hash-baz, (i. e.
Haste to the spoil, quick to the prey.*) for before the child
shall have knowledge to cry, my Father and my Mother, the
riches of Damascus, and the spoil of Samaria, shall be taken
away before the king of Assyria," viii. 3, 4. He then proceeds
to say, in the name of the Lord, that because the people refused
the waters of Shiloah, meaning terms of peace, the king of
Assyria would come up, as a torrent, against them, and "the
stretching out of his wings shall fill the breadth of thy land,
O Immanuel," v. 8. What is meant here? Will any orthodox
critic affirm, that the prophet apostrophises Christ? If there
be, let him enjoy his fancy—to deprive him of it would be
cruel—and he might exclaim with one of his old classic ac-
quaintances:—

> Pol me occidistis, amici,
> Non servastis, ait; cui sic extorta voluptas,
> Et demptus per vim mentis gratissimus error.
> HOR.

> Ah! cruel friends! he cried,
> Is this to save me? Better far have died,
> Than thus be robb'd of pleasure so refined,
> The dear delusion of a raptured mind.
> FRANCIS.

The word Immanuel occurs again in 10th verse, but there it
is translated "God is with us."

Trinitarians rest great weight on another passage of Isaiah,
ix. 6, applied by that prophet to Hezekiah also, "Unto us a
child is born—unto us a son is given: and the government shall
be upon his shoulders: and his name shall be called Wonderful,
Counsellor, the Mighty God, the Everlasting Father, the Prince
of Peace." "The words Everlasting Father," says Dr. Clarke,
"are very ill rendered; for it is absurd to say of the Son,
that he is the Everlasting Father, the Father of himself. The
phrase ought to be translated—the Father, or Lord of the age to
come." This is well, and it might be added, that no prophet
could affirm of the Father, meaning God, that he had ever been
a child, or was born. But on what authority, save that of orthodox divines, are they applied to Christ at all? They may
certainly be used as descriptive of the character of him who was
so truly the Prince of Peace—but nothing was farther from the
mind of the prophet who wrote them than such a reference. They
were applied by him to the same son of Ahaz, whom he names

---

* Lowth.

X

Immanuel. Such lofty hyperbolical epithets are perfectly in
accordance with the style of oriental description, particularly
prophetic and poetical description. Moreover it was customary
with the Jews to give names to individuals expressive of some
event or circumstance of their lives: and such names were frequently associated with that of God, in a manner which may
excite the surprise of those who have thought the title of Immanuel, when applied to Christ, demonstrative of his Deity. Thus
Hezekiah signifies "God my strength."—Israel, "Prince of
God."—Elijah, "God the Lord;" or the strong Lord.—Elisha,
"Salvation of God; or, God that saves."—Jotham, "Perfection
of the Lord."—Ishmael, "God who hears."—Lemuel, "God
with them." The word Immanuel, therefore, even if it belonged
exclusively to Christ, which it did not, yields no support to the
cause for which it is adduced as an auxiliary.

As to the appellation *Jehovah*, there is no place in the sacred
volume by which it can be clearly shewn that our Lord Jesus
Christ was ever so denominated—and even if there were, it
would be no argument for his Deity, since it is an appellation
shared in common by angels, by men, and by places. The angel
of the Lord who appeared to Moses in the bush, is called *Jehovah.*—Exod. iii. 2, 3, 4. The sons of Seth called themselves
by the name of Jehovah.*—Gen. iv. 26. Abraham named the
place where he caught the ram, *Jehovah-jireh*—Gen. xxii. 14.
Moses built an altar and called the name of it *Jehovah-nissi,*—
Exod. xvii. 15. Gideon built an altar unto the Lord and called
it *Jehovah-shalom.*—Jud. vi. 24. The city to be possessed by
the tribes of Israel was to be *Jehovah-shammah.*—Ezek. xlviii.
35.† The text Jer. xxiii. 6. "This is his name whereby he
shall be called, the Lord (Jehovah) our righteousness," is supposed, by the orthodox, clearly to establish the Deity of Christ,
though in fact it has no more reference to Christ, than to
William the Fourth, King of Great Britain and Ireland. Every
reader of ordinary intelligence, who will read it in the connexion
where it stands, will find that it must apply to some temporal
ruler, and not to him whose kingdom is not of this world. The
text states, that he of whom the prophecy is written, "shall
reign and prosper, and shall execute judgment and justice on the
earth." Our Lord, on the contrary, so far from reigning and
prospering, was a man of sorrows, who had not where to lay
his head. Instead of executing judgment and justice; he asked
the young man who wished him to arbitrate between him and
his brother, "who made me a judge or a divider over you?"—

---

* See Calmet's Dictionary.

† "It is fortunate," says Rammohun Roy, "that some sect has not
hitherto arisen, maintaining the Deity of Jerusalem, or of the altar of
Moses, from the authority of the passages just mentioned."

Luke xli. 14. "In his days," says the text, "Judah shall be saved, and Israel shall dwell safely." But so far are these words from applying to Israel in the days of Christ, that it was then she filled up the measure of her iniquity, and laid a train to the mine which blew her to pieces. The prophecy applies to Zerubbabel, "son of Salathiel, of the royal race of David; to whose care Cyrus committed the sacred vessels of the temple when the Jews returned from captivity; who laid the foundations of the temple, and restored the worship of the Lord, and the usual sacrifices." The same prophecy is repeated in the 33d chapter, 15, 16 verses of the same prophet—but that part of it, which has attracted most special attention, is not here applied to a man, but to the city of Jerusalem. "This is the name wherewith SHE shall be called, *Jehovah our righteousness.*"— Dr. Blaney, who has favoured the world with a new and much esteemed translation of Jeremiah, renders c. xxiii. 6, thus, "This is the name by which Jehovah shall call him, *our righteousness.*" "I doubt not," says he, in a note, "but some persons will be offended with me for depriving them by this translation,* of a favourite argument for proving the divinity of our Saviour from the Old Testament. *But I cannot help it.*" It is to be wished, that all translators and commentators were under the same kind of moral necessity, and that they *could not help* publishing the truth in defiance of orthodoxy and the fear of giving offence. Let them fear God,—be valiant for the truth, and not include themselves in the condemnation of those false prophets that "speak a vision of their own heart, and not out of the mouth of the Lord—which think to cause my people to forget my name by their *dreams*, which they tell every man to his neighbour, as their fathers have forgotten my name for Baal."—Jer. xxiii. 16, 27.

Since Mr. Pope thinks a name, or title, of so much importance, it may be well for him to consider, how many titles are given to the Father which are never applied to the Son. The Father is termed the King eternal, immortal, invisible, incorruptible; the only wise, living, and true God; the blessed and glorious Potentate, who only hath immortality; the one who alone is good. None of all these titles is given to Christ in the Scriptures.—Neither is he denominated the High God—the highest— the mighty one—the blessed—the God of Abraham, of Isaac, and of Jacob—the God of Glory—God who quickeneth, or giveth life—God our Saviour—the Majesty on high—Δεσπότης, or Sovereign Lord. Nor is the designation "who is, and who was, and who is to come," equivalent to the term Jehovah, ever once ascribed to the Lamb, though mentioned so frequently in the

---

* The proper application of the prophecy deprives them still more effectually.

book of Revelation. These titles belong exclusively to the Father, as does also Παντοκρατωρ Almighty. This name is given to the Father alone, not only in Scripture, but in all creeds—for truth will sometimes assert her right, and triumph in spite of all the inventions of man to suppress or conceal it.

One text, Rom. ix. v. 5. "Of whom, as concerning the flesh, Christ came, who is over all, God blessed for ever,"—Amen ;— is supposed to afford ample proof, that one, at least, of the foregoing titles, is applied to Christ. But this is a text which, in the opinion of the most learned critics, admits of a very different interpretation. The ascription, in this solitary instance, of a title to Christ, which is given to him no where else, and which belongs peculiarly to the Father, naturally leads us to suspect an erroneous reading. Grotius informs us, (Ex Syro) that ancient copies had not the word God—but ran thus, ὁ ων επι παντων ευλογητος which reading, he observes, is more consistent with Paul's style ; for when he speaks of Father and Son together, he terms the former God, and the latter Lord. He farther remarks that according to Erasmus, this was the reading of the old copies of Cyprian, and that it was followed both by Hilary and Chrysostom. Hence there is sufficient reason to conclude that there has been some corruption or dislocation of words in the text ; and we are led still more strongly to this conclusion by the subject itself. It seems strange that the Apostle, in enumerating to the Jews their peculiar privileges, should omit the greatest of all, that of having God himself, in a special manner, for their king, and supreme legislator, the God of Abraham, of Isaac, and of Jacob. It has accordingly been suggested that the transposition of two little words ὁ ων to ων ὁ,* the participle now becoming the genitive plural of a pronoun, the same as that which twice precedes it, will probably restore the original reading ; supply the omission which has been remarked ; complete a noble climax agreeable to the Apostle's style of composition, and certainly add great force and beauty to the passage. It will then read in connexion with the preceding verse, thus: *Who are Israelites, of whom was the adoption of Sons, and the glory, and the covenants, and the institution of the law, and the service, and the promises.*

---

* Slitchtingius, Whitby, and Taylor, approve of this as a conjectural reading. A similar construction occurs in Callimachus Γμν, ης ΔΙΑ. 73. See Belsham in loc.—Dr. Clarke and other learned critics say that the words, as they stand at present, are of " ambiguous construction," and may be rendered, " God, who is over all, be blessed for ever, Amen." Rammohun Roy considers it as a pious ejaculation, and observes, that "it was customary with Jewish writers, to address some abrupt exclamations to God, while treating of other subjects, and for proof refers us to Psalms lxxxix. 52. civ. 35.

*Of whom were the Fathers ; of whom was the Christ according
to the flesh ; of whom was God, who is over all, blessed for
evermore. Amen.*

"Where," asks Wakefield, who has given us this version,
" shall we find a more striking selection of the principal circumstances, (one great source of the sublime) or a more just and
majestic gradation?—What? Is it possible then, that Paul, himself a Jew and proud of his descent, in enumerating the exclusive privileges of the Jewish nation, and setting forth the vast
superiority, which their *Theocratic* polity gave them over the
communities of the earth; is it possible, I say, that he should
overlook their pre-eminent distinction, the very characteristic of
their constitution—that is, the *peculiar relation* in which they
stood to their king Jehovah? He was *their God*, and they were
his people; he was their Father, and they were the *sons* and
daughters of the *Lord Almighty.*—Such an omission is equally
incredible and unaccountable.

Supposing the original text not to be corrupted, the passage
may be rendered thus: " God who is over all; or He, who is
God over all, *be* blessed for ever, Amen. The words ὁ ευλογητος,
THE BLESSED are applied so exclusively to the Father, that the
High Priest when interrogating our Saviour, did not employ the
word God, but said, "Art thou the Christ, the Son of THE
Blessed."—Mark, xiv. 61. The word *blessed* is used in praising
the Father, or as an epithet peculiarly his own;—Luke, i. 68.—
Rom. i. 25.—2 Cor. i. 3. and xi. 31. Also in Ephes i. 3.
and 1 Peter, i. 3. but in not a single instance is it applied
to Christ in all the New Testament. In four of the places referred to, the Greek εστω *be* is understood—and accordingly our
English version has the word *be* printed in Italics, to indicate that
it is supplied. We are led by a principle of fair criticism, to
conclude that the last clause of the verse under discussion, supposing it to contain the *ipsissima verba*, the very words which
the Apostle wrote, should be translated with the aid of the same
supplementary verb. Some critics allege that the *Amen* at the
end of the verse, proves the last clause of it to be a doxology;
similar to that which occurs in the 25th v. of the 1st chap. and
elsewhere. Whiston observes truly, that there is no instance of
such a doxology to any but God the Father in all Scripture.
Hopton Haynes says, that the grammar, and the style, and the
sense of the whole New Testament is against the Tritheists in
this place; and he might have added, in every other place. Had
the words been intended to apply to Christ, they would have
been ος εστω instead of ὁ ων. For so the Apostle " uses the relative ος.—Rom. i. 25, and three times just before this passage, referring his readers to the Israelites of whom he had been speaking."

But laying aside Greek criticism, though the farther it is
pursued, the more it betrays the weakness of the supports on
which Trinitarianism leans, let us for a moment, attend to another

argument which may be deemed of superior force. It is put to the good sense of the reader to consider, whether it is at all probable that the Apostle in writing to the Jews, endeavouring to overcome their prejudices and reconcile them to the Christian dispensation, would designate as the Supreme Deity, a person who came to them in *the flesh*, or by *natural descent*. Would he call a descendant of the house of David—the everlasting Father?—a crucified man—the ever-blessed God? Even supposing the doctrine to be as true, as we contend that it is false, is it consonant to his usual mode of introducing an obnoxious subject, to bring it forward in a style that to a Jew would be so offensive? Is it in such a mode that the author of the Epistle to the Hebrews exalts Christ above Moses, and the other angels or inspired messengers of God? So great a master of the art of persuasion would have said nothing about natural descent, had he wished to inculcate a belief that the Messiah was Jehovah. The very idea would have exasperated the Jews, and crushed the whole structure of the Apostle's reasoning. As for the usual subterfuge, that Christ had two natures, and that the expression, "as concerning the flesh," intimates this, we might as well be told that Paul had two natures, since he speaks only two verses before this, (v. 3.) of his own " kinsmen according to the flesh." But where it is applied, (v. 5.) to Christ, the κατα σαρκα has the article το before it, and the use of this, it seems, is to remind us that Christ had a higher nature! Of what prodigious importance are *articles* to the arcana of theology! Dr. Carpenter justly observes, that "the employment of the article here is obviously founded on the fact, that Jesus was of the Israelites as to *natural* descent only, and that as to spiritual descent he was the Son of God—that he had his commission, his doctrine, and his miraculous powers by immediate communication from his God and Father."[*]

Even admitting the common version to be in all respects, correct, it would not prove the Son consubstantial and coeternal, and possessed of equal power with the Father; for the same Apostle who has written this, tells us elsewhere, 1 Cor. xv. 27. that when he says *all things*, HE is excepted who *did put* all things under him.

Parkhurst contends against Dr. Clarke, that another of the foregoing epithets, viz: Δισποτης is applied to Christ, and says that the master of the house spoken of in 2 Tim. ii. 21. may

___

[*] " Those persons manifest little regard to truth and candour who assert that the Unitarians (or Socinians as they are pleased to term us) maintain that Jesus was a *mere* man. *We believe with the Apostle Paul,* that as to nature, *Jesus was a* man, descended from David, but that as to the divine communications *of knowledge and power which God made to him for purposes the most important, he was the Son of God; and as such we revere his authority, and own his claims upon our implicit and submissive obedience.*"—Dr. Carpenter.

most naturally be *referred* to him.—The Lord, or master of any house, was so denominated, and Christ uses the word in conjunction with οἴκου in that sense.—Mat. x. 25. But no one is termed Δεσπότης, in the supreme and absolute sense, but Jehovah alone. Nor can the author find that our Lord is ever accosted by this title, even in a subordinate sense; for his authority over the disciples was not that of the master of a house over his slaves, but of an instructor over his pupils. When Peter II. Ep. ii. 1. speaks of "false teachers, bringing in damnable heresies, and denying the Lord Δεσπότην that *bought* them;" Parkhurst refers us, to learn *who he is*, to Gal. iii. 13. and to the Hymning Elders in Rev. v. 9. Whitby thinks it most reasonable to interpret it of God the Father, and as we profess to adopt what is most reasonable, we do not choose to follow the direction of the learned lexicographer in this matter, especially as he could have referred us to texts much more in point, which would inform us *who he is* without any ambiguity. We learn from Deut. xxxii. 6. that it was the Everlasting Jehovah *who bought them.* "Do ye thus requite the Lord, O foolish people and unwise? Is not he thy Father, that *hath bought thee*?" And from Exod. xv. 16. " that it was Jehovah who *purchased* his people Israel." See also Cor. vi. 19, 20.

Parkhurst would willingly apply to Christ τὸν μόνον Δεσπότην in Jude, 4, "denying the only Lord God, and our Lord Jesus Christ." He thinks that the want of the article τὸν before Κύριον shews that Jesus Christ is there styled the only Lord; but he is refuted by Grotius and Woltzogenius; or, if, says he, with several MSS. we omit the word Θεόν God, altogether, the application to Christ will be still more evident. No doubt. But since the meaning is perfectly clear, since no good reason can be assigned for any change, since our version of it, as Whitby affirms, "is without any exception," since it is in perfect harmony with the great doctrine of Scripture, that God alone is Deity supreme, and, above all, since it most clearly marks the distinction which no Christian should ever forget, between the only Lord God, and our Lord Jesus Christ, the Unitarian desires that the text may not be mutilated.

When any two objects are declared to be in all respects similar and equal, whatever can be predicated of the one, can also be predicated of the other. Their properties, qualities, appearances must be all alike, insomuch that no difference can exist between them. A single adjunct belonging to the one and and not to the other, destroys their equality. Now let us apply this argument to the question before us. It has been just shewn that certain titles and epithets are given to the Father Almighty, which are never given to the Son. On the other hand, certain titles and epithets are given to the Son, the ascription of which to the Father would confound every believer whose belief does not extend as far as that of the Patripassians, who maintained that the Father himself suffered on the cross; or of Gregory Nyssen, who said, that there was "a whole Father in a whole Son, and a whole Son in a whole Father." The titles which our Saviour gave himself were Καθηγητα; guide, director, or teacher.—Κυριο; Lord—Διδασκαλος instructor or master—"a man that hath told you the truth."—John, viii. 40. The Son of God, and the Son of man. The last is the appellation by which he designates himself when speaking of his coming in all his glory, with the celestial hierarchies, to judge the world. See Mat. xvi. 27, and xxvi. 64. None of these titles is ever given to the Father. It cannot be predicated of him that he is the Son, the Son of man, nor the Son of God, nor the receiver, nor the sent, nor the well-beloved, nor the only begotten, nor he that is in the bosom of the Father, nor the great Prophet, nor he which was dead and is alive, nor the sanctified and ordained, nor a high-priest in things pertaining to God, nor a mediator, nor an intercessor, nor the Messiah, the anointed, or the Christ. God does all things by his own sovereign will—his own undivided authority. Christ does nothing but in obedience to the will of him who sent him. With what consistency then, can it possibly be maintained that those two Beings are one and the same, whose attributes and offices are so exceedingly distinct, and whose grand characteristics are so far from being reciprocal, that the very idea of ascribing to the one, those which belong to the other, puts reason to the blush, and "shocks all common sense?"

SECTION SIXTH.

No proof of the Deity of Christ to be found in the Epistle to the Philippians.

Few texts are quoted more frequently in support of Christ's imagined equality to God, and consequently subjected to the ordeal of more rigorous criticism than Philip, ii. 6. "*Who being in the form of God, thought it not robbery to be equal with God;*"— a verse which rightly translated and properly understood, has a meaning totally different from that assigned to it by Trinitarians. The Apostle's object is to inculcate humility and benevolence by the example of Jesus.

"Let nothing, says he, be done through strife or vain glory; but in lowliness of mind let each esteem other better than themselves. Look not every man on his own things, but on the things of others. Let this mind be in you, which was also in Christ Jesus: who being in the form of God, thought it not robbery to be equal with God: but made himself of no reputation, and took upon him the form of a servant, and was made in the likeness of men: and being found in fashion as a man, he humbled himself, and became obedient unto death, even the death of the cross."

The tritheists contend that the phrase, *being in the form of God*, means being really and essentially Jehovah! They might

With equal good sense and meaning contend, that when the Prophet describes the carpenter with his rule and line, his plane and compasses, shaping a piece of timber, "after the figure of a man, according to the beauty of a man," he makes a real human being: or that when the Apostle declares of some hypocrites, that they have the "form of godliness," he means the substance of all piety and virtue. though he adds in the next clause, "denying the power thereof." In no other connexion, would they betray such a total disregard to sense as to confound the shadow with the substance, or the reflection with the object that reflects. But the word "being," υπαρχων, they affirm, implies that Christ was, by *his original nature*, in the form of God. Before they rest in this conclusion, let them answer Dr. Carpenter's question, "Did the Apostle mean to represent himself as, by his original nature, 'zealous towards God,' when he says, (Acts xxii. 3.) ζηλωτης υπαρχων του Θεου? To what hollow and miserable expedients are they obliged to have recourse? As to the word μορφη form, Parkhurst renders it *outward* appearance; and he has the honesty to say that, in his apprehension, it does not in this place refer to Christ being real and essential Jehovah. To what then does it refer? Not as the sturdy tritheist affirms, to essence; nor as the anthropomorphist might, with equal reason, affirm, to outward shape; but to his divinely delegated powers, in the exercise of which, for the benefit of others, he manifested a disposition truly godlike. Being in *the form of God* no more implies that he was really God, than being in the *form of a slave* implies that he was really a slave. The one phrase is opposed to the other, and each means that Christ was in a certain state of similitude. In the power and authority with which he was invested by his heavenly Father, and in the mode in which he employed them for the temporal and eternal good of mankind, he bore a striking resemblance to the Deity.* In his simple and precarious mode of life, in his deprivations and sufferings, he resembled one in the condition of a slave. Had he been so disposed, he might have reigned as a king, and triumphed as a God. But such was his humility, that he did not assume even the name *Elohim*, though so much better entitled to that appellation than Moses and all the other Jewish legislators to whom it was given. He had none of that pride of heart which led the Babylonian potentate to boast, "I will exalt my throne above the stars of God: I will be like the Most High." He thought his similitude to God, his το ισαι ισα Θεω, a phrase evidently pa-

---

* It was the belief of a heathen philosopher, that in no respect could men approach so near to the Gods, as in giving health to the sick. *Neque enim ulla alia re homines proprius ad Deos accedunt, quam salutem hominibus dando.* Cic.—How closely to God then did he approximate, who went about doing good, and healing all manner of sickness, and all manner of disease among the people?

rallel to ·μορφη, was no prey (αρπαγμον)* or spoil, like the booty, taken in war, a prize won and seized by his own right hand, but a gift or *trust* committed to him by the giver of all. So far, therefore, from making an ostentatious display of his similitude to God, much less of claiming equality with Jehovah, he emp- tied or divested himself, on numerous occasions, of the use of the power which he possessed, and rejected the honours which were proposed to him, and which he might have justly claimed and enjoyed; declaring that he came not to seek his own glory, but the glory of him by whom he was deputed. In- stead of accepting the kingdoms of the world, which were offered to him by the Tempter—or occupying the throne of David, when the people would have made him their king— or calling down twelve legions of angels to destroy his enemies— or retaining that bright resemblance to an inhabitant of heaven— in which he appeared at his transfiguration,—he lived a life of poverty, "a man of sorrows, and acquainted with grief." He humbled himself from the similitude of a God to the similitude of a slave—and in this station ministered unto his disciples, even unto the washing of their feet—being among them *as one that serveth.* Nay, more—*he was made*—or, more simply, *being,* γενομενος, in the likeness of men, ανθρωπων of common men—and *being found,* i.e. *being,* in fashion, or in external guise and condition as an ordinary† man, and "with all the contingencies of human nature," for he was, in all points, tempted like as we are, yet

---

* The word αρπαγμον is of rare occurrence in classical authors. Grotius says it is a Syriac phrase, and he quotes a Syriac litany, in which John the Baptist objects to baptize Christ, saying in Syriac, as translated by Grotius, *non assumam rapinam,* I will not take the spoil, meaning, I will not be guilty of such a predatory, or robber-like act, as to assume the honour of bap- tizing one so much my superior. "Christ glorified not himself to be made an high-priest,"—Heb. v. 5, is an expression of similar import. He received the appointment to that office as an honour, not as a right or spoil, "*quasi honori, non præda.*"—SALLUST. *Non habuit præda loco simi- litudinem cum Deo.* h. e, *non ea, qua poterat uti majestate divina, cupide utendum esse existimavit; seu, non semper eam fecit conspicuam, interdum ab- stinuit ab ea.*—SCHLEUSNER. How the words were understood by early writers may be learned from the 5th book and 2nd. chap. of the Church History of Eusebius. "The ancient fathers, both Latin and Greek," says Whiston, "never interpret Phil. ii. 6, to mean an equality of the Son to the Father—Novatian says, "he, therefore, though he was in the form of God, did not make himself equal to God, *(non est rapinam arbitratus equalem se deo esse,)* for though he remembered he was *God of God* the Fa- ther, he never compared himself to God the Father, being mindful that he was *of* his Father, and that he had this because his Father *gave it him.*" Suppose the equality contended for, established, it would make two dis- tinct independent beings, for equality is not identity. See Priestley's Cor- ruptions of Christianity.

† The candid Dr. Price objects to the application of the epithet *ordinary.* But surely he could not require to be told that ανθρωπος does mean a com- mon or ordinary man, and that it is so used in the Septuagint and contrasted

without sin, he submitted to the most cruel and humiliating indignities, to be tried as a perverter of the people, to be mocked,
buffetted, scourged, spat upon, and, finally, he became obedient
to the *servile* and ignominious death of the cross.

What constitution of mind does it require to believe that all
this is predicated, by an inspired Apostle, of the ever-living,
ever-blessed, Omnipotent Jehovah? Wherefore do they who
hold such a belief, speak with pity or contempt of those who
believe in the incarnations of Bramah and Vishnu?

> " O judgment! thou art fled to brutish beasts,
> And men have lost their reason."

The Apostle having shewn the great humility and conde-
scension of our Lord, next proceeds to shew how those virtues
were rewarded. "Wherefore," says he, *i. e.* in consequence of
his great humility and obedience, God also hath highly, or exceedingly, exalted him, and given him, or kindly bestowed upon
him, a name which is above every name, that at (*w in*) the
name of Jesus every knee should bow *** and that every tongue
should confess that Jesus Christ is Lord, *to the glory of God
the Father.*

This is a most beautiful and affecting lesson on humility, and
an admirable illustration of the truth of our Lord's doctrine,
that he who humbleth himself shall be exalted. The meaning
is perspicuous throughout, and in perfect conformity with the
Apostle's design. But if we understand the passage, in the
Trinitarian sense, we shall find that it perverts his meaning,
contradicts his design, and turns the whole passage into absolute
nonsense. Let us see. " Who being in the form of God," *i. e.* as
Trinitarians understand the expression, being the Supreme God,
did not think it any act of rapine or robbery to be equal with
the Supreme God! Christ, being Jehovah, deemed it his fair,
legitimate, and unquestionable, right, to place himself on a perfect
equality with Jehovah!—From this mode of interpretation, it
would appear that the Apostle was exhorting the Philippians

---

with αν̣ηρ. In Isaiah, li. 9. ανθρωπος, אדם, denotes *a mean man*, and
αν̣ηρ. איש, *a man of elevated rank*, "and the mean man, (ανθρωπος)
bowed down, and the great man humbled himself" εταπεινωθη αν̣ηρ. See
Schleusner, and Dr. Carpenter's " *Unitarianism the Doctrine of the Gospel.*"
The very argument of the Apostle required that he should speak of Christ
as ανθρωπος and not as αν̣ηρ. "It is natural," says Dr. Price, "to ask
here, when did Christ divest himself of the *power* of working miracles.
The gospel history tells us, he retained it to the last." But who affirms
that he divested himself of the *power*? The humility of Christ appeared in
refraining from the *exercise* of the power which he did possess. Had he
not possessed, and had he not retained the power, it would be absurd to
propose him as an example of humility. I can find nothing in the whole
passage that either requires or indicates the truth of the Arian hypothesis.

not to be humble, but ambitious! BUT thinking such equality no robbery, he made himself of no reputation. Here the disjunctive particle *but* expresses no opposition, though both the meaning and expression are highly antithetical.* Christ being the Supreme God, emptied himself of his glory, and was made in the likeness of men, and in consequence of his incarnation, abasement and crucifixion exalted him the Supreme God, viz: himself, and gave him a name, which is above every name; that every tongue should confess that Jesus Christ who is the Supreme God, is Lord, that is the Supreme God, to the glory of God the Father, that is of the same Supreme God!†

Assuredly no one who will lay aside human systems of theology, and suffer himself to be guided by a single spark of reason, can suppose the Apostle capable of expressing aught that leads to such incomparable absurdity. In vain do the Tritheists endeavour to give a consistent explanation of the passage on their principles, though they torture language and call to their aid the new unscriptural *revelation of the two natures*. What idea have they of the "High and lofty one that inhabiteth eternity, whose name is holy," that he can make himself of no reputation or divest himself of his glory? The thing is impossible. We might as well suppose he could cease to exist. "I, saith the Lord of hosts, am Jehovah—I change not."—Mal. iii. 6. "To whom then will ye liken me, or shall I be equal saith the holy ONE."—Is. xl. 25. "I am Jehovah, and there is none else; there is no God besides me."—Is. xlv. 5. Again, it is stated of Christ, that in consequence of his obedience, "God hath highly exalted him, and given him a name." How can this be predicated of the Omnipotent? To whom is he who rules in the

---

* "The argument of the Apostle," says Wakefield, "according to the usual translation of the passage, and the Trinitarian exposition of it, is inconsequent and completely absurd. *But*, is a conjunction employed to introduce a proposition, or assertion, which answers and explains another correlative to it, for example. " *The healthy need not a physician*"—By no means; it were useless to affirm it. Who then? The contrary to these— BUT the sick, Matt. ix. 12. *Jesus Christ thought it no robbery to be equal with God.* By no means, it were untrue to affirm this. What then? The contrary to thinking it a robbery; BUT *he emptied himself.*

Who does not see that this is absurd, and that the power of *but* is not preserved? To give the conjunction its proper force, and to preserve the paragraph from nonsense, it should be thus stated :

Jesus Christ thought it no robbery to be equal with God; by no means; it were untrue to affirm this. What then? The contrary to thinking it a robbery; BUT he steadfastly *maintained* and *insisted* upon this equality.

Let us now try the translation above proposed.

Jesus Christ did not think his resemblance to God, a thing greedily to be asserted; BUT the contrary to this, *he emptied* himself of it.

This, methinks, looks a little like sense and argument; and therefore the opposite interpretation is evidently absurd."

† See Whitby's last Thoughts.

armies of heaven, and among the inhabitants of the earth, obedient? To what, or by whom can he be exalted? Away with
the most unscriptural, most unhallowed imagination!

> "It is he that sitteth on the circle of the earth;
> And the inhabitants are to Him as grasshoppers:
> That extendeth the heavens, as a thin veil;
> And spreadeth them out as a tent to dwell in."
>
> LOWTH'S ISAIAH, xl. 22.

"Thine, O Jehovah, is the greatness and the power, and the
glory, and the victory, and the majesty; for all that is in the
heaven and in the earth is thine. Thine is the kingdom, O Jehovah, and thou art exalted as head above all."—1 Chron. xxix. 11.

SECTION SEVENTH.

No proof of the Deity of Christ to be found in 1 *Tim.* iii. 16.
1 *John,* v. 20. *nor in John,* xx. 28. xiv. 9.

Another text which claims our attention as being deemed
by some, of great importance in this discussion, is to be found in
1 Tim. iii. 16.

"Without controversy great is the mystery of Godliness: God was manifest in the flesh, justified in the spirit, seen of angels, preached unto the
Gentiles, believed on in the world, received up into glory."

All Biblical critics know, or ought to know, that the word
God, Θεος, in the original, of this verse, is rejected by the most
eminent scholars as a corruption, and particularly by Griesbach,
who instead of Θεος reads ος, and alleges that the critical rules by
which he corrected the text required such a reading. "*Postula-
bant enim hoc leges criticæ * * * quas doctissimi critici suo
assensu comprobarunt.* Sir Isaac Newton, in the second of his
Letters to Le Clerc, affirms that all the churches, for the first
400 or 500 years, and the authors of all the ancient versions,
Jerome, as well as the rest, read "great is the mystery of godliness *which* was manifested in the flesh." He farther informs
us that Hincmarus, who lived above 800 years ago, states the
fact out of Liberatus, that Macedonius, Bishop of Constantinople,
was banished by the emperor Anastasius, for falsifying the text
of the gospels; *quoniam falsarit evangelia.* In the above text
he changed the Greek letter O into Θ, and thus the word which
before was ΟΣ *(he who)* became ΘΣ the abbreviation of ΘΕΟΣ
God. But the original text, Newton says, was not ΟΣ but Ο,
and "as the corruption lay in a letter, it was the more easily
spread abroad in the Greek MSS. than the testimony of the
three in heaven, in the Latin ones." He mentions a great number of the most distinguished advocates of Athanasianism, but
cannot find one who quotes this text, to prove his doctrine, "and
in all the times of the hot and lasting Arian controversy, it never
came into play." This statement is corroborated by Whiston,

who observes that " this text so agreeable to the Athanasian was yet so far from being taken in an Athanasian sense by the ancients, that as Dr. Mill himself, with great surprise, observes it was not once cited by the Athanasians against the Arians, til A. D. 380, by Gregory Nyssen. Nor is it certain that it was even in Nyssen's own book, much less that it was in St. Paul's text itself, as some of the most inquisitive persons do find upon examination."

Suppose we were for a moment to gratify the modern Athanasian, and admit, contrary to the most approved rules of criticism, and to universal testimony, that " God manifest in the flesh," is the true reading, what will he gain by the admission? Will he have the hardihood to affirm that it will favour his Doctrine of the Trinity? The Unitarian finds nothing in the expression but what he can receive in perfect consistency with his principles. He believes that God is every where "manifest." That the Spirit of God

> " Warms in the sun, refreshes in the breeze,
> Glows in the stars, and blossoms in the trees."

And, if a couplet may be added,

> Spake by the Prophets, by the Saviour taught,
> And warmed and brightened in the deeds he wrought.

God was "manifest in the flesh," when Jesus cast out devils by the finger of God; and well might the people who heard his heavenly discourses, and witnessed his miraculous deeds, say "a great Prophet hath risen up," and that by sending such a Prophet "God hath visited his people." But that "God assumed a real, corporeal, visible, and tangible, form, is a supposition to be paralleled only by some of the old incarnations of Jupiter. How can they who have read that God is a spirit, that he fills the heavens and the earth, and that the heaven and the heaven of heavens cannot contain him, believe that he was tabernacled in a pavilion of human clay—that the King of heaven who sitteth on the throne of his holiness, and all whose works are truth, was "justified in the spirit,"—that he who is clothed with honour and majesty, who hath prepared his throne in the heavens, and whose kingdom ruleth over all—was " received up into glory?" Shame on such carnal, impious imaginations!

With the former text may be classed another which suffers much from modern Athanasian persecution.

" We know that the Son of God is come, and hath given us an understanding, that we may know him that is true, and we are (в) in him that is true—ву by or through his Son Jesus Christ. This is the true God and eternal life."—1 John, v. 20.

" This is the true God." Who? He whom the Son of God hath given us an understanding that we may know. Nay, exclaims the Tritheist—it is the Son of God himself. For this refers to the immediate antecedent which is Jesus Christ.—And to whom does *this* refer in the following text ?—2 John, 7.

"Many deceivers are entered into the world, who confess not that Jesus Christ is come in the flesh. This is a deceiver and an anti-christ."

Who is a deceiver and an anti-christ? The tritheist, if he follows any consistent principle of interpretation should answer Jesus Christ, for he is the immediate antecedent. But any one though superficially acquainted with the Scriptures, must know that the pronoun and relative frequently refer not to the proximate, but the remote antecedent, as in the present instance. See also, John, vi. 50. 1 John, ii. 22. Acts. i. 22. We must be guided by sense and reason, not by mere rules of grammatical arrangement. It requires no aid from syntax to learn that by *him that is true*, we must understand the only living and true God. This, our Saviour himself renders perfectly plain, when he says, " This is life eternal, that they might know thee, the *only true God*, and Jesus Christ whom thou hast *sent*."—John, xvii. 3. The Apostle, most probably, had this sentiment in his remembrance, when he wrote the words on which we are commenting. They are in fact but an elliptical expression of the same thought. We maintain then, that the words *this is the true God and eternal life*, refer solely to God, the Father—who has revealed the life to come by our Lord Jesus Christ. The distinction between the Father and the Son is clearly marked in the verse itself; and it is paying a poor compliment to the judgment of an inspired Apostle, to suppose that he would say of Christ that he was the Son of God, and the true God, in the same sentence, and affirm that the one came to give us an understanding of the other, if both were identically one.

No Christian prior to the Council of Nice, appears to have understood this verse in the Trinitarian sense. The Father Almighty alone was universally acknowledged to be the true God. Whiston says,

" The Athanasians shew no citation or interpretation of it in their sense, before the days of Athanasius. Nay, somewhat after his days, his great admirer Ephiphanius, who was incomparably a more honest and learned Athanasian, than he whom he admired, evidently appears to have been an entire stranger to that exposition : having plainly let us know that he had never heard of any text whatsoever that called the Son the true God ; though for want of such a text, like a thorough Athanasian, he pretends to prove he might be so called, by *consequence of his own making*."

The Athanasians find a similar proof of the Deity of Christ in John, xx. 28.

" And Thomas answered and said unto him, my Lord and my God."

Thomas was a Jew—a believer in the one invisible and immortal God—a disciple of Christ—incredulous—a sceptic who required no less than ocular and palpable proof that the body of Christ had become re-animated and arisen from the dead. Our Lord condescended to give him the proof required, on which

occasion he uttered the words just quoted. Now, what do we
learn from them? The Athanasians would have us believe that
this incredulous Apostle who would not credit the testimony of
his fellow disciples as to a plain matter of fact, passed in a moment to the belief, of which he had not the least previous hint
or conception, that in the crucified Jesus, whose flesh he handled,
and whose wounds he felt, he saw, touched and addressed the
infinite and incomprehensible Jehovah, whom he had been taught
to think no man could see and live! That he whom he had so
lately beheld nailed to a cross, and mortally wounded by a Roman spear—was Jehovah of hosts—the Lord God of Israel, who
liveth and reigneth for ever and ever! Verily, the credulity of
the Athanasians exceeds, the incredulity of Thomas! But the
Saviour's address to his disciple sufficiently proves the gross folly
and absurdity of such imaginations. "Jesus said unto Thomas,
because thou hast seen me, thou hast believed." Believed what?
That of which he had previously doubted,—Christ's resurrection.
Our Lord continues, "blessed, or happy, (μακαριοι) are they who
have not seen, and yet have believed."—Not seen and yet believed what? Not seen Christ personally, as Thomas had seen
him—and yet believed that he was actually risen. There is not
the slightest ground for any of the Athanasian whims in the whole
passage. Thomas, under the influence of excited and wonder-
struck feeling, gave way to his emotion, as was perfectly natural,
by apostrophizing God. All men under such impressions, express themselves in language precisely similar. Thus, when
Gideon saw that one with whom he had been conversing was an
angel of Jehovah—he said, "Alas, O Lord Jehovah! for because
I have seen an angel of Jehovah, face to face."—Judg. vi. 22.
Thus, Jonathan in the ardour of his friendship, "said unto
David, O Jehovah God of Israel, when I have sounded my
Father, &c."—1 Sam. xx. 12. Had Thomas been capable of
embodying all his feelings in words, he might have uttered some
ejaculations like these, in addition to "my Lord and my God."
It is then true! I doubt no longer! Here is proof! I yield
to conviction! O my God, how great is thy power, how wonderful thy deeds! Now, I see, now I believe that thou hast indeed raised from the dead, thy holy child Jesus! That our
Saviour understood him thus is evident from his address to the
disciple.—Milton refers the words my Lord to Christ, and my
God to the Father, who had testified that Christ was his Son, by
raising him from the dead. The whole comment of this great
genius on the passage before us, is well entitled to the readers serious consideration. He regards the words of Thomas as an
abrupt exclamation in an exstacy of wonder, and deems it incredible—

"That he should have so quickly understood the hypostatic union of that
person whose resurrection he had just before disbelieved. Accordingly
the faith of Peter is commended—blessed art thou, Simon—for having only
said—thou art the Son of the Living God,—Matt. xvi. 16, 17. The faith of

Thomas, although, as it is commonly explained, it asserts the divinity of Christ in a much more remarkable manner, is so far from being praised, that it is undervalued, and almost reproved.—*Thomas, because thou hast seen me, thou hast believed: blessed are they that have not seen, and yet have believed.* And yet, though the slowness of his belief may have deserved blame, the testimony borne by him to Christ as God, which if the common interpretation be received as true, is clearer than occurs in any other passage, would undoubtedly have met with some commendation; whereas it obtains none whatever."

Our Saviour's declaration to Philip is also frequently advanced by advocates of the Trinity, as a strong proof of their doctrine. But like all their other texts, when weighed in the balance of fair criticism, it will be found wanting. Let us try. Our Lord said unto Thomas,

"I am the way, the truth, and the life; no man cometh unto the Father but by me. If ye had known me, ye should have known my Father also; and from henceforth ye know him and have seen him. Philip saith unto him, Lord, shew us the Father and it sufficeth us. Jesus saith unto him, have I been so long time with you, and yet hast thou not known me Philip? He that hath seen me hath seen the Father; and how sayest thou then, shew us the Father?"—John, xiv. 6, 9.

There are only two ways of understanding these words, literally or figuratively. If we take them literally, they will prove too much, like many other texts, viz. that Christ is the Father—and the Father of himself! Moreover, they will deny that Jehovah is the *invisible* king, "whom no man hath seen, nor can see," as he is denominated in 1 Tim. i. 17. vi. 16. and contradict the indisputable truth, "that no man hath seen God at any time." They are to be understood then figuratively, and the meaning is this: Had ye known me, or formed a right judgment of those divine virtues which have been so conspicuous in my words and actions, ye would have acquired a just knowledge of the perfections of God; but from henceforth ye both know him, because I have more fully revealed him; and have seen him, because I have presented his character more closely to your contemplation. Philip, not apprehending his true meaning, said, "shew us the Father and it sufficeth us," our Lord's interrogatory reply conveys some rebuke to Philip's hebetude in misconceiving him so grossly, and in making so extravagant a request. "Have I been so long time with you, and yet hast thou not known me, Philip?—He that hath seen me, hath seen the Father." His language now becoming so much more palpably figurative, that even Philip, it is presumed, could not mistake him as intending to convey the idea that he who saw Christ, saw as close a similitude of God as can be presented to the mind of man; even the "express image" of the invisible Jehovah. And to prevent all farther possibility of misconception, he adds, "Believest thou not that I am in the Father and the Father in me," in the same sense as John, when he says, "he that dwelleth in love, dwelleth in God, and God in him." "The words that I speak unto you, I SPEAK NOT OF MYSELF, but the Father

66

SECTION NINTH.

No proof in Scripture that Christ is eternal and self-existent.

They who maintain what they call the Supreme Deity of
Christ, miserably torture and misapply Scripture to support their
hypothesis. But in vain do they labour to shew that he was
possessed of any single attribute which properly belongs, in the
highest sense, to Jehovah. The first proof of this position shall
be taken from their attempts to prove him eternal and self-
existent, by a passage in the first chapter of the Hebrews.
The object of the author, in this chapter, being to exalt Christ
above all the preceding prophets and inspired messengers of
God, he asks unto which of them did God at any time, say,
" Thou art my Son, this day have I begotten thee? *And again,*
I will be to him a Father and he shall be to me a Son? *And*
again, when he bringeth in the first-begotten into the world, he
saith, and let all the angels (or inspired messengers) of God
worship him, (or do him homage.) And of the angels, (or messengers) be (or rather the Scripture) saith, who maketh his angels
spirits (winds,) and his ministers a flame of fire. *But unto the*
Son he saith, thy throne, O God, is (or God is thy throne)
for ever and ever : a sceptre of righteousness is the sceptre of
thy kingdom." Thus are intimated the stability and equity of the
Messiah's reign. The next verse assigns the reason of Christ's
exaltation, and of his favour with the Father. *Thou hast loved*
righteousness and hated iniquity ; therefore God, even THY GOD,
hath anointed thee with the oil of gladness above thy fellows.
Here ends the supposed address of the Father to the Son.—
The author of the Epistle then bursts into an apostrophe to Jehovah, borrowed from the 102d Psalm. *" And thou, Lord, in*
the beginning, hast laid the foundation of the earth, and the
heavens are the works of thine hands : they shall perish ; but
thou remainest ; and they all shall wax old as doth a garment ;
and as a vesture shalt thou fold them up, and they shall be
changed : but thou art the same, and thy years shall not fail."
These words, Trinitarian writers inform us, are applied to Christ,
but by whom, except by themselves, is not very apparent. If
they are to be considered as a continuation of the Father's
address to the Son, then does one eternal being tell another
eternal being, the palpable truism that his years shall not fail!
Reason and common sense cannot discover any meaning or object in this ; to say nothing of the unscriptural idea involved in
such a supposition, that instead of the Eternal *One,* there are
Eternal *Two.* We conclude then that the passage is not a continuance of the Father's address to the Son, but an apostrophe
of the writer to the Father. The connexion of the ideas, indeed,
is by no means perspicuous. The style is very elliptical, often

ing to Josephus, said of him while yet a child, "that he was (μορφη θυος) in form, divine," an expression precisely similar to that of the Apostle, who says that Christ was in the form of God, how would such expressions have been tortured to prove the identity of the Son with the Father!

It is written of man himself that he is formed in the image of God. But this is only a figurative mode of speaking; for even a heathen philosopher knew the nature of God too well to suppose that he could be represented by any object of sense, and that man bears a closer similitude to the Deity in his virtues than in his form.* Such was the purity—the holiness—the boundless benevolence of the Saviour's character, independently of his miraculous powers; that he might well be said to be not only the image, but the express image of him whose love fills the universe.

SECTION EIGHTH.

The beginning of John's Gospel contains no proof of the Deity of Christ.

The Evangelist, John, informs us distinctly with what view he wrote his gospel, when he says, " These are written that ye might believe that Jesus is the Christ, the Son of God; and that believing, ye might have life through his name."—John xx. 31. Assuredly none of the evangelical writers, gives us such numerous proofs of the supremacy of the Father. Notwithstanding, the beginning of his gospel has been deemed favourable to the Trinitarian scheme. Others find in it nothing that cannot be much better explained on Unitarian principles. It informs us that "*in the beginning was the word.*" The *word*, in the opinion of Lardner, Priestley, Lindsey, Fox, and other distinguished Unitarian authors, is but another name for that reason, intelligence, or wisdom, which is an essential attribute of the Deity. They allege that it is spoken of in such a manner by the Evangelist, as fully to justify them in affirming that he imitates that well-known passage of the Book of Proverbs, in which Wisdom is so beautifully personified. "The Lord possessed me in the *beginning* of his way, before his works of old. I was set up from everlasting, *from the beginning*, or ever the earth was. I was *by him*, as one brought up with him."—Prov. viii. 22, 23, 30. Thus John affirms that the divine principle which he calls *logos*, existed from the beginning—that it dwelt with God—nay, that it was virtually God himself—for that all the works of creation, and all the operations of his providence were made and con-

* Cicero de Natura Deorum.

ducted by its agency and influence. All things were made *εσνο*
by *it*—not by him: for as Dr. Campbell, who was a Trinitarian,
observes, "it is much more agreeable to the figurative style here
employed to speak of *the word*, though really denoting a person,
as a thing, agreeably to the grammatical idiom, till a direct intimation is made of its personality:—The way of rendering here
adopted is agreeable to the practise of all translators except
the English." But the Bishop's Bible—the Bible vulgarly known
by the name of the *Breeches Bible*—the black letter translation
with the paraphrase of Erasmus, and all other versions which
preceded the common one, as far as Dr. Campbell was able to
discover, uniformly employed the neuter pronoun. In French
and Italian, the pronoun is feminine—in the Vulgate and in the
German, neuter; corresponding respectively with the gender of
the noun signifying *word*. "*In it was life, and the life was the
light of men*." Thus Wisdom says, in Proverbs, *he that findeth
me, findeth life*. The divine intelligence imparted life to mankind, and gave them a light from heaven to guide them to immortality—*and the light shineth in darkness, and the darkness
comprehended it not*. (*ου κατιλαΐιν hath not overtaken it.*) It
beams brightly on mankind to dispel their ignorance and lead
them to happiness and to God.

"*And the word was made (νγινττο was,) flesh*." What is meant
by this? If we cannot give a rational interpretation, let us
abandon it as unintelligible or beyond our comprehension. But
let us not apply to it, the crude heathen invention that the
infinite Jehovah became incarnate. The Evangelist no where
gives us ground for such an idea, or if he does, it is where he
says, "if we love one another, *God dwelleth in* us."—1 John,
iv. 12. This is just as strong a text in proof that God becomes
incarnate in every pious man, as any, in all revelation, that he
was incarnate in the person of our Lord. He does not say that
Jehovah the Father Almighty, the Eternal Spirit, became flesh.
This would be a species of transubstantiation as difficult as it
would be horrible to imagine. But he says, *the word was flesh*;
which is a brief figurative mode of saying that the divine wisdom was manifest in a human being—it appeared in the character, the discourses, and the ministry of our Lord Jesus Christ,
insomuch that he is justly denominated *the wisdom of God*—
as he is also called *the power of God* on account of the miracles
which he wrought—for, says the Apostle Paul, he "of God, is
made unto us *wisdom*, and righteousness, and sanctification,

* "The word κατιλαμΐανω is often used of the day and night and their
vicissitudes. Of this application of it there are many examples in Wetstein's
note upon the place; an example of it occurs in John xii. 35, and in
1 Thes. v. 4.—There is not a more common hebraism than to express the
same thing both positively and negatively. There are several examples in
this very chapter."—See Cappe's Critical Remarks.

58

and redemption."—1 Cor. i. 24, 30. *And dwelt* (ισκηνωσι tabernacled) *among us, full of grace and truth.* Here is a plain allusion to the *Shekinah*, or visible glory by which Jehovah manifested his presence in the temple and tabernacle of the Jews. If by that appearance God was represented as dwelling among them, much more might the divine wisdom be said to dwell among us in the person of Jesus Christ, by whom it spoke, and promulgated the oracles of salvation. *And we beheld his glory, the glory as of the only-begotten of the Father.* We saw him invested with such wisdom, and power—heard him uttering such gracious and important truths—and witnessed him performing such miraculous deeds of mercy, as convinced us that he was the well-beloved Son of God, the promised Messiah.

It is objected that the λογος of John is not the same as the σοφια of Solomon. But wherefore might not John choose to render the Hebrew of wisdom, *Cachema*, by λογος as well as the Seventy by σοφια? Calmet's Dictionary, on the article " word," says, the Memra, *(i. e. the logos)* answers to the *Cachema*, or Wisdom of Solomon; and Dr. Campbell observes that " there is such a coincidence in the things attributed to each, as evidently shews that both were intended to indicate the same divine personage—*(attribute)* and that plausible arguments might be urged for rendering λογος, in this passage, *reason.*" In the words quoted from Paul, we have seen that Christ is denominated *the wisdom of God,* Θεου σοφιαν.—Λογι; is a word of similar meaning with σοφια, and signifies reason, understanding, intelligence: λογοι sunt *præcepta sapientiæ ac prudentiæ.*—Schleusner. In Acts, xviii. 14. it is translated *reason,* and it is elsewhere found in a great variety of significations, as doctrine, message, command, divine communication, reckoning, *teacher.* The lexicographer just quoted, gives *doctor* as one of its meanings, *abstracto posito pro concreto, ex usu loquendi Hebræorum.* τις ὁ λογος ουτος, *qualis est hic doctor?*—Luke, iv. 36. In our translation, *what a word is this!* He thinks this mode of interpretation may be applied to John, i. 1. 14.

The sacred writers speak repeatedly of the Word of God as of other attributes, and describe it as the great agent of the Almighty to create and destroy—to instruct, exhort, and prohibit. It is thus sublimely personified in the Wisdom of Solomon, xviii. 15, 16. "Thine Almighty Word leaped down from heaven out of thy royal throne, as a fierce man of war into the midst of a land of destruction, and brought thy unfeigned commandment as a sharp sword, and standing up filled all things with death; and it touched the heaven, but it stood upon the earth." Similar agencies being ascribed to the Word, as to the Wisdom of God, is it surprising that they should be considered as synonimous? Our Saviour himself appears to use the expression *Wisdom of God,* (Luke, xi. 49.) as tantamount to the *Word of God.* Shall we hence assert the distinct personal existence of

Wisdom, and invest her with the attributes of the Eternal? A ___
apocryphal writer would correct such folly by telling us, th___ at
"God *created* her, and saw her, and numbered and poured he___
out upon the earth." If we would not make Wisdom a godde___
to be adored, neither should we deify the Word, and seat ___ it
on the throne of heaven. We must not confound qualities wit___
substance—attributes with person—nor the herald with his kin___
"The spirit of Jehovah spake by me" says David, "and hi___
word was upon my tongue." Should any one hence infer tha___
David was Jehovah? The spirit of Jehovah spake more fully b___
Christ, and the word was so richly and copiously on his tongue___
that he is called, κατ' ἐξοχην, *The Word.* Does it therefore___
follow, that Christ is Jehovah? This conclusion is not a title___
more valid in the one case than in the other.

That the character of *the word,* belongs to Christ not as ___
God but as man, is sufficiently plain from the declaration *the* ___
word was flesh—and also from the commencement of John's
first epistle, where he speaks of *the word of life* which he
had *seen, heard, looked upon, handled with his hands.* But
he tells us in the 4th c. 12 v. that *no man hath seen God at
any time.* Whence it is clear that he had not the most remote idea that in speaking of the word, he was speaking of
the Deity. Christ, therefore, is denominated *the word,* because
he spoke the oracles of God; and *the word of life,* because he
taught the doctrine of immortality—and Θεος, *Elohim, a God,*
or God, in a subordinate sense—for if those to whom the word,
the wisdom, or the counsel of God, was but partially communicated, bore that title; much more should it be borne by him
to whom the Spirit of God was imparted without measure.—
Erasmus, in his paraphrase, says well—

" As holy Scripture calleth God that moste excellente minde, which minde
is bothe greater and better then all thinges that can bee imagined : even so
it calleth his onely Sonne, the woorde of that minde. For although the
Sonne be not the same that the Father is, yet he is so very like the Father,
that a man may see the one in the other. * * He is called the worde bee-
cause God, which in his own proper nature can no wales be comprehended,
woulde be knowen to us by him."

The *Fratres Poloni,* Polonian Brethren, and some English
Unitarian writers, of whom Simpson, who has written so learnedly on the language of Scripture, may be esteemed one of the
most eminent, consider the *Logos,* not as an attribute of God,
but an appellation of the man Christ Jesus; and explain the
first verses of John's Gospel as descriptive of the *new moral*
creation of which Christ was the divine instrument—beautifully
and consistently—whether in exact conformity with the Evangelist's meaning, the reader, if he can, may determine for
himself. They understand the words *in the beginning* as speaking of the commencement of the public life of Jesus, and support their opinion by numerous parallel texts, in which the same

55

words, unquestionably, refer not to the origin of the world, but to the first promulgation of the gospel—and it can be proved by innumerable instances, that the substantive verb ειμι, both in the present and past tenses, must signify to *represent*. "Thus when Christ says, this bread εστι *is* my body—this cup, εστι *is* my blood; and when Paul says, Gal. iv. 25, this Agar εστι *is* Mount Sinai in Arabia; and v. 26, the Jerusalem from above εστιν *is* Sarah; εστι in all these places, means *represents*.—Θεος ην ὁ λογος must signify that *the word* was only a representative of God, or spake and acted in his name, and by his authority; whether the term Θεος be understood of the true God, or of one commissioned and empowered by him.—If it be maintained that the Apostle John's assertion Θεος ην ὁ λογος proves the Word or Jesus Christ to be truly God, the affirmation of the Apostle Paul, 1 Cor. x. 4, ἡ δε πετρα ην ὁ Χριστος, *that rock was Christ*, equally proves him to be an inanimate rock; and the assertion of Christ αυτος εστιν Ηλιας *this is Elias*, proves John the Baptist to be really Elias."

Whatever views Unitarian writers take of this subject, they have the merit at least of being intelligible. Not so our Athanasian friends. The instant they approach the first verses of John, they plunge headlong into an abyss of absurdities. They at once ascribe personality and Supreme Deity to the word, and thence it follows, that we must understand the Evangelist thus, *In the beginning was the word*, which word was the Supreme Deity; *and the Word*, that is the Supreme Deity, *was with God*— that is with the Supreme Deity. *And the Word was God*, that is the Supreme Deity was the Supreme Deity! What man of common sense can suppose that the Apostle wrote to be understood thus? If the Word was a person and that person God, he must be God in a different sense from that God with whom he was, or else he was God in the same sense, a coequal and associate. This seems to be admitted and maintained, for we are told that one of them is God the Son, and the other God the Father—and each of them is God Supreme! Whence, it indubitably follows, that we have two Gods Supreme, (where is the third?) contrary to the whole tenor of Scripture, which teaches that we have but one. Moreover, to affirm that one God was *with* another God, is to contradict the positive declaration of Jehovah himself that *with* him there is no God. "*I*, even *I*, am ΠΕ, and there is no God *with* me.—Deut. xxxii. 39. The Lord he is God; there is none else *besides* him."—iv. 35. "Thus saith Jehovah—I am the first, and I am the last; and besides me there is no God; *I* know not *any*."—Isaiah, xliv. 6, 8.

abstruse; nor is it easy to trace in it an uninterrupted current of thought. Notwithstanding, some circumstances lead us very decidedly to affirm that the verses in question, are addressed here by the author, as they were originally by David, to Jehovah. Their object in the Psalm from which they are borrowed, was to confirm the truth, "*that the children of thy servants shall continue, and their seed shall be established before thee.*" With a similar view are they cited here, to prove from the permanence and immutability of the eternal ONE, the durable nature of the spiritual kingdom which he established by the agency of the Son. What Hebrew, and the Epistle is to Hebrews, could possibly suppose them applicable to any one but his own Jehovah, the Father everlasting, who, in the beginning, created the heavens and the earth—"who stretcheth forth the heavens *alone*, that spreadeth abroad the earth by *himself?*—Is. xliv. 24. Emlyn observes that this, though a new citation, is not prefaced with *but unto the Son he saith*, as v. 8, or with *and again*, as v. 5, 6, and ii. 13, but barely, *And thou Lord.* Now the God last mentioned was Christ's God who had anointed him; and the *author* thereupon, addressing himself to this God, breaks out into the celebration of his *power*, and especially of his *unchangeable duration*." The same learned divine proceeds to shew "that no one ancient writer ever applied the words to Christ, during the three first centuries; and Dr. Waterland does not pretend that they were ever so applied till the fourth or fifth." The verses which precede the passage in question show, as clearly as language can well express, the inferiority and subordination of Christ. They tell us that God hath spoken by him, and of course he is God's agent or minister. whom he hath *appointed* heir of all things—by whom he hath made the Æons, or Ages,* not the worlds composing the material system, as some erroneously imagine, but that particular dispensation of which Christ was the author; a truth of some im-

---

* Heb. i. 2—"*By whom also he made the worlds*," This translation may mislead the English reader, not only into a belief that Christ was the instrument by which the Creator formed this earth, but also a plurality of worlds; where the word Αιωνα; has been clearly shown not to refer to the material system at all, but to that particular dispensation of which Christ was the author. Wakefield and Doddridge render the term *ages*, and the Latin Vulgate, and the Latin rendering of the Syriac and Arabic, is " *sæcula.*"

"Αιων in the New Testament, whether in the singular or plural, always denotes some portion of time. The plural number is often used by the Hebrews for the singular superlative; and in the epistle to the Hebrews it is often used to express the superior excellence of many particulars relative to the Christian covenant. In four chapters of this epistle the Greek plural is rendered *nine* times in the singular in the English version. Αιωνας in Heb. i. 2, should also be rendered in the singular, viz. *the age*, by way of eminence and distinction, meaning the age of the Messiah." See this subject fully and most satisfactorily illustrated by Simpson, in his Essays on the Language of Scripture.

portance for us to understand. Even the address of the Father to the Son, in the 8th and 9th verses, demonstrates the superiority of the former. This address is borrowed from the xlv Psalm, and was originally a part of Solomon's Epithalamium, on his marriage with Pharaoh's daughter; and a small portion of this " Song of Loves,"* as it is characteristically entitled, is, in this chapter of the Hebrews, very properly *accommodated* to Christ, who, as well as Solomon, was a son, or descendant, of David. If the words were applicable to Solomon, much more were they applicable to Christ, for " behold a greater than Solomon is here!" Dr. Young,† a scholar and divine, not less distinguished by profound erudition than by elegance of taste, renders the words in the Psalm, " thy throne, O PRINCE;"‡ and this translation, assuredly, conveys the meaning of the original much more truly than our common English version.

However just and appropriate the application of these verses to Christ, they can have none to the Eternal and Almighty ONE. HE has no God—he cannot be appointed to any office;—appointment implies a greater and a less; he cannot be made the agent of any other—he cannot be anointed—and he can have no fellows.

Trinitarians find a proof of CHRIST'S SELF-EXISTENCE in his declaration to the Jews, John viii. 58, *before Abraham was, I am.* This expression, when properly understood, will be found incapable of affording even the shadow of an argument in favour of that doctrine. What is meant by " the lamb slain from the foundation of the world?" Rev. xiii. 8. What does the Apostle teach when he says, " God hath chosen us *before* the foundation of the world?" Eph. i. 4. And again, he affirms of God, that he " hath saved us and called us, with an holy calling, not according to our works, but according to his own purpose and grace, which was given us in Christ Jesus before the world began." 2 Tim. i. 9.

---

* With what propriety it is called a *song of loves* שיר ידידת let the reader determine after he has contemplated its rich and glowing imagery—the bridegroom clad in his royal panoply, and the bride in her robes of wrought gold and needle-work, exhaling perfumes of myrrh, aloes, and cassia—the palace of ivory, and the bridal train of virgins. This Psalm is applied, like Solomon's song, by mystic divines, to the mystic union of Christ and his church. " The bridegroom," says Horsley, " is the conquering Messiah, the bride, the church catholic, or, perhaps, the church of the converted Jews, become the metropolitical church of all Christendom, and the virgin's companions are the other churches!" How erudite and instructive the lucubrations of mystic theology!

† From being a Fellow of Trinity College, Dublin, he was promoted to the bishopric of Clonfert but unfortunately for the cause of Biblical learning, did not long live to enjoy his episcopal honours.

‡ The original word is *elohim*, commonly translated God. It is a striking instance of the application of the term to men of rank and distinction. As it is rendered God, in Heb. i. 8, it also happily exemplifies the subordinate sense in which the word *God* is sometimes to be understood.

How, it may be asked, could the lamb be slain before the creation, or we be chosen, called, and saved, and have grace imparted to us, before we came into existence? An orthodox writer, Dwight, shall answer. "Every being and every event which has been, or will be, with all their qualities and operations, *existed in his* (God's) *mind;* or in the beautiful language of David, were written in his book, and what day they should be fashioned, when as yet there was none of them." Yes, the inspired writers too, speak of that which in past ages was ordained to be, as having actually occurred; because its occurrence being determined by the immutable counsels of God, was as certain as if it had already come to pass. To a prophet under the influence of inspiration, what has been, and what shall be, *is.* To his gifted vision, those scenes which lie far behind, or far forward in the pilgrimage of time, seem to be brought nearer. The cloud brooding over them is, for a moment, dispersed. He contemplates them amidst a coruscation of celestial light, and he describes them not as the images of the past or future, but as the realities of the present.

Even in ordinary discourse, future events, deemed certain, are spoken of as already present. Jonathan said to David, "to-morrow *is*, (will be) the new moon." 1 Sam. xx. 18. Thus our Lord says, "Ye know that after two days *is* (will be) the passover, and the Son of Man *is* (will be) betrayed." Mat. xxvi. 2. "*Ye have been* (ητε, literally, *ye are*) with me, from the beginning." John xv. 27. Past events are also spoken of as present, particularly by poets, historians, and all descriptive writers, and animated speakers. Thus, Stephen, speaking of the miracles wrought by Moses in achieving Israel's redemption from the bondage of Egypt, says, "This *is* that Moses." Acts vii. 37. Thus our Lord says, "Elias, indeed, doth first come," or is coming; for in the original, the present tense is used, and not the future, as in the common version, (Mat. xvii. 11;) whereas Elias, or John the Baptist, of whom the disciples understood that he spake, had long since arrived. Wakefield says, that "the peculiar use of the present tense, in the usage of Scriptural expressions, is to imply determination and certainty:" and therefore our Lord says, *I am**

---

* Id est *eram*, præsens pro imperfecto, *Eram*, Syrus: εγω πιλον [ego eram] Nonnus. Sic in Græco Psalm, xc. 2. Πρω τα ορη γεννηθηναι ου η, [Antequam fierent montes tu es] Fuerat ante Abrahamum Jesus divina constitutione, infra, xvii. 5. Apocal. xiii. 8—1 Petr. L. 20, Constat hoc, quia de ipso ipsiusque Ecclesia mystice dictum erat, recente humano genere, futurum *ut semen muliebre contereret caput serpentis*, ut exponitur, Rom. xvi. 20. Unde simul intelligitur huncce hominem Iesum majorem esse Abrahamo; quod ipse innuere quam prædicare mavult. Grot in loc.

"The reference which ειμι has to the conjunction πρω in John viii. 58, clearly shows, that the verb, though in the present tense, should be interpreted of the past, in which sense it frequently occurs."—SIMPSON.

instead of *I was*, to intimate that his mission was certain and determined before the birth of Abraham. In the preceding verses, he says, not that he saw Abraham, but that Abraham saw (i. e. foresaw) his day; for it had been declared to the Patriarch, that in his seed should all the nations of the earth be blessed, and "he died in faith, not having received the promises, but having *seen* them afar off."—Heb. xi. 13.

These words "I AM," afford a striking instance, out of hundreds, how Trinitarians are led by sound and not by sense. They affirm, but without even a shadow of authority, that when our Saviour uses them in the foregoing passage, he employs the words used by the Almighty himself, Exod. iii. 14. where he asserts his self-existence: "I AM THAT I AM." Our Saviour made no allusion to those words whatsoever, nor are either the Greek or the English words a translation from the Hebrew.* The Hebrew should be rendered thus, "THE BEING WHO IS BEING;" in Greek, but not very correctly, εγω ειμι ὁ ων, I am the *existing* or *he who exists*. In John, the words are εγω ειμι I am.—They form the termination of a sentence, and do not, like the Hebrew, stand either as an unconnected absolute declaration of self-existence, nor as the agent of any verb. Some word must be understood to complete the sense; and that is Christ, or the pronoun HE, *viz:* I am, or I was, *he*, or *the Christ*. This is sense;—but an absolute assertion of self-existence including all time, would not accord well with the words, "before Abraham;" nor form a very pertinent answer to the question of the Jews; "Thou art not yet fifty years old, and hast thou seen Abraham?" The Apostle Peter leads us to the true meaning of the expression, when he affirms that Christ "was *fore-ordained*, before the foundation of the world, but was manifest in these last times."—1 Pet. i. 20.—The words εγω ειμι *I am*, are by no means of such rare occurrence that there should be any argument about them. We find them in the 24th verse of the very same chapter, "Unless ye believe that *I am*, ye shall die in your sins." That I am what? is naturally enquired, and the translators have given the answer, by the insertion of the word *he*, viz: the Messiah. This is clear as demonstration itself. So also, in his conversation with the woman of Samaria, our Saviour uses the same elliptical expression,

* *Ehjeh ascher ehjeh*—rendered by Geddes, "I will be what I will be," as well, perhaps, "*I will be what I am*," a form of words expressive of the eternal existence and unalterable nature of Jehovah. The LXX do not represent the phrase amiss by *I am the Existing*, or *he who exists*; that is, *Jehovah, the living God*. And afterwards they have not *I am*, but *the Existing* hath sent me. To make, therefore, the *I am* of the Evangelist a reference to the passage of the Pentateuch, is a most idle fancy, unsupported by the original, and what is more to the purpose, by the Septuagint, the text book of the Gospel writers."—WAKEFIELD.

I am: he, is supplied by the translators.—John, iv. 26. When it was doubted whether the man born blind was he who sat and begged; he said *I am?* What? *he* is supplied here also, as it ought to have been in the verse under consideration—John, ix. 9.

Suppose the words *I am* to mean Jehovah, the verse would be totally destitute of meaning, as will appear evidently by substituting the one for the other. *Before Abraham was— Jehovah.* Here, there is no connecting link between the former and the latter clause;—no copula, as logicians term it, between the subject and the predicate. A grammarian would say, that they formed no sentence, for they express no thought. The word *Jehovah* stands completely insulated, and has no manner of connection with any thing either preceding or coming after it. The Trinitarian reader in order to make sense of the words *I am*, must impose on his own understanding, by affixing two meanings to them. He reads them as if they were *I am that I am*, the former *I am* signifying *I exist;* the latter as the name of the self-existent One; and thus he contrives to extort a meaning from them which they will not bear, and which they were never intended to express.

When the eternity of Jehovah is spoken of in the Scriptures, it is not in dark and ambiguous terms. Our knowledge of it is not conveyed by a couple of monosyllables the meaning of which may be disputed. They assert, in language most intelligible and distinct, " that Jehovah is the high and lofty ONE that inhabiteth eternity."—Is. lvii. 15. " He is the living God, and an everlasting King."—Jer. x. 10. " Before the mountains were brought forth, or ever thou hadst formed the earth and the world, even from everlasting to everlasting thou art God."—Ps. xc. 2.

On the text, " Jesus Christ, the same yesterday, to-day, and for ever," Trinitarians found their doctrine of Christ's IMMUTABILITY, though it is not intended to teach us any thing about either his person or his nature, as is evident from the context. It is found amidst a series of moral instructions, and forms part of an exhortation to be stedfast in the faith· " Remember them, (says the Apostle, Heb. xiii. 7, 8, 9,) that have the rule over you, and have spoken unto you the word of God, whose faith follow, considering the end of their conversation *with what constancy and perseverance they continued in the faith, and sealed it with their blood, in hopes of that crown of glory Christ had promised to them that were faithful to death, even that Jesus Christ, who, both as to his doctrines and his promises,* is the same yesterday, to-day, and for ever. Be not carried about with divers and strange doctrines." The lines in Italics are Whitby's, written by him before his last thoughts had shaken his orthodoxy; we hope, therefore, they will escape the common accusation of being a Socinian gloss. But lest they should not, we shall defend our interpretation by the authority of the redoubtable Calvin;

" Apparet *non de æterna Christi essentia* apostolum disputare, sed de ejus notitia, quæ omnibus seculis viguit inter pios, ac perpetuum ecclesiæ fundamentum fuit—ideo dico ad qualitatem, ut ita loquar, referri hunc sermonem *non ad essentiam.*"

Dr. Samuel Clarke also observes, " that this is here spoken, not of the *Person*, but of the *Law* of Christ, appears from the words immediately following, with which it is connected." The same learned writer says, that

" God, in respect of his essence, is absolutely unchangeable, because his being is necessary, and his essence self-existent; for whatever *necessarily is*, cannot but *be*, so it cannot but *continue* to be *invariably what it is.* That which depends *upon* nothing can be affected *by* nothing, can be *acted upon* by nothing, can be *changed* by *nothing*, can be *influenced* by no *power*, can be *impaired* by no *time*, can be *varied* by no *accident.*"

All this inevitably follows from God's being the great I AM, the self-existent ONE. But how can any such assertions be made of him *who had a Father?* and who by the very admission that he had, is declared not to be self-existent—of him who was obedient—who came not to do his own will—who declared of himself that he spoke, acted, *lived* by the Father? Where is he denominated the immortal King—the incorruptible, impassible God?—or introduced in holy writ, like him who is,—asserting his immutability, and declaring, " I am Jehovah, I change not?" Overboard! then, with an invention, as unphilosophical as it is unscriptural, that would synchronize a son with his father, and transfer to the creature the incommunicable attributes of the Creator.

SECTION TENTH.

No proof in Scripture that Christ possessed the Divine attribute of Omnipresence or Omniscience.

That the infinite, self-existent Jehovah, whose presence fills the boundless universe, became incarnate in the person of a man, and lived upwards of thirty years in the condition of an humble Galilæan, till he allowed himself to be crucified as a malefactor, and ascended into heaven in the same corporeal form in which as a man, he, the ever-blessed, ever-living God, had suffered and expired—this is, indeed, a doctrine so tremendously stupendous, that we are at some loss to conceive by what omnipotent force of evidence its credibility could be established. With more facility could we imagine the whole unfathomable ocean to be contained in a lady's thimble, or all the orbs which compose the solar system revolving in the tiny sphere of a nut-shell— Did revelation propose for our adoption, any doctrine so marvellous, we should naturally expect with it some proof, or positive assertion, at least, of its truth, especially as it teaches us, at

considerable length, and with great variety of proofs and illustrations, doctrines much less difficult of credence. But it
would seem that the belief of our Athanasian worthies, is always in the inverse ratio of the evidence; and when a doctrine
becomes altogether absurd and impossible, to adopt and believe
it, is the most sublime exercise of their faith!

What is the proof that Christ was *Omnipresent?* As usual,
we discover that it is *inferred.* And from what? From a
text and a half of Matthew! viz.

"Where two or three are gathered together *in my name,* there am I in the
midst of them." xviii. 20.

"And, lo, I am with you alway, even unto the end of the world."
xxviii. 20.

To understand these texts literally involves one of two great
errors, either that Christ did not ascend to heaven, but still
remains on earth; or that he descends from heaven really and
corporally, whenever two or three are gathered together in his
name. Moreover, it contains a virtual denial, that in heaven his
dwelling-place, he presides over his church and people, with
such power and efficacy as take away the necessity of personal
manifestations, and gives up one of the strongest arguments
against the *real presence* of Christ in the Eucharist, a concession for which the infallible church would, no doubt, be
grateful.

Orthodox commentators on the former text, give an emphatic sense to *Am I,* and affirm that it refers to Christ's divine
presence at all times and in all places. A short time ago, they
referred "*I Am,*" to his self-existence, and we shall not be
surprised if we find them referring it again to any of the
other attributes. When we object that it would be superfluous for Christ to say, that he would be present with "two
or three," if by the very necessity of his nature, he must be
present at all times, and on all occasions, not with his disciples
only, but with Jews and Gentiles; we are told, in contradiction
to the preceding orthodox statement, that the words refer, not
to his general, but his *special* presence, the particular object of
which is to intercede for them to the Father!

But, in fact, our Lord makes no claim to personal or essential
ubiquity. Some modern critics have concurred with Chrysostom,
and other ancient Fathers, in thinking that the words were limited in their application to the Apostles, and had a special
reference to the gifts of the Holy Spirit, which were to be communicated to them after our Lord's departure. They are,
however, capable of a more extensive application, and they seem
to convey an important truth to the disciples of all ages. Our
Lord had been speaking of offences and of the conduct to be
observed towards an offending brother—he is thence led to
make unanimity a condition of their success in prayer. "If
two of you shall agree on earth, as touching any thing they

shall ask, it shall be done for them *of my Father* which is in heaven." The reason of this promise is annexed. " For where two or three are gathered together *in my name*, (or, as my genuine disciples,) there am *I*," not personally, not essentially; the disciples were not so absurd as to understand him in either sense, but virtually—in that harmony, union, and Christian spirit, which characterise their conduct and dictate their petitions. Their prayers ascend accepted to the throne, and you may confidently trust, that what they ask shall be done for them *of my Father*, as surely as if I myself were the petitioner,* and present in the midst of them.

Here the courteous reader is requested to enquire how were the words understood by the Apostles? How did Peter, in particular, understand them ? Peter was a man of ardent temperament, all alive to every thing novel and surprising. Here then was something to excite the admiration of the most phlegmatic mind, if it was what Trinitarians represent it ; but Peter, instead of betraying the least emotion, or appearing to suspect that he stood face to face before the Omnipresent God, in the person of his master, an idea that would have confounded and overwhelmed him, cooly draws nearer to Christ, to ask a question relative to the subject on which he had been discoursing.

In the text Matt. xxviii. 20. instead of *end of the world*, we should read *end*, or consummation *of the age*, viz. of the Jewish dispensation, which terminated with the destruction of the temple. Until that period, Christ was present with his Apostles, in the special manner of which he gave them intimation when he declared that he would not leave them comfortless, but that he would come to them again. "These things have I spoken unto you," said he, "*being yet present with you*," intimating that he was about to be *absent from them ;* and to console them, added, " the Comforter, which is the Holy Spirit, whom the Father will send *in my name*, he shall teach you all things, and bring all things to your remembrance, whatsoever I have said unto you." After his ascension into heaven, he came to them no more personally ; but the influence of the Holy Spirit which inspired them to preach, and enabled them to work miracles, supplied his place, and ratified his promise. He who could pray to the Father, with a certainty of being heard, for twelve legions of angels, might well promise to be *with* his disciples, or to

---

* *Adesse alicui dicitur qui ei favet, auxiliumque præbet.* He who favours and assists another, is said to be present with him. Grotius, who makes this observation, says, that our Lord's declaration is very similar to a saying of the Jews, " Where two sit discoursing concerning the law, the *Shekinah*, or symbol of the divine presence, is among them." A metaphorical mode of expressing the approbation with which they were regarded by heaven, when engaged in such pious topics of conversation.

impart to them all needful aid, without laying claim to that Omnipresence, which is an attribute of the Supreme Deity alone.

Christ may still be said to be virtually present in every assembly congregated for Christian devotion. In sooth, he is present by his ministers, says Calvin: *revera adest per suos ministros.* But he is present only on the condition that they assemble *in his name,* with motives, objects, hopes, and wishes all in unison with the spirit of Christianity. For "*if any man have not the spirit of Christ, he is none of his.*—Rom. viii. 9. With him Christ is not present, Nor can any one who does not participate in the same exalted views of the Father of all, and the same philanthropic affections, which appeared in the thoughts, and wrought in the actions of our blessed Lord, be a true disciple, though his professions be eloquent as if they flowed from the tongue of an angel, and his faith so ardent that it would lead him " to give his body to be burned."

When Abraham replied to the rich man, Luke, xvi. 29. " They have Moses and the Prophets ; let them hear them." Did he mean to affirm that they were omnipresent?

Or did the author of the Epistle to the Hebrews intend any similar intimation of Abel, when he wrote that by faith, he, " being dead, yet speaketh ?"—Heb. xi. 4.

Would Paul have us to understand that he was possessed of ubiquity, when he wrote to the Corinthians? I, v. 3, " I, verily, as *absent in body, but present in Spirit,* have judged already, as though I were present." Or when he wrote to the Colossians? ii. 5. " Though I be absent in the flesh, yet am I *with you in the Spirit,* joying and beholding your order and the stedfastness of your faith in Christ."

How do the Scriptures speak of the omnipresence of the Deity ? Do they impart a knowledge of it in a few doubtful expressions? are we obliged to take one or two clauses of a text, and stretch them on a theological rack, to extort from them a confession, false as it is reluctant ? No. But they announce to us the truth which they have to impart, voluntarily, and with a clearness, a copiousness, and a decision worthy of a revelation from the Most High. They speak with a sublimity that surpasses the conception of the uninspired, and, at the same time, with a simplicity that is understood by children. Hear So-LOMON,

" Will God, indeed, dwell on the earth ? Behold, the heaven, and heaven of heavens cannot contain thee." 1 Kings, viii. 27.

Or JEREMIAH, xxiii. 23, 24 .

Am I a God at hand, saith JEHOVAH,
And not a God afar off?
Can any one hide himself in secret places
So that I shall not see him? saith JEHOVAH.

> The heavens and the earth
> Do not I fill? saith JEHOVAH.*

Or Amos, ix. 2:

> If they dig down to the grave,
> Thence shall mine hand take them :
> If they climb up to heaven,
> Thence will I bring them down.†

Or DAVID, Ps. cxxxix. 7, 12:

> Whither can I go from thy spirit,
> Or whither can I flee from thy presence ?
> If I climb the heavens thou art there ;
> If I make a bed of the abyss, behold thou art there also ;
> If I lift my wings towards the morning,
> Or dwell beyond the bounds of the sea,
> Even there shall thy hand lead me,
> And thy right hand shall hold me.
> If I say, surely darkness will cover me ;
> Even the night shall be light about me.
> Yea, the darkness hideth not from thee,
> But the night shineth as the day ;
> As is the darkness, so is the light."‡

Such is the lofty and glowing style in which the Scripture speak of the Omnipresence of Jehovah. The truths here revealed are readily admitted by the mind of man, for they correspond with all that reason, in her most sublime investigations teaches. If affirmed of any other being whatsoever, we should expect them to be taught not only with equal, but with superior force and perspicuity. But where is our Lord spoken of in a style which has any parallel to the passages quoted? Instead of receiving the evidence required of a doctrine so stupendous, we are referred to the fragment of a text, which not only admits, but demands, an interpretation that affords no support to the doctrine.

As to the question of our Lord's OMNISCIENCE, it has been already settled by himself with all the clearness which any reasonable enquirer can wish. He informed the disciples after his resurrection, that "*the times and the seasons, the Father hath put in his own power.*"—Acts, i. 7. Meaning by the times and seasons, as the context shews, a knowledge of futurity. On another occasion, as we have already seen, (p. 20—note,) he declared that he knew not when the day of judgment would arrive; and this single declaration furnishes an unanswerable argument, which every suckling in the knowledge of Divine truth, may wield to the utter confusion of all the sophistry that would invest the Saviour with omniscience. And here we cannot refrain from once more expressing our wonder at the

---

* Blayney's translation.   † Newcome's translation.
‡ Dr. Young's translation.

disrespect with which the disciples of Athanasius treat the language and the character of the Saviour, by their irreverent contradiction of his words, and their unrighteous attempts, abortive as they are unscriptural, to rob Jehovah of his glory, by ascribing to another, those attributes which belong to himself alone. To prove their contradiction of the Saviour well-founded, in the present instance, they quote Jeremiah, xvii. 9, 10, where Jehovah is represented as saying, "The heart is deceitful above all things, and desperately wicked; who can know it?* I, Jehovah, search the heart, I try the reins, even to give every man according to his ways, and according to the fruit of his doings." Then they find in the Apocalypse, ii. 23, Christ represented as saying, "all the churches shall know that I am he which searcheth the reins and hearts: and I will give unto every one of you according to your works." These passages, they affirm, directly identify the Saviour with the heart-searching God.

Such is another striking instance of the summary mode in which orthodoxy rushes to her conclusions. It is quite enough that the same thing be affirmed of two beings to constitute their identity, though their characters and offices are perfectly distinct. God searches the heart, and Christ searches the heart, therefore, they are the same! But every examinator, in a judicial capacity, searches the heart of the accused; and though no eye, but the eye of God supreme, can perfectly see the secret workings of the human heart, there are many to whom he has given such faculties of discernment that they can detect the springs of action, through the thickest veil of hypocrisy. Some of the prophets were thus remarkably endowed. Ahijah knew the thoughts of Jeroboam's wife.—1 Kings, xiv. 5, 6. Went not the heart of Elisha with Gehazi to detect his falsehood and avarice? and did he not tell the king of Israel the words spoken in the bed-chamber of the king of Assyria?—2 Kings, v. 25, 26, vi. 12. When the prophet fixed his countenance stedfastly on Hazael, he read not only what was passing in his soul, but the long catalogue of crimes which he was about to commit, viii. 11, 12. Daniel knew, by experience, that there is a God in heaven that revealeth secrets, when he told the thoughts that came into the mind of Nebuchadnezzar on his bed.—Dan. ii. 28, 29. Peter also knew the thoughts of Ananias and Sapphira, when he convicted them of lying not unto men, but unto God.—Acts, v. 4. The knowledge of men's thoughts possessed by the Prophets and

---

The heart is wily above all things;
It is even past all hope; who can know it?—BLAYNEY.

This is a favourite text with the Calvinists, by whom it is grossly misunderstood and misapplied to support their infernal doctrine of man's total and innate depravity.

Apostles, was communicated to them by the Almighty; and so was
was that possessed by Christ as guardian of the churches, and
the judge of mankind. It is expressly declared, at the beginning
of the book of Revelation, that it is "the Revelation of Jesus
Christ which God GAVE unto him," and this is quite sufficien
to overturn all the arguments that are found in any part of it
in support of the grand orthodox fiction. It is added that i
was given him " to shew his servants things which must shortly
come to pass." This, therefore, as Lindsey observes, "limits his
knowledge to the particular subjects specified in the book.
When he says that he searches the hearts, he alludes particu
larly to the faculty he had received of detecting, in the church
of Thyatira, the concealed principles and misdeeds of certain
false teachers, whom he designates by the appellation of Je
zebel, who corrupted Israel by her lewd and idolatrous prac
tices."*—The same person who says, " I am he that searcheth,
says also in the first chapter, 18 v. " I am he that liveth and
was DEAD." But who dares to affirm this of the living God
though this is the conclusion which those who identify him who
searches the heart, in Rev. ii. 23, with Jehovah, can by no pos
sibility evade?

Again, we are told that Christ must be omniscient, for Peter
" said unto him, Lord, *thou knowest all things*." But the evan—
gelist who records this, applies the very same expression to all
faithful disciples, " *Ye* have an unction from the Holy One,
and *ye know all things*."—1 Ep. ii. 20. Are all faithful disci
ples therefore, omniscient? Did the woman of Tekoah believe,
or mean to affirm, that David was omniscient, when admiring
his penetration, she said, " my Lord is wise according to the
wisdom of an angel of God, *to know all things* that are in the
earth."—2 Sam. xiv. 20. The Jews were not so extravagant
as to take in a literal sense, the hyperbolical language of surprise and admiration. They thought their prophets might possess a high degree of supernatural knowledge without ceasing to
be men, or being invested with the attributes of Jehovah. Thus
when the woman who was a sinner, washed the Saviour's feet
with her tears, the Pharisee said, within himself, "this man,
if he were a prophet, would have known who and what manner of woman this is that toucheth him."—Luke, vii. 39. When
our Lord told the Samaritan woman, some incidents of her life,
she said, " Sir, I perceive that thou art a prophet." She afterwards said to the men of the city, "come, see *a man*, which
told me *all things* that ever I did: is not this the Christ?
A very important question, which, coupled with the first part of
her speech, shews clearly what opinions were then entertained
of the Christ with respect to his nature. Neither Samaritan

---

* Lindsey's examination of Robinson's " Plea."

nor Jew harboured an idea that he was to be essentially one
with the Father. They believed, and they believed truly, that
omniscience is an attribute of none but God Supreme.* "Thou,
even thou ONLY," says Solomon, "knowest the hearts of all
the children of men."—1 Kings, viii. 39. When the Scriptures
speak of the wisdom and knowledge of Jehovah, it is not in the
way of allusion and inference. They do not put us off with
two or three ambiguous or mysterious phrases, the meaning of
which can be extracted only by adepts in occult theology. But
they tell us plumply, in such terms as carry instantaneous conviction to the heart and mind, that he is "perfect in knowledge
and infinite in understanding." The Psalmist, in a noble appeal
to the natural reason of man, asks, "he that planted the ear,
shall he not hear? He that formed the eye, shall he not see?
He that teacheth man knowledge, shall not he know?"—Psalm,
xciv. 9. "O Lord, thou hast searched me and known me.
Thou knowest my down-sitting and mine uprising: Thou un-
derstandest my thoughts afar off. Thou compassest my path,
and my lying down, and art acquainted with all my ways. For
there is not a word in my tongue, but, lo, O Lord, thou knowest it altogether."—Ps. cxxxix. 2, 4.

Such is the copious and perspicuous style in which the Scriptures speak of the omniscience of Jehovah. They take care
also to inform us that his knowledge is not *given* nor derived.
"Who hath directed the Spirit of the Lord, or being his counsellor, hath taught him. With whom took HE counsel, and
who instructed HIM and taught him in the path of judgment,
and taught him knowledge, and shewed to him the way of understanding?"—Is. xl. 13, 14.

SECTION ELEVENTH.

Christ not the Creator of the Universe—not Omnipotent.

The attribute of OMNIPOTENCE, like that of omniscience, was
disclaimed by the Saviour. As there were certain events of
which he declared that he knew not when they were to happen,
so were there certain acts which he confessed his inability to
perform. Notwithstanding, they who admire what they are
pleased to call a "triplicity in the Godhead," are fond of ascribing to him omnipotence, but with no more success than they
ascribe to him omniscience and omnipresence. To prove this
point, they allege that Christ was the Creator of the physical
system of the universe, and thence *infer* that he must be Almighty.

---

* See "*Omniscience an attribute of the Father only*"—an excellent discourse by the Rev. Dr. Hutton of Leeds: and "Christ's knowledge of all
things," by the Rev. Edw. Higginson, Jun. of Hull.

Supposing, for a moment, this statement capable of bein verified, must it not appear very strange and unaccountable, th Christ himself, in all his numerous discourses both to friends an foes, never made the slightest allusion to his having such power never did he drop a hint that might lead the disciples to su pect they were conversing face to face, with the Creator A mighty of heaven and earth. Frequently did he take image and illustrations from the works of nature—but he referred a the beauty and glory of those works to the Father. If he speak of the sun and the shower, it is the Father, he declares, tha causes the one to shine, and the other to descend. If he speak of the flowers of the field, it is the Father who clothes them if of the birds of the air, the Father feeds them.

We repeat it then, that we deem it most marvellous, if Chris were the Creator, that he should not only drop no hint of it but that he should ascribe all to the Father: and that three of the Evangelists who have recorded his history, have been so silen on the subject, that its most orthodox supporters cannot extor from them one syllable in their behalf. But, they find it written in John, i. 10, κοσμος δι' αυτου εγενετο which rendered literally means, *the world, through him, was.* Was what? *Made,* say the Trinitarian. We contradict the assertion, and affirm that, in this place, εγενετο does not signify *made originally,* or *out of nothing created*—nor, though used above 700 times in the New Testament, can any one decisive instance[*] be adduced in which it must bear that signification. We admit, indeed, it has been so rendered by able Unitarian, as well as Trinitarian, writers, in the 3d verse, in connexion with the *logos;* but if, in that connexion, such rendering be true, it only furnishes a reason for objecting to it here, since the Apostle after telling us that "all things were made by him (or it) and without him (or it) was not any thing made that was made," would scarcely sink into the anticlimax and tautology of informing us that the world was made by him. The phrase is manifestly ellip-tical, and the ellipsis is to be supplied by something in the context. The preceding verse says, "That was the true light, which *lighteth* every man that cometh into the world." It is then stated, that he, viz: the true light, was in the world—and the world, through him, *was.* Was what? we ask again, and we think the intelligent and unprejudiced reader, will reply *enlightened.* Such ellipses are frequent in Scripture.[†] Thus,

---

* Simpson thinks there are two, James, iii. 9—Heb. iv. 3. "It does not appear to Dr. Carpenter, that either of these cases is fully in point." With him we agree.

† Thus in Matt. xxv. 13. "Watch therefore; for ye know neither the day nor the hour." Here the sentence in Griesbach, and in the Douay Testament, closes. *Wherein the son of man cometh*—was added by some one to fill up the ellipsis, and thence it crept into the text. The next verse, begins

the Apostle Paul in reply to the Roman captain, (Acts, xxii. 28.)
said, " *But I was born.*" (εγω δε και γεγεννημαι) The ellipsis is
supplied by the word *free* inserted in the translation. This is
good sense ; but the ellipsis would be more correctly filled by
the words *a Roman citizen,* for they are obviously in reply to the
question in the 27th verse, *art thou a Roman?* as well as to
the captain's declaration that he had purchased his freedom with
a great sum.*

The word κοσμος *world,*† Simpson remarks, occurs of-
tener in John than in any other of the sacred writers—about
seventy-eight times in his Gospel, and twenty-four times in his
Epistles, and yet it is applied in only two instances to original
creation. In the verse under consideration, it occurs three
times, and once in the verse immediately preceding. If it
means the world in a physical sense, that is, the material system,
then must we understand the passage thus, " He was the true
light which lighteth every man that cometh into the material
system. He was in the material system, and the material system was made by him, and the material system knew him not."
This, like many a similar clinking concatenation of words, may
tinkle sweetly in the ears of orthodoxy, but it sounds in the
ears of reason and common sense not unlike what is y-cleped nonsense. Can either knowledge or ignorance be attributed to

---

* " for *the kingdom of heaven is,* as a man travelling." Here all the words
in Italics are supplied, for they have no representative in the original, and
the translator has been obliged to go back to the beginning of the chapter,
no fewer than thirteen verses, for words to complete the sense. In the
17th verse of the same chapter, we read, " he that *had received* two, he also
gained other two." Two what? The reader must look to the foregoing
verse for an answer—*had received* is the translator's, not the evangelist's.
In Heb. iii. 16. We read, ' he took not on *him the nature* of angels,' and
in II Thess. ii. 3. ' Let no man deceive you by any means ; for *that day shall
not come,* except, &c.' The words in Italics here, and generally throughout
the common version, are inserted as necessary to render clear the sense.
When such writers, therefore, as Dr. Wardlaw, express surprise at the word
enlightened not being expressed in John i. 10, but left to be supplied from
the preceding verse, they only betray ignorance of scriptural phraseology.
The Doctor, as quoted by Dr. Carpenter, observes that " there are not a
few unnecessary, and there are some injurious supplements in our ordinary
English version." True. Thus in Acts, vii. 59, the word *God* is thrust in
where it is not wanted—and in John, viii. 58, *he* is wanting, though the
sense absolutely requires it. But in neither case have the interests of orthodoxy been overlooked. We are glad to receive the above acknowledgment from a Calvinistic divine. It shews the necessity of having a new
version, or the old one revised and corrected.

* See Dr. Carpenter's " Unitarianism the Doctrine of the Gospel."
† " The term κοσμος, world, is often used by Christ, as it was natural it
should be, concerning the body of the Jewish people. By Paul, the same
term is used concerning the Jewish dispensation."—Gal. iv. 3.—Coloss. ii.
8, 20.—Cappe. No intelligent reader can require to be told in what numerous senses it is used in our vernacular language.

that which is inanimate? What object could the Evangelist have in telling us that the Creator of the world was in the world? Could he be out of it? Or, was Apostolical authority necessary to confirm so indubitable a truth? *He came to his own, and his own received him not.* The creator of the material system, came to his own! What a hideous bathos! What egregious folly! "The earth is the Lord's and the fulness thereof; the world, and they that dwell therein: for he hath founded it upon the seas, and established it upon the floods."

Let us now turn from the inconsistencies and tortuosities of Trinitarian expounders, and see whether a Unitarian exposition does not do more justice to the sentiments of the inspired author. The true light, *was in the world,* among mankind—or, more particularly, among the Jewish people—*and the world through him was,* mankind were enlightened by the beams of his heavenly truth—but, notwithstanding, *the world knew him not,* mankind did not duly acknowledge and appreciate him as the true light, which the Father of all had sent to illuminate their minds, and purify their hearts. *He came to his own, and his own received him not.* He appeared among his own countrymen, in their towns and villages, their streets, and their synagogues, with tidings of joy, and promises of immortality, but far from prizing him and his doctrines, as became them, they ungratefully rejected both. All, however, were not so perverse. *But as many as received him, to them gave he power to become the sons of God.*

Here, if we mistake not, there is something that can be understood. Let the judicious reader determine whether this plain explanation is not more worthy of acceptance, and more in accordance with the simplicity of gospel truth, than the strained and perplexing incongruities of what is falsely called the " orthodox" doctrine.

The CREATIVE AND OMNIPOTENT POWER of Christ is inferred from an ill-translated and worse understood text of Coloss. i. 16, 17.

" By him (*εν αυτω* in him) were all things created that are in heaven, and that are in earth, visible and invisible, whether *they be* thrones or dominions, or principalities, or powers ; all things were created by him, (*δι' αυτου* through him) and for (*εις* to) him ; and he is before all things, and by (*εν* in) him all (these) things consist."

These words, as they stand insulated, may, certainly, to a superficial reader, appear to convey the meaning attached to them by dogmatic theologists. But if any one will take due pains to acquire a knowledge of the language of Scripture, and consider the context of the passage, he will discover that the moral and religious, not the physical, creation, must be understood here; that great change which was effected, by the introduction of the gospel, both in the civil and ecclesiastical polities of the Jews. In the language of Scripture, and particularly in that of the Prophets, the terms earth and heaven are employed to represent these two states. Thus, in Is. lxv. 17, 18. Jehovah is introduced saying, "Behold, I create new heavens and a new earth—I create Jerusalem a rejoicing, and her people a joy." The Apostle adopts the ideas, and the language of the prophets, and speaks of the new dispensation as of a new creation. "If any man be in Christ, he is a new creature; old things are passed away; behold, all things are become new. And all things are of God, who hath reconciled us to himself by Jesus Christ." 2 Cor. v. 17, 18.

Tyrwhitt,* in his brief but very comprehensive Essay, entitled, "An Explanation of St. Paul's Doctrine, concerning the Creation of All Things by Jesus Christ," justly observes, that

"The term created is frequently used by St. Paul, as well as by the writers of the Old Testament, in a figurative, or secondary sense, in which it signifies not to give being, or to bring into existence, but to confer benefits and privileges, or to place in a new and more advantageous state of being. The Apostle tells the Ephesians, ' That they are the workmanship of God, created by him in Christ Jesus, unto good works; that they who, in their Gentile state, were formerly afar off from God, are now brought nigh unto him by Christ, who hath made both Jews and Gentiles one, and hath broken down the middle wall of partition between them, that he might create of twain one new man, which new man is also said to be created in holiness and righteousness, after the image of God who created him.' Eph. ii. 10—17; iv. 24; Col. iii. 10. Here is plain mention of a creation, distinct, not only from that by which the heavens and earth were made, but from that also by which the Jews had before been created the people of God; and in opposition to the latter of these, it is called the new creation, in the same manner that the covenant of God with all mankind, through the mediation of Christ is called the new covenant, in opposition to the former covenant which God had before made with the children of Israel, by the mediation of Moses."

In a verse preceding the passage under consideration, the Apostle informs us, " that we have been delivered from the power of darkness, and translated into the kingdom of his (God's) dear Son," whom he denominates the image of the invisible God, the first born of every creature (πάσης κτίσεως of the whole creation.) For as Adam was the first created man in the old physical creation, so was Christ the first created, or the first born, in the new moral creation. The power of darkness, from which we have been delivered,

---

* A short biographical sketch prefixed to the essay, informs us, that the Rev. Robert Tyrwhitt was a Fellow of Jesus' College, Cambridge, and grandson of the learned and pious Dr. Gibson, Bishop of London. On the deliberate conviction of his mind, that ' God the Father is the sole object of religious worship,' he resigned his fellowship, gave up all hope of preferment, and lived cheerfully on a very narrow income, till by the death of his brother, Clerk to the House of Commons, he came into possession of a property, which enabled him to act up to the dictates of a generous heart. He was the friend of the late Bishops Law and Watson, and, more intimately, of the amiable and accomplished Dr. John Jebb, who has testified of him, that " his character may be justly said to be above all praise. His strong abilities, extensive learning, strict integrity, and most amiable manners, united with sol judgment, and determined resolution, would reflect lustre on the most distinguished station." He breathed his last on the 25th of April, 1817.

K

is not a physical, but a spiritual power; the kingdom into which we have been translated, is not an earthly, but a heavenly state. The Apostle is evidently highly figurative throughout. That by such expressions as *things that are in heaven, and things that are in earth*, he does not mean the material frame of the universe is evident, from the 20 v. of this very chapter, in which he states, that God by Christ "*reconciled* all things (*i. e.* all men) to himself; by him, I say, whether they be things in earth, or things in heaven," (*i. e.* whether they be Jews or Gentiles.) Will any orthodox man affirm, that the Apostle here means that God reconciled the sun, moon, and stars unto himself? By things visible and invisible, he intends the external state of the evangelized world, and the unseen felicities and exalted honours of its members, whether they be represented by thrones, of which the Saviour himself gave intimation, when he told the disciples that they should sit upon twelve thrones judging the twelve tribes of Israel; or dominions, or principalities, or powers, to the possession of which, men annex their highest conceptions of happiness. All this new spiritual state was created through the agency of Christ, and for his peculiar glory. He is before, or superior to all its other agents, and in him all the various arrangements of its constitution subsist.* The Apostle continuing to rise in his ideas, (it is never his habit to sink,) says, *He is the head of the body, the church:* an expression, which at once conveys to us in what sense we are to understand his previous figurative language—then he adds, *who is the beginning*, viz. of this new moral creation, *and the first born from the dead;* appellations which can by no means be given to the omnipotent, ever-living Jehovah: that *in all things* connected with this new creation, *he might have the pre-eminence; for it pleased the Father that in him should all fulness dwell.*

Dr. Doddridge, with other commentators of his school, is indignant at the application of Col. i. 16, 17, to "the new creation in a *spiritual* sense." Yet the spiritual sense is the noblest and best. "The letter killeth, but the spirit maketh alive." But though the Doctor, in this place, prefers the *material* and carnal sense, because it is best suited to his system, when he meets with *principalities and powers*, again, in ii. 15 of the very same epistle, he begins to *spiritualize*, and would have us, by those expressions to understand "our spiritual enemies, and especially the formidable spirit of darkness." In a note also to Rom. viii. 38, he quotes Elsner as authority for understanding by *principalities* (αρχας) magistrates, (*magistracies*,) and refers us to Titus iii. 1, where it occurs in a sense indubitably similar. Does the Apostle Paul speak of physical or metaphysical existences, in that sub-

---

* Lindsey and others think the Apostle makes particular allusion to the oriental hierarchy or demonology, a belief of which had begun to prevail among the Jews.

lime declaration, in which he personifies death and life, and principalities and powers, and height and depth, and things present, and things to come? Rom. viii. 38, 39. No one, we presume, could be preposterous as to answer the former. Wherefore then be so preposterous as to infer from similar expressions elsewhere, that Christ was the Creator, in contradiction to the Scriptures, which affirm that this appellation belongs only to Jehovah? How would it sink our ideas of the grandeur and majesty of the Omnipotent, to suppose he could have any partner or coadjutor in the work of creation! We challenge our adversaries to produce a single text to justify such supposition. We defy them to shew any one instance, in which it is asserted of Christ, as of Jehovah, in the commencement of the Bible, that in the beginning he created (ברא, εποιησε Sept.) the heavens and the earth. Or in which any inspired Apostle has applied to him such language as Paul applied to that God whom he revealed, on Mars' hill, to the men of Athens; the God that made (ὁ ποιησας) the world and all things therein—the Lord of heaven and earth, who hath made εποιησε) of one blood all nations of men, Acts xvii. 26—28; or addressed him in such terms as the primitive disciples addressed Jehovah, when they said, "Lord, thou art God, which hast made (ὁ ποιησας;) heaven, and earth, and the sea, and all that in them is." Acts iv. 24. Until such Scriptural proof be placed before us, to convict us of error, we beg to be excused for adhering to the original faith, and believing with Moses and the prophets, with the Apostles and primitive disciples, and the framers of the creed called the Apostles', that God the Father Almighty is the maker of heaven and earth.

It may be here objected, that in Heb. i. 2, it is stated that God by him *made the worlds* τους αιωνας; εποιησε: —true, the worlds. The word, however, which we demand is not worlds, but *heaven, earth, and sea.* The Jews knew nothing of any world but one; and the word here rendered *world*, as we have had occasion to remark before, p. 57, does not mean the globe of earth, or the visible frame of nature, but the age, or dispensation, in the plural, *ages*, which, according to the Hebrew idiom, is used as the singular for the sake of emphasis and particularity. It means here the new dispensation, which was communicated through Christ; and it is perfectly accordant with the context, that the author should speak of the new dispensation, which it was his object to magnify and recommend, and not of the material creation with which his subject has no manner of connexion.

In a subsequent part of the Epistle, (iii. 2,) it is expressly affirmed, that God *made* Christ* τῳ ποιησαντι αυτον. This, in our

---

* Whiston informs us, on the authority of Philastrius, *De Hæret.* c. 41. That in the fourth century, this doctrine was reckoned so heterodox, that, in some places, the Epistle was seldom read in public, partly out of the dread of such an expression—a striking proof how it was understood.

him extensive power over both animate and inanimate nature. Paul says, " I can do *all things* through Christ who strengtheneth me." Is Paul therefore omnipotent? No. The meaning is, that he can bear all afflictions and reverses of fortune with patience. Again, he informs us, that God has given Christ to be head over *all things* to the church; and that he upholds *all things* by the word of his power. Is Christ therefore omnipotent? No. The Apostle affirms no more, than that Christ orders or conducts the whole of the Gospel dispensation, by virtue of the authority imparted to him by the Almighty. He acts in subordination to the Father. " *He that built all things* (in the widest sense) *is God.*"

Even granting that Christ was the Creator of the material frame of nature, which we confidently deny, as contradictory to the most unequivocal declarations of Scripture, he was only the agent of omnipotence. The verse preceding the passage quoted to prove him possessed of that attribute, demonstrates the contrary. It denominates him " *the image* of the invisible God—the *first born of every creature.*" The *image,* therefore not the reality—*born,* therefore not self-existent—*a creature,* therefore not the Creator, consequently dependent, therefore not omnipotent.

In support of the doctrine here impugned, Phil. iii. 21, has been also quoted:—

" The Lord Jesus Christ, who shall change our vile body, that it may be fashioned like unto his glorious body, according to the working whereby he is able even to subdue all things unto himself."

A common reader who has no system to support, would suppose that the ascription of a body, though a glorious body, to Christ; and the declaration that the bodies of the righteous shall be fashioned like his, should effectually preclude all ideas of confounding him with Jehovah, who is a Spirit, and to whom there can be no corporeal similitude. More sublime was the idea of God in him who wrote,—

" All are but parts of one stupendous whole
Whose body nature is, and God the soul."

But the words, *subdue all things,* sound like an ascription, of omnipotence, and to some writers, that is enough both for premises and conclusion! The power attributed to Christ, however, is not infinite nor underived, but limited to a particular object, and delegated to him by the Father Almighty, till the final consummation, when death shall be destroyed, and all the just shall be raised incorruptible and immortal. A parallel passage occurs in the xv. 27 of 1st Cor. " He (viz. God) hath put all things under his feet. But when he saith *all things* are put under him, it is manifest, that *he is excepted, which did put* all things under him. And when all things shall be subdued unto him, (even) then shall the *Son also himself be subject* unto him that put all things under him, that God may be all in all." Can the subordination and subjection of Christ, in his highest state of future glorified existence, be expressed in terms more strong and distinct? It would almost seem that the Apostle had some inspired anticipation of the attempts that would be made, in a future corrupt state of the church, to identify the Son with the Father; and that he had taken particular pains to express the supreme dominion of God alone, in such a manner as to prevent the possibility of their succeeding for a moment. " The head of the woman is the man,. and *the head of Christ is God.*" 1st Cor. xi. 3.

Some orthodox writers think the miracles wrought by our Saviour an ample proof of his omnipotence; and they dwell on them with peculiar energy, as if they were fully demonstrative of his being the Almighty himself, though it is evident from our Lord's own words, that his wonderful works were only the tests of his divine mission.* They also discover in the style of his language, a similarity to that which is ascribed to Jehovah. Thus, God said, " let there be light, and there was light." Christ touched a leper and said, " I will; be thou clean; and immediately his leprosy was cleansed." Mat. viii. 3. Hence they argue, that the Creator of light, and the healer of the leper, must have been the same individual being. But here again, they only afford evidence of their bad reasoning. The people who saw our Lord's miracles performed, never reasoned thus. The same chapter which records the cure of the leper, tells us of another miracle still more calculated to excite astonishment. Being asleep, on board of a vessel, he was roused by the cry of the disciples, " Lord, save us—we perish! And he saith unto them, why are ye fearful, O ye of little faith? Then he arose and rebuked the winds and the sea; and there was a great calm." This was one of the most stupendous miracles wrought by our Lord; and it may well be supposed that if any thing could create, in those who beheld it, the belief of a present Almighty power, it would be an act like this. But how did *they* reason upon it? Was it in the style of modern orthodoxy? They were not so stultified. They only " marvelled, saying, *what manner of* MAN is this, that even the winds and the sea obey him!" As to the mere exertion of physical power, so far as its display may seem calculated to produce a belief of high supernatural agency, our Lord did not stand alone among the prophets of God. If he commanded the stormy winds and waves to be still, Moses cleft the billows of the red sea, and led the Israelites in triumph through the heart of the deep, before

---

" Though our modern writers do endeavour to prove from the miracles our Saviour did, that he was the same supreme God with the Father, yet Christ himself doth only use them to prove, that he was sent by the Father, and had commission from him to deliver this message to the world: as is evident from these words, John v. 36; for the works which the Father hath given me to finish, the same works that I do, bear witness of me, that the Father hath sent me."—WURRER'S *Last Thoughts.*

the pursuing host of Pharaoh. If he raised the dead, so did
Elisha, so did Peter, and so did Paul. If Christ said to the fig-
tree, "Let no fruit grow on thee henceforward, for ever :" Joshua
said in the sight of Israel, " Sun, stand thou still upon Gibeon ;
and thou, Moon, in the valley of Ajalon." Our Lord declared
to the Apostles, "verily, verily, I say unto you, he that believeth
on me, the works that I do, shall he do also ; and *greater* works
than these shall he do, because I go unto my father," John xiv. 12.
If with seven loaves and a few little fishes, Christ fed four thousand
men, besides women and children ; Elisha caused the widow's
barrel of meal not to waste, and her cruise of oil not to fail. If
Christ mounted the skies in serene majesty till a cloud received
him out of the sight of the disciples ; Elijah, with the chariot of
Israel and the horses of fire, went up by a whirlwind into heaven.
Our Lord, therefore, did not prove himself to be the Omnipotent
by the miracles which he wrought, nor was it in the exercise of
physical power that his superiority to other prophets consisted ;
but in what was infinitely more important, the moral beauty,
dignity, and sinless perfection of his character. In this respect
he stood above them all, unrivalled and alone. In this respect he
bore the untarnished image of the Invisible God. But he gave
frequent sufficient indications that he was not God Supreme. He
was tempted by Satan—he hungered—he wept—he prayed. But
Jehovah cannot be tempted by Satan, since he could annihilate
him by a breath ; he cannot hunger, for he has no corporeal appetite ;—he cannot weep, for though most compassionate and
merciful, he is far superior to those sensibilities which characterise
human nature ;—neither can he pray since he has no superior,
but reigns the Sovereign, undisputed Lord of all. The beloved
Disciple tells us, that Jesus being *wearied* with his journey, sat by
Jacob's well, John iv. 6. But "hast thou not known, hast thou
not heard, that the everlasting God, the Lord, the Creator of the
ends of the earth, fainteth not, neither is weary ?" Is. xl. 28.

SECTION TWELFTH.

*No Proof in Scripture that Christ was worshipped as the Supreme
God.*

The advocates of " *The Triplicity*" affirm, that divine honours
were paid to Christ, and thence they *infer* once more, that Christ
was the supreme Deity.

Negatur. We deny that divine honours were ever paid to
Christ by any of his contemporaries upon earth ; nor have all
those who affirm it been able to establish it by any satisfactory
proof ; though there is no position in divinity, which they have so
strongly arrayed their forces to maintain. To a mere English
reader who does not take pains to ascertain the exact meaning of

words, it may appear otherwise from those passages of the New Testament, in which Christ is said to have been *worshipped*. But let him pause to enquire into the proper signification of this word, and he will find that in all cases, except where it is joined with the name of God, it means the act of paying respect, homage, obeisance, such as was and still continues in the east, to be paid to kings and men of distinction, by those of inferior rank. In this sense, and it is not yet obsolete, the words "worship" and "worshipful," were formerly used in English; and examples could be brought from Coke and Littleton, and other writers learned in the law, to shew, that it means civil homage, *terrene honor*. An instance occurs in the language of our blessed Savior himself, Luke xiv. 10, " When thou art bidden (or invited to a feast) go and sit down in the lowest room, that when he that bade thee cometh, he may say unto thee : Friend, go up higher ! then shalt thou have *worship* in the presence of them that sit at meat with thee."

What is meant by the priest, when in the form of solemnizing marriage in the Church of England, he instructs the bridegroom to say to the bride, " With my body I thee *worship ?*"

In Ps. viii. 5, of the Psalter, appointed to be sung or said in Churches, we read, "to crown him (man) with glory and *worship.*"

The sanctity apparent in all our Saviour's conduct, and the benevolent manner in which he exercised the miraculous power which the Father had given him, excited strong feelings of gratitude, and drew forth the most respectful homage of those whom he benefited. But not one of them all ever considered him as God, or offered him divine adoration. Not one of them all, from the highest to the lowest, from Nicodemus to the leper, regarded him as more than a prophet; no, not even when he was in the act of performing the most astonishing miracles. When he fed five thousand with five loaves and two fishes, they said, of a truth, this is THAT PROPHET that should come into the world. The blind man, whose sight was restored, said he is a PROPHET; and Nicodemus, " Rabbi, thou art a TEACHER come from God, for no man can do those miracles which thou doest, except God be with him." Even they who knew and acknowledged him to be the Messiah, never said, nor had they ever been taught to believe, that he was Israel's God. This is plain from the language of Philip to Nathanael, " We have found him, of whom Moses in the law, and the prophets did write—Jesus of Nazareth, the son of Joseph." The admiration of the people, excited as it was, by his wonderful works, and accompanied with all the warmth of eastern feeling, imagination, and gorgeous magnificence of diction, never rose to such a height as to give him epithets that belong only to Jehovah. " It was said of some, that John was risen from the dead ; and of some that Elias had appeared, and of others, that one of the old prophets was risen again." Luke ix. 7, 8. When he restored to life the widow of Nain's son, "there came a fear on all, and they glorified God, saying, that a GREAT PROPHET is risen up among us, and that God hath *visited* his people." Luke vii. 16. The latter expression is, by some sturdy Trinitarians, applied to Jesus, with what reason let the reader decide. When Zacharias, at the birth of the infant Baptist, burst into the pious ejaculation, "Blessed be the Lord God of Israel, for he hath *visited* and redeemed his people;" Luke i. 68. who visited them, since Christ was not yet born? What did David mean when he asked, "What is man that thou art mindful of him; or the son of man that thou *visitest* him?" Ps. viii. 4. Or the Apostle James, when he said, "Simeon hath declared, how God at the first, did *visit* the Gentiles, to take out of them a people for his name?" Acts xv. 14. The original verb is ἐπεσκέψατο, which signifies *he looked upon or regarded.* Primate Newcome renders it by the latter word, both in Luke i. 68, and in vii. 16; and every sciolist in Greek must know that this is a more literal translation than *visited.* But the word *visit* suggesting the idea of corporeal manifestation, affords loose thinkers and wordy declaimers, a specious argument in behalf of a favourite established error. But no Jew could ever be guilty of confounding the GREAT PROPHET with Jehovah, nor of entertaining the gross and heathenish idea, that the Almighty had veiled himself in a human form, and was come to sojourn among men. Such an imagination did not enter the minds of the multitude in the highest enthusiasm of their admiration, even when they conducted Jesus into Jerusalem, as they would have conducted one of their kings of old; spreading their garments and branches of trees in the way, preceding and following him with acclamations of triumph. They shouted "Hosanna to the Son of David; blessed is he that cometh in the name of the Lord; Hosanna in the highest!" And when he was come into Jerusalem, all the city was moved, saying, "who is this?" And what did the multitude reply; that multitude (*qui stupet in titulis,*) which delights in high-sounding epithets and hyperbolical descriptions? They said, "this is Jesus, the prophet of Nazareth of Galilee." Mat. xxi. 8, 11. Nor were their ideas, or their language, more exalted, when they saw him make such a display of his authority in purging the temple, and healing the lame, and the blind, for the children still continued to shout, "Hosanna to the Son of David!"—to the great displeasure of the high priests and scribes, who were as far as the multitude from recognising a present Deity in the person of our Lord. What admiration could not excite on the one hand, neither could apprehension on the other. Even the guilty, superstitious, conscience-stricken Herod was incapable of so monstrous an absurdity. For when he heard of the fame of Jesus, instead of exclaiming that Jehovah had descended to take vengeance of his crimes, he said, "This is John the Baptist; he is

L

risen from the dead; and therefore mighty works do shew forth themselves in him." Mat. xiv. 2.

There is another personage, whose testimony on the present occasion is valuable. It must be esteemed inestimable, indeed, by the Calvinists, and others who gift him with omniscience and omnipresence. The DEVIL himself did not know Christ to be God, though he knew full well that he was the Son of God, and, in the temptation, addressed him repeatedly by that title. But this ghostly potentate, with all his knowledge of things invisible—with all his skill in logic, and in drawing *inferences,* in which he might have foiled the Stagirite himself, did not identify the Son with the Father, nor *infer,* that because the Father was God supreme, the Son must be God supreme also. The dialectics of theology were not so well understood then, even by the devil, as they have become since, under the discipline of Athanasius and Calvin. He makes a clear distinction between the Father and the Son, and says, "If thou be the Son of God, cast thyself down, for it is written, HE (God) shall give his angels charge concerning thee." Again, he promised magnificent gifts to Jesus—no less than the kingdoms of the world and the glory of them, if he would fall down and worship him;—a proposition, which, with all his unparalleled audacity, he could scarcely be suspected of making, had he known he was accosting Jehovah. We suppose the frequently needful device *of the two natures* will be called for in this extremity; and that we shall be told, it was only in his human nature Christ was tempted! But, the "Archangel ruined" knew nothing about *the two natures,* that invention being long subsequent; and he tempted Christ not as the son of man, but as *the Son of God.*

We are told that a leper came and *worshipped* Christ, Mat. viii. 2; or, as some quote it, *adored.* The Unitarian prefers our common translation, because *adore* conveys an erroneous notion to the English reader, and leads to a false doctrine. The leper, on seeing our Saviour, came, and, in the usual oriental mode of asking a favour, rendered him homage by crossing his hands on his breast, by bowing low, by kneeling, or prostration, and besought Christ to cleanse him from his disease. But he did not pay him divine honours. He was not so ill-instructed, nor so little of a Jew, as to adore any but God alone.

The same species of worship was paid to Elijah: "As Obadiah was in the way, behold, Elijah met him; and he knew him, *and fell on his face* and said, art thou that my Lord Elijah?" 1 Kings xviii. 7; and to Daniel, "then the King Nebuchadnezzar fell on his face and *worshipped* Daniel, and commanded that they should offer an oblation and sweet odours unto him." Dan. ii. 46.

It was also paid to kings: thus, Nathan the prophet, "when he was come in before the king, he bowed himself before the king with his face to the ground." 1 Kings, i. 23. In 1 Chron. xxix. 20, it is written, "that all the congregation blessed the Lord God of

their Fathers, and bowed down their heads and *worshipped* the
Lord and the King." Their act, as applied to God, was religious
homage—to David, civil obeisance.*

Joseph was *worshipped* by his brethren: "Joseph's brethren
came and bowed down themselves before him (in the Septuagint :
Grabe : Oxon. MDCCVII. *worshipped*) with their faces to the
earth." Gen. xli. 6.

Moses *worshipped* his father-in-law." Exod. xviii. 7. Solomon's
bride is admonished, in Ps. xlv. 11, to *worship* her Lord, the king.

The sheaves of his brethern *worshipped* Joseph's sheaf.

" Your sheaves stood round about, and made obeisance to (in
the Sept. *worshipped*) my sheaf." Gen. xxxvii. 7.

The sun, the moon, and the eleven stars, made obeisance to (in
the Sept. *worshipped*) Joseph in his dream. Jbl. 9.

Origen, who flourished at the beginning of the third century,
and who, for talents, learning, and knowledge of the Scriptures,
was distinguished above all his contemporaries, most clearly asserts, that prayer is to be made to the Father alone, and argues
strongly and convincingly against addressing it to the Son. The
curious reader may see the subject discussed at length in the 50th
and 51st sections of his Treatise on prayer. (περι ευχης.†) He
also answers the objection of those who, as a reason for praying to
the Son, quote the Septuagint version of Deuteronomy, xxxii. 43.
" Let all the angels of God worship him." This text is not in
our English version of Deuteronomy, but may be found in Heb. i.
6, applied to our Saviour. He says, that the prophet Isaiah in-
troduces Jehovah addressing Jerusalem or Zion, saying, " Kings
shall be thy nursing fathers, and their queens thy nursing mothers;
they shall worship, or bow down to thee, with their face toward
the earth (επι προσωπον της γης προσκυνησουσι) and lick up the dust
of thy feet ; and thou shalt know that *I* am the Lord." Is. xlix. 23.
He continues, " How did our Lord reply to him who called him
good ? ' Why callest thou me good ? no one is good but one, God
the Father.' What was his reply, but to say, why prayest thou to
me ? It behoves thee to pray to the Father alone, to whom I also
pray, which you may learn from the Holy Scriptures." Is it to
be supposed, that he who refused a divine title, would receive
divine honours ?

Bishop BULL, (in his discourse concerning the existence and
nature of angels,) says,

" It is to be observed, that in the Clementine Liturgy, (so called,) which
is by the learned on all hands, confessed to be very ancient, and to contain

---

* Sozomen praises a Christian who *worshipped* the Persian King, as a
customary honour due to royalty ; but afterwards refused the same species
of homage, when informed that it would be deemed a mark of apostacy from
his faith.

† Oxford Edition, 1686.

the order of worship observed in the churches before the time of Constantine;—*all the prayers are directed to God*, in the name of his Son Jesus Christ." And again, "In the *first* and *best* ages, the Churches of Christ directed all their prayers according to the Scriptures, to God only, through the *sole* mediation of Jesus Christ our Lord."*

And the learned Dr. WAKE,

" The Lord's prayer teaches us, that we should pray to *God only*, and to him as our Father, through Jesus Christ our Lord."

And the honest and candid Dr. PRIESTLEY :—

" The practice of praying *to the Father*, was long universal in the Christian Church. The short addresses to Christ, as those in the Litany, *Lord have mercy on us !—Christ have mercy on us !* being, comparatively, of late date. In the Clementine Liturgy, the oldest extant, contained in the Apostolical Constitutions, which were, probably, composed about the fourth century, there is no trace of any such thing. Such hold has established custom on the minds of men, that, excepting the Moravians only, whose prayers are always addressed to Christ, the general practice of Trinitarians themselves is to pray to the Father only."

Notwithstanding, it is contended that our Lord did receive such worship as an Apostle refused, and therefore it must be understood in a higher sense than customary homage. We are told in 10th chap. of Acts, 25, that as "Peter was coming in, Cornelius met him, and fell down at his feet and worshipped him. But Peter took him up, saying, Stand up, I myself also am a man." Now let it be remembered, that Cornelius was a Centurion of the Italian band; a Roman, not a Jew; a devout man, however; one but recently instructed, perhaps, in the knowledge of the God of Israel ; and who, prior to this, had been accustomed to worship hundreds of deities, and to believe that they often came down to the earth in human form. Thus, the people of Lystra, on seeing a miracle wrought by Paul, exclaimed, " The Gods are come down to us in the shape of men !" They called Barnabas Jupiter, and Paul, Mercury, and could with difficulty be prevented from offering sacrifice. Cornelius had a vision, in which an angel appeared to announce the approach, and prepare him for the reception of Peter. Accordingly, when the Apostle drew nigh, Cornelius being predisposed by the vision to encourage a delusion, mistook him for a being of superior nature; Peter saw this, and very properly rectified the heathenish mistake, by telling him that he was a man like himself. The argument founded on this circumstance falls by its own weakness; but lest any one should deem it valid, our Lord himself will lend us a demonstration of its invalidity. He tells us of a servant who being unable to discharge his debt, fell down at his master's feet and *worshipped* him, Mat. xviii. 26. The master did not reject the worship, and there-

* This and the following paragraph are quoted from Dr. Clarke's Scripture Doctrine of the Trinity, p. 435, 3rd. edition, London.

fore, according to the Trinitarian mode of making clear "logical solutions," the master received divine honours, and should be adored as God!

This "solution" is like many of the Rev. Wm. Jones's, a favourite and distinguished champion of the Trinity; and of Dr. Burgh's, whose work on that subject is pregnant with false reasonings, and the most hideous distortions of Scripture,*

If divine worship were to be offered to Christ, is it not marvellous that we are not told so expressly, and in terms about the meaning of which there can be no dispute? With respect to the worship of the Father, there is no difference of opinion; for though it is one of the plainest dictates of reason, it is taught by the Scriptures so clearly and so strongly, that no one ventures to question its propriety. Another deity besides God, being proposed by revelation as an object of worship, it is inconceivable, on any principle of common sense, why it is not enjoined in terms at least equally clear as those which enjoin prayer to God supreme. The less obvious any truth, the stronger evidence does it demand. The more obscure an object, the more light should be poured upon it to render it distinct. The reverse is the case here, and that, too, in a revelation from the God of all wisdom! The inspired volume makes it the first and greatest of all its injunctions, to serve and worship the Lord God alone; and here is another doctrine, which, if true, would be of equal importance; a doctrine which reason never could discover—which is novel, and at variance with the first injunction, and which therefore requires ten-fold evidence, left in such obscurity that many of the keenest, most candid and learned investigators of Scripture truth, have never been able to find it; nay, deny it altogether as a human fiction! This is

---

* Wakefield gives us the following example as an "exact specimen of the curious manner, in which Dr. Burgh and such writers, constantly reason in defence of the Trinity.

Make *a cheerful noise* to the God of Jacob. Ps. lxxxi. 1. Whatsoever things are of *good report*, think on these things. Phil. iv. 8.

The Psalmist exhorts us to make *a cheerful noise*; and Paul recommends as a Christian virtue, whatsoever is of *good report*; therefore a cheerful noise is a Christian virtue, Q. E. D.

For nonsense like this, delivered in a strain of the most indecent buffoonery, and accompanied by every symptom of the most profound ignorance of these subjects, was our theologian complimented with the dignity of LL.D. as a reward of his high deserts, as a controversialist and a divine, by one of the most renowned Universities in Christendom!"

According to Burgh's mode of reasoning, David might be proved to be a bird, an insect, and an inanimate quadruped; for he compares himself to a pelican, an owl, and a sparrow. Ps. cii. 6, 7, and says, that he is a flea, and a dead dog. 1 Sam. xxiv. 14.

Burgh's school of theology is by no means extinct. It has still many hopeful pupils, who would certainly not suffer even Burgh to bear away the palm, without a desperate syllogistic conflict.

"When Greek meets Greek, then comes the tug of war."

strange. It amounts to a demonstration of the absolute nullity of the doctrine, or of the necessity of an infallible church, invested with power, not only to decree rites and ceremonies, but to open the eyes of the blind, to give a clear perception of invisibilities, and work miracles in every exigency.

This argument derives considerable force from the reflection, that the Gospel was designed for the poor and illiterate, as well as for men of education; and that the doctrines necessary to the formation of the Christian character, and to eternal salvation, lie on the surface, and are not to be explored with difficulty through the dark profundities of theology. They depend not on the inferences of metaphysicians or subtle disputers and dialecticians, but may be found in the luminous pages of Scripture without note or comment. No man of plain understanding, unsophicated by articles, and creeds, and confessions of faith, will ever find in the Gospel that it is his duty to pray to any being but the Father Almighty. We are told in Luke xi. that "one of the disciples said to our Saviour, Lord, teach us to pray, as John also taught his disciples." Our Lord, with his wonted promptitude, immediately complied with their wish, and desired them to say, "Our Father, which art in heaven." On other occasions also, he told them *how*, *to whom*, *for what*, they should pray, and *for what* they should not pray; but he never desired them to address a Trinity, nor to accost himself by the appellation of God the Son. He said to the woman of Samaria, " The hour cometh, and now is, when the true worshippers shall worship."—Whom? Not God the Son, not God the Holy Ghost, not a "holy, blessed, and glorious Trinity, three persons and one God;" but "THE FATHER, in spirit and in truth; for the Father seeketh such to worship him;" and, as if the Saviour meant to guard against all mistake on a subject so important, he adds, "God is a Spirit;" i. e. one Spirit, not three Spirits; and repeats the declaration which he had just made, to give it double efficacy—"they that worship *him* (not them) must worship him in spirit and in truth." John iv. 23, 24. The woman, without expressing any opinion on what she had just heard; but with that intuitive acuteness of perception by which the female mind is often distinguished, probably suspecting that Jesus was the Christ, and at the same time commingling with her suspicions, a little address to discover whether they were well-founded, said, " I know that Messiah cometh, which is called Christ; when he is come, he will tell us all things;" all things relative to the subject of their conversation. Our Lord saw and rewarded her address by informing her that *he* was the Messiah, consequently implying, that she might have unbounded confidence in the truth of what he had said. The woman appears to have given him full credence, for when she met the men of the city, she said, " Come and see *a man* which told me all things that ever I did.—Is not this *the Christ?*" The men went, and having heard our Lord discourse, they entered fully into her sentiments, and requested him to sojourn among them. He gratified them by remaining two days, during which time " many more believed because of his own word, and said unto the woman, Now we believe, not because of thy saying ; for we have heard him ourselves, and know that this is indeed the Christ, the Saviour of the world." But though they had such high veneration for the character of our Lord, and saw clearly that he was the long-expected hope of Israel, they did not pay him divine honours; nor would it have evinced that they were much edified by his conversation, if after being so expressly told that the Father is to be worshipped, they had dishonoured his instructions by offering adoration to himself.

Our Lord was instant in prayer to " his Father and our Father, to his God and our God." But is there any instance of his having preferred a petition to any being but Jehovah ? Or is there any Evangelical authority for those fearfully solemn adjurations by which his own name is so frequently invoked ? The Unitarian cannot find, either from the precepts or example of the Saviour, that any being whatever is to be adored, save God alone. If told that he ought to address Christ in prayer, he replies, that he has received no such instructions in the Gospel ; for not only did Christ never desire that prayer should be made to him, but, on the contrary, forbade it. " *In that day*," viz. in the time of his highest exaltation, " *ye shall ask me nothing*," said he. " Verily, verily, I say unto you, whatsoever ye shall ask the Father in my name, he will give it you," John xvi. 23. But here we are told that the first *ask*, in Greek ερωτησει, signifies to ask questions—and the second αιτηστι to beseech. But the former verb occurs in one or another of its tenses, in numerous places of Scripture in the sense of *praying, entreating, and beseeching*. Luke xiv. 18. xvi. 27, *I pray.*—In John xiv. 16. Christ himself says, *I will pray*, ερωτησω. No fewer than three times does he use the same verb in the same sense, in John xvii. 9, 15, 20. In Philip. iv. 3, it is rendered, *I entreat*. Thrice in the two Epistles to the Thessalonians, *beseech*, I. iv. 1, v. 12.—II. ii. 1. In 2 John 5. *beseech*, and in 1 John v. 16, αιτιω is translated *ask*, and ερωτα *pray*. Doddridge is one of those who think that the latter verb in John xvi. 23, should be understood as an interrogatory, for no very apparent reason, except that if it be rendered *pray*, it is fatal to his doctrine. Accordingly his paraphrase runs thus, " When I have sent the Comforter, you shall *not enquire any thing of me*." But if they were not to *enquire*, much less, *a fortiori*, were they to *pray* to him, as is sufficiently clear from the context, for he immediately subjoins by a solemn asseveration, that if they would, ask, or pray to the Father, in his name, their prayers would be heard. Again, when John fell down to worship the angel, Rev. xxii. " See thou do it not," said he, " for I am thy fellow-servant, and of thy brethren the prophets, and of them which keep the sayings of this book : worship God." The angel before whom

John fell down was he who said in the 7th verse, "Behold I come quickly"—and in the 9th, See thou do it not—worship God."—Again in the 12th verse, we have the same words, "Behold I come quickly." Was it the same angel who uttered these words, or another? The same, as their very repetition indicates; and in the whole passage there is but one agent who is designated by the pronoun *he*, and no intimation whatever of any change of persons, or the introduction of any new interlocutor. The same person who says "I come quickly," in the 7th and 12th verses, says in the 13th, "I am Alpha and Omega, the beginning and the end, the first and the last,"—or in other words, the first born of the new creation, the author and finisher of our faith—and in the 16th, "I Jesus have sent mine angel to testify unto you these things in the Churches." It is demonstrated then, that this Jesus was he who refused the worship of John, and prohibited all worship that is not paid to the Father. But though there should be some subterfuge from this conclusion, it cannot be denied, on any pretext, that the positive command, whether pronounced by Jesus or an angel is "WORSHIP GOD." The Unitarian having the fear of God before his eyes, and a just dread of the curse denounced in the 18th verse against "any man who shall add unto these things," dares not add a syllable to that command, nor join any other object of adoration whatsoever to the Holy One of Israel, the God and Father of our Lord Jesus Christ. As for the words at the close of the volume, "Even so, come, Lord Jesus,"—they are only a pious ejaculatory wish.

The Apostles followed the injunction and example of their divine Master: they neither prayed to Christ themselves, nor did they desire the disciples to pray to him. We have several of their prayers in the Acts, addressed to the Father, the Creator of heaven and earth; and every one must observe a most marked distinction in them between God and his holy child Jesus. Great stress has been laid on the invocation of Stephen in his last moments, as if it were an infallible rule to which we were commanded to conform. But to what does it amount? The ideas which Stephen had formed of our Lord, were not such as would justify an act of adoration, as appears from the account which he himself gives of his vision.—"Behold I see the heavens opened, and the *Son of man standing at* the right hand of God."—"And they stoned Stephen, calling upon (God is not in the original) and saying, Lord Jesus, receive my spirit." Nothing could be more natural than such an invocation to the Saviour whom he saw, or had just seen. But what example can it be to us, unless we should be placed in similar circumstances, and gratified with a similar vision? Christ, not Stephen, is the example for us to follow, and Christ always prayed to the Father.

The conduct of Stephen has furnished the Socinians with an argument for praying to Christ. Hence, of course, the Unitarian disclaims the appellation of Socinian. He does so, moreover, nor because he thinks that denomination of Christians more erroneous than many others in their belief; nor because he would dread to incur the uncharitable denunciations by which they are so commonly anathematized; but because he thinks their creed unsound; and in spiritual things, he calls no one his master. Socinians, though a constant theme of obloquy with those who know nothing of them but the name, and classed with deists and infidels, were, notwithstanding, steady believers in the truth of Christianity, and they have illustrated the Scriptures by many works of great piety and learning, to which some of the most orthodox writers have not disdained to be indebted. The grand error of their creed was their believing in the simple humanity of Christ, and at the same time worshipping him as a God. This was certainly a great inconsistency; an inconsistency, however, in which they were not singular. Some of those who vaunt their orthodoxy, and are most forward to malign Socinians and their creed, would do well to examine their own belief, and ascertain whether they may not be guilty of the very heresy which they condemn. Does not a well-known orthodox church in its Litany, invoke Christ thus? *"By thine agony and bloody sweat; by thy cross and passion; by thy precious death and burial; by thy glorious resurrection and ascension; and by the coming of the Holy Ghost, Good Lord deliver us."* Will some of those who repeatedly join in this invocation, have the goodness to declare to whom it is addressed? Is it to Christ in what they call his divine, or in his human nature,—to God or to man? The Unitarian feels reluctant to suppose that it is to the former; for "the agony and bloody sweat" of God—the "cross and passion—the death and burial" of God, would be to him most revolting ideas. There is nothing in popery more abhorrent from the simplicity of Gospel truth. The crucifix alone is wanting to give it full effect—If it be to the latter, is it not evident that he who employs it, is one with the Socinian, and that both pay their adorations to a deified man? And, should not this consideration mollify the wrath of the Athanasians against their Socinian brethren, and induce them to pause, before they brandish and hurl the hissing red-hot thunderbolts of damnation on the heads of their fellow-worshippers?

The Unitarian can understand and appreciate the feelings which lead men of devout minds, to ascribe to the Son all that is due to the Father. But there are errors of excess as well as of deficiency. Many pious women feel all the ardours of devotion in praying to the Virgin Mary: and seem to think that they are more likely to obtain the object of their petition from the tenderness and compassion of a divinity of their own sex, than from either the Father or the Son. Protestants wonder at this, and condemn the practice, for the best of all reasons, that it has no Scripture authority. For the same reason, the

M

Unitarian objects to all worship that is not paid to the Father; and dislikes such phrases as God the Son, and God the Holy Ghost, as much as the orthodox Protestant dislikes to hear Mary termed the mother of God. Popery is the origin of both. And yet the objections of such Protestants as believe Christ to be the Deity, to hear Mary called the mother of God are certainly very unreasonable. For Mary being his mother, if he were God, the obnoxious conclusion is unavoidable; and wherefore should she be refused her title?* The Roman Catholic who calls her the Queen of Heaven and the Mother of God, as she was called in the days of Cyril, and *decreed to be* in the councils of Ephesus and Chalcedon, is consistent. But the Church-of-England-man who refuses her the latter appellation at least, is not only inconsistent, but a dissenter from one of the most landed bishops of his own church; even from Bull—the great Bull, the Lord Bishop of St. David's, who wrote in defence of the Nicene creed. Nelson the biographer of this redoubtable orthodox bishop, informs us, (page 487) that "in his Sermon concerning the Blessed Virgin, he asserts and vindicates her peculiar title of the MOTHER OF GOD; which was not invented by the Fathers of the third general council at Ephesus, convened against Nestorius, but approved by them as what belonged to her, since it *was the language of Scripture, and the style* of the Apostolical age." Another Church-of-England divine, but of a very different stamp, says, that "some of the fathers of the Nicene council would have had no difficulty to give the superiority or precedence to the Virgin Mary, in making her the third person of the Trinity."† The council of Ephesus, A.D. 431, received her as a *supplement* to the Trinity, under the appellation of *Theotokos*, Mother of God—Mosheim thinks it an innocent term; but his translator, Dr. M'Clean, truly observes that the use of such mysterious terms, as have no place in Scripture, is, undoubtedly, pernicious to true religion.

Some one may ask, are we not commanded to honour the Son, even as we honour the Father? Yea, verily, friend. But we are now discoursing, not of honour, but of religious worship. We are commanded to honour our father and mother, not to worship them;—we are commanded to honour the king, not to adore

---

* "Also, James ought to be called the ʼBrother of God,' but such phrases are highly derogatory to the character of the Supreme Author of the Universe; and it is the use of phrases similar to these, which has rendered the religion of the Hindoos so grossly absurd and contemptible."— *Rammohun Roy*, p. 254.

† "This, says the Rev. H. Taylor, Vicar of Portsmouth, the learned author of the Letters of Ben Mordecai, (p. 191) we learn from *Elmacinus & Patricides*." Hottinger, Hist. Orient, l. ii. p. 227.

him; to honour all men, not to deify them; and to honour the Son of God, not to hail him as the supreme Jehovah. We should honour him, indeed, in a very exalted sense, for the reason which he has himself assigned—because the Father "*hath committed* all judgment unto the Son, that all men should honour the Son (καθως) as they honour the Father"—in the same manner, not in the same degree. Thus, we are enjoined to be merciful, as (καθως) our Father also is merciful. Luke iv. 36. "He that honoureth not the Son, honoureth not the Father *who hath sent him.*" He that would honour the king, must honour his ambassador. We honour Christ, not by praying to him, but by listening with reverence to his precepts and doctrines; not by exclamations of Lord! Lord! but by doing the will of his heavenly Father. We dishonour him by giving him attributes which he disclaimed; by torturing his language, to favour creeds of human fabrication; by contradicting his own positive declarations that he was neither omnipotent nor omniscient; and by imputing to him that *duplicity* of character involved in the doctrine of what is called "the two natures."

If prayer to Christ were an evangelical duty, we should have evangelical instruction for its performance. Those who advocate it are challenged to produce a single text in which the Saviour *commands* prayer to be addressed to a Trinity, or to himself, and to shew where certain terms ascriptive of religious homage to Jehovah, are equally applied to the Son. It has been already shewn that προσκυνω, a verb expressive sometimes of divine worship, and sometimes of civil respect, is used in conjunction with the Saviour's name, as with that of kings and prophets. But αινω, I praise, used in the worship of the Eternal God, is not applied to Christ: nor λατρευω I serve. "Thou shalt worship the Lord thy God, and HIM ONLY shalt thou serve."—λατρευσεις. Let the defenders of Trinitarianism produce a text like this for the worship of the Son, and the contest will be at an end. Σεβομαι I worship, in the true religious sense, is also applied to God, but not to Christ. Thus Mat. xv, 9, and Mark, vii. 7. "In vain do they worship me, σεβονται με, teaching for doctrines the commandments of men." Paul speaking of the corruptions and idolatries of the Gentiles, says, εσεβασθησαν και ελατρευσαν, Rom. i. 25. they worshipped and served, or paid religious homage to the creature more than the creator. We find no such expressions connected with the name of Christ. Luke also, Acts, xvi. 14. says of Lydia the seller of purple, that she was one σεβομενη τον θεον worshipping God—and of Justus, c. xviii. 7. σεβομενη τον θεον who worshipped God; and v. 13, persuaded men σεβεσθαι to worship God; and again, Acts, xix. 27. where Demetrius speaks of Diana, whom all Asia and the world worship. ἡ σεβεται σεβεται. Mark what a distinction the Apostle makes. (Philip, iii. 3.) between God and Christ; and the *worship* due to the one, and the *joy* inspired by a sense of the blessings conveyed by the other: "We are the circumcision, says he, which *worship* God in spirit, and *rejoice* in Christ Jesus," οἱ πνευματι Θεῳ λατρευοντες, και καυχωμενοι εν Χριστω. When Peter and John were suffering persecution from the Jews, they addressed their prayers not to Christ but to God—and clearly marked in what light they contemplated Christ, when they prayed "that signs and wonders may be done by the name of thy holy child *(servant)* Jesus." αγιε Παιδος Ιησυ, *servi tui.* GROTIUS.

To quit verbal criticism; this part of the subject shall be concluded by one general argument, to which the candid reader is requested to give particular attention. It will be admitted that no people, on the face of the earth, were ever more tenacious than the Jews, of their religious principles; or more jealous of any infringement on the honour and worship due to Jehovah. A belief in one God was the grand discriminating feature of their religion. They considered the God of Israel as peculiarly their own, and looked with ineffable contempt and abhorrence on every species of strange worship; insomuch, that after their return from the Babylonish captivity, we never hear of their relapsing into idolatry. Now, let the following questions be fairly answered.—Wherefore did the Jews never accuse either Christ or his Apostles, of introducing any species, or any object, of worship to which they had not been accustomed? Were they, with all their national prepossessions; their boasted patriarchal covenants; their special interests with heaven; their commandments written by the finger of God, and sanctioned by so many threats and promises; their positive laws directed against all idolatry, and guarded not only by the sword of the legislature, but by the interests of a vigilant, vindictive, and intolerant priesthood; were they, after all, less regardful of the purity of their worship, than the idolatrous Athenians who put Socrates to death, on the pretext that he had corrupted their religion? Why did they not bring forward a similar charge against Christ, and accuse him of having advanced the unheard-of claim to the second place in the Godhead, and demanded the same adoration as the Father? This would have been a glorious accusation for the priests. It would have sacrificed their victim, and preserved their popularity: and, it cannot be doubted that if they had found, either in the words or actions of our Lord, the smallest point on which they could rest such a charge, they would have seized it with malignant avidity. But that was an invention of which, with all their iniquity, they were guiltless. No suspicion of it ever glanced across their minds. For though the Saviour taught them more just notions than they had entertained of the benignant and paternal character of God, it was the God of their fathers whom they jointly worshipped—and in all their accusations of blasphemy, they never said that he claimed a right to be adored. We have already seen that the high priest adjured him to declare, not whether he had assumed the character of deity, but whether he were the Christ; and when he was brought before Pilate, by the elders, the chief priests and the scribes, of what did they accuse him? We found this *fellow*, said they, perverting the nation.—Luke, xxiii. 2. What kind of perversion did they mean? Political or religious? The former decidedly: to the latter they did not even allude. Nor did they, nor could they allege, though it would have served their purpose well, that any body of men, or any individual of all the thousands who had congregated to hear him, ever paid him divine honours. They dared not to affirm that he attempted to seduce them from the worship of the God of their fathers. For when the multitude saw the dumb to speak, the maimed to be whole, the lame to walk, and the blind to see; they glorified, not the agent by whom these wonders were wrought, but "the God of Israel," who had imparted such power to work them.—Mat. xv. 31. When he cured the sick of the palsy, the people "marvelled, and glorified God, who had *given such power unto men;*" (ανθρωποις) Mat. ix. 8. that is, according to the Hebrew idiom, *to a man.* During the whole scene of his trial and crucifixion, he was never once accused of having either claimed or received adoration. When he hung upon the cross, and the mob, the soldiers, the priests, and the thieves, or one of the thieves at least, seemed to contend with each other, who should revile him most, they never touched upon this topic. One of the groupes said, "if thou be the Son of God, come down from the cross. He *trusted in God,* let him deliver him if he will have him, for he said I am the Son of God." But amidst all their revilings and derisions, they never confounded his claim to the title of the Son of God with that of God himself; nor charged him with the impiety of usurping divine honours; for the plain reason that he had never afforded them the slightest pretext for such an accusation; nor did they dream of any one in human shape making such extravagant pretensions: and if they had, our Lord's exclamation, "MY GOD, *my God,* why hast thou forsaken me," would have dispelled the delusion.

Once more—Why were the Apostles in all their bitter persecutions and trials before the grand council of the Jews, never in any one instance, accused of introducing strange worship? Stephen was arraigned for speaking blasphemous words against Moses, against God, the temple and the law, and of saying that Jesus of Nazareth would destroy their city, and change the customs or institutions which Moses delivered unto them.— Acts, vi. 14. But he was not taxed with any attempt to introduce a new deity. The ritual of the Jews might be changed, but the object of their worship was eternally the same. The Apostle Paul, after his conversion, declares, Acts, xxiv. 14. that he worshipped the God of his fathers—"I thank God," (says he, 2 Tim. i. 3.) "whom I serve, (ω λατρευω) from my forefathers." He sojourned at Ephesus for three years, and during that time, "shunned not to declare *the whole* counsel of God"—but we are no where informed that he ever taught the Trinitarian doctrine. The Jews accused him of being a pestilent fellow, a mover of sedition, and a ringleader of the Nazarenes—but they could not tax him with the more heinous offence of making a deity of Christ. They formed a conspiracy to assassinate him; but they did not charge him with an attempt to turn the people to idolatry. Both in his preaching and his writings he most strictly maintains the divine unity. "There is none other God but one. For though there be that are called Gods, whether in heaven or in earth, (as there be Gods many, and Lords many,) but to us, (Christians) there is but *one God, the Father; * * * * * and one Lord, Jesus Christ.* 1 Cor. viii. 4, 5, 6. And again—"There is one God, and one mediator between God and men, the man Christ Jesus."— 1 Tim. ii. 5. The adoration of Christ, like the doctrine of the Trinity, is founded neither on Scripture, nor on reason and common sense, but on tradition and the infallible church.

SECTION THIRTEENTH.

The Trinity a human invention—a mystery, and therefore no subject of Christian belief.

After quoting a long series of texts, which carry no proof of the doctrine he advocates, to such as understand them right, Mr. Pope comes to the conclusion that the TRINITY IS A MYSTERY. In this conclusion he has the felicity of agreeing with all who have espoused his side of the question. One of the fathers terms it "a tremendous doctrine,"* and never was any appellation more appropriate. It originated in darkness, has been propagated by terror, and upheld by the sword. The term Trinity was not known in the Christian Church for nearly 200 years, and when it was first used by Theophilus, a convert of Antioch, it was in a sense very different from that which it afterwards assumed. The fathers of the three first centuries, and consequently all the ancient Christian people for 300 years P. C. till the Council of Nice, were generally Unitarians.† This may be learned from the testimony even of the most decided

* "The *tremendous* Deity," says Dr. Waterland, "is all over mysterious." Surely this must be meant of some heathen deity; not of him whom the Scriptures have *revealed* to us as our Father, and whose tender mercies are over all his works.
† Priestley.

Trinitarian authors. Bishop Bull says, that "almost all the Catholic writers before Arius's time, seem not to *have known any thing* of the *invisibility* and *immensity* of the Son of God, and they often speak of him in such a manner as if, even in respect of his divine nature, he was finite, visible, and circumscribed."* And again, " the Catholic writers, both they that were before, and they that were after the Council of Nice, have *unanimously declared* God the Father to be *greater* than the Son ; even according to his divinity."†

Whiston, after a minute examination of the Antenicene evidences, affirms ;

"That the Son was not an underived, unoriginated independent, and in that sense, an *eternal* Being, but truly derived from and produced or begotten by the Father, is the unanimous voice of all Christian antiquity, both in and after the apostolical age; and is not directly denied by any Athanasian at this day. Now, how a confessedly derived, produced and begotten Being, and only begotten Son, should be really *co-eternal* with his underived, unbegotten and necessarily existing author, producer, and Father, I cannot possibly understand."‡

Mosheim also observes, " that the doctrine of the three persons in the Godhead, during the three first centuries, had happily escaped the vain curiosity of human researches, and had been left undefined and undetermined by any particular set of ideas." And " Jurieu, whose zeal against heresy," says Jortin, " is well known, assures us that the fundamental articles of Christianity

---

* Ben Mordecai. Def. Fid. Nic. § 1. c. iii. Bulli. Quippe, ex ipsorum (viz. primævorum Doctorum) sententia, Deus Pater nemine unquam, ne per assumptas species, visus est, aut videri potest. A nullo ille ortus principio, nulli subjectus est: neque magis ab alio missus, quam ab alio natus dici potest. Contra, filius Dei, qua ex Deo Patre natus, eo certe nomine Patri *suam omnem auctoritatem acceptam* refert.

Bulli opera: Sectio, iv. c. iii, § 4, p. 268.

The same author makes the following concession to Socinus, almost at the very beginning of his work. " Cum dicit veteres omnes, usque ad concilium Nicænum, credidisse, *Patrem solum* Jesu Christi esse *unum illum verum Deum ;* si de Patris prærogativa, qua ipse solus a seipso Deus verus est, intelligatur;* *verissimum esse illud fatemur."* Id. p. 2, § 4.

† Idem, Cap. ii. Thesis secunda. The translation is by Nelson, the bishop's biographer, who also states that he hath learnedly and solidly confuted the unreasonable and uncatholic notion of the moderns, which maketh the Son a self-dependent principle of divinity (and by consequence another God,) by asserting and defending, that he might *properly* be called αυτοθεος as well as the Father is, and that he is truly God of himself, and not *God of God*, as the Nicene fathers confess him. This opinion (MARK reader MARK !) was first of all started by Calvin against the judgment of the Catholic Church to this very day, and even of the first reformers, Luther and Melancthon, as Petavius and our Author have sufficiently shewn."—BULL's LIFE, p. 317.

‡ Whiston's Letter to the Earl of Nottingham, concerning the eternity of the Son of God and of the Holy Spirit—pp. 27, 28.

(viz: of *his* Christianity) were not understood by the Fathers
of the three first centuries; that the true system began to be
modelled into some shape by the Nicene bishops, and was immensely *improved and beautified* by the following synods and
councils." The learned theologian should have completed the
climax by saying that the Apostles were ignorant of Christianity,
which they certainly were, if Christianity consists either in the
inexplicable dogmas of succeeding councils, or the sanctimonious
jargon of certain advocates of "peculiar doctrines" at the
present day, which are as repugnant to the word of God,
as they are insulting to common sense. At length came the
struggle between Arius and Athanasius, the one loaded with
every epithet of abuse which an intolerant and triumphant faction could invent; the other a falsifier, a forger, and the author
of a new system of divinity, whose language, at least, and prac-
tices, if not notions, were certainly unknown to the early ages
of Christianity.* Their rival claims were discussed by the
Council of Nice, A.D. 325. and the stronger and more numerous party, of course, prevailed. But even that celebrated
Council left its unhallowed work incomplete. We have the
orthodox testimony of Jurieu for affirming that "the mystery
remained without its right form or shape until the Council of
Constantinople;† and this in two points, the *temporal generation* of the second person, and his *inequality*; both which were
unanimously professed by all the ancients of the three first
ages." Petavius, as quoted by Whiston, alleges that the very
first Synod which expressly decreed that the Holy Spirit should
be esteemed God, was that of Alexandria, where Athanasius
was President, A.D. 363. After various defeats and successes,
Athanasianism became finally triumphant, and erected its thrones
and its tripods on the ruins of gospel truth. The Saviour had
declared that his kingdom is not of this world, but Athanasianism formed an indissoluble alliance with the potentates of the
earth, laid the cross of Christ beneath the footstool of imperial
power, and found that the arm of flesh and the sword of steel
would serve its cause more effectually than "the sword of the
spirit, which is the word of God." Having obtained dominion
on earth, it boldly laid claim to supreme authority in heaven
and hell, and pretended to be in possession of the keys of both.
Belief in its dogmas, was made the passport to the one, and disbe-
lief doomed to the irremediable everlasting torments of the other.
The "tremendous doctrine" was fortified by all the strength
of the civil and ecclesiastical powers; by all the hopes and

* Whiston's Preface, p. 98.
† "A council of gladiators held in an amphitheatre, would be as venerable
as that of the Constantinopolitan Fathers, if Gregory Nazianzen may be
believed."—JORTIN.

fears which are created and fostered by pride, ambition, avarice and servile submission to human authority. Tradition interposed a shield to guard it against every shaft from the quiver of divine truth; common sense lay crushed under the hoof of superstition; and if reason presumed to mutter, she was awed into silence by the clank of chains and the crackling of faggots.

Mr. Pope having acknowledged that the divinity (meaning the deity) of Christ is a mystery, proceeds to defend it, by asking, "Is it therefore to be renounced? The union of soul and body is a mystery—do we therefore disbelieve it? The growth of the humblest blade of grass is inexplicable—shall we therefore withhold our assent from it?" From what?

Such is a specimen of Mr. Pope's reasoning powers, and of the mode frequently adopted to end embarrassing inquiries, and establish "tremendous doctrines." Better to let them rest undisturbed on the basis of tradition, than try to support them by such reasons as these. An argument is drawn from our ignorance of one subject, to enforce our adoption of some absurd opinion on another. Because my limited faculties are unable to form any adequate idea of the divine nature which is incomprehensible; I am told to embrace notions concerning it from which my understanding revolts. If I persist in starting unanswerable objections, I am desired to "prostrate my understanding," and told that I should not question but believe; that the subject is mysterious; that we must give credence to many things equally beyond our comprehension, and that it is the part of infidelity alone to doubt them. Such a minatory process has often served the purpose intended. It may repress a vexatious curiosity, and impose silence on children; but it will not satisfy a fearless searcher after truth, who wishes to build his faith on a solid foundation; nor prevent those who have taken the Apostle's advice, "in understanding to be men," from boldly pursuing their inquiries. A mystery is a secret thing, and "secret things belong unto the Lord our God; but those things which are revealed, belong unto us and to our children for ever, that we may do all the words of this law.—Deut. xxix. 29.—Revelation and mystery are contradictory terms. Behold, says the Apostle, I shew you a mystery;—he did so, and it was a mystery no longer; the secret was revealed.—I believe in revelation; of mystery I form no opinion, for what can I think of what has not been unfolded? I cannot believe what I do not understand. I can no more adopt an article of faith because it is a mystery, than because it is impossible. *Credo quia impossibile* was once deemed the most sublime effort of faith. It may be so still, but I have no capacity to admit it.

Mystery is a being of magical power in theology, a reconciler of absurdities, and the inseparable companion of priestcraft, fanaticism, and superstition. She would willingly be received as a descendant of the skies; but in features, dress, manners, and language, she betrays more of an origin from below. There is no spark of heaven in her eye. She wants the cloudless brow, and the voice of celestial music. Her mantle is a pall, and she wears an amulet of dead men's bones.—Truth, the real daughter of heaven, delights to walk abroad in the full blaze of day—but mystery "loves darkness better than light, because her deeds are evil." She creeps into her labyrinths of woods and caves to mutter her spells, and pore over her hieroglyphics; while reason is reading the attributes of God in the volume of nature, in the starry letters of the firmament, and the luminous page of inspiration. Mystery detests such words as reason and common sense, and calls them carnal and unchristian. She deems it presumptuous to utter them along with her "peculiar doctrines," which are a tissue of paradoxes, contradictions, and impossibilities—and gladly would she exclude them by an *index expurgatorius* from all pious vocabularies. Over the weak, the ignorant, and all whom the prejudices of custom and education have subjected to her controul, she exercises a tyrannical domination. But men who know and dare to assert their rights, will neither be silenced nor spell-bound by her terrors. They burst into the unhallowed circle which she draws around her, and with the torch of reason and of gospel truth, dispel the mists in which she is shrouded, and expose her impositions to the scorn they merit.

Was not MYSTERY the name inscribed on the forehead of the woman in the Revelations—who was arrayed in purple and scarlet, and drunk with the blood of the saints, and with the blood of the martyrs of Jesus?*

---

* "It is surprising that mankind should suffer themselves to be *mocked, abused, and insulted,* by certain dealers in hard words, who, when they are driven, by men of spirit, out of every other fort, retire to the impregnable one of MYSTERY, where they think themselves secure, and impudently defy all the attacks of human understanding and common sense. Like the philosophers of old, who when they were puzzled to account for any phenomenon in nature, resolved it easily by the convenient term of OCCULT QUALITY."

An attempt to explain the words Reason, Substance, Person, p. 208, by a Presbyter of the Church of England.

The able work from which this passage is extracted, was written by the Rev. Dr. Wm. Robertson, born in Dublin, 1705. Like Lindsey, he resigned his living in the church established by law; preferring poverty and a pure conscience, to the loss of his Christian liberty—and to the hope of advancement in the church, which hope, his learning, piety, and the friendship of Primate Stone, and of Dr. Robinson, Lord Bishop of Ferns, might have justly encouraged him to indulge. When he waited on his patron, under scruples, he was told, "you are a madman; you do not know the world." True. But he had some of that wisdom which passeth the understanding of worldlings; and might say with Paul, that he was "determined not to know any thing among you, save Jesus Christ and him crucified." For a farther interesting account of this "voluntary martyr," see Belsham's Life of Lindsey.

Mr. Pope seems not to have considered that there can be any difference between a physical fact, and a theological mystery. I cannot tell how soul and body are united; but that they are united, every creature possessing a rational soul, intuitively knows. *How* they are united is another question. The growth of a blade of grass is inexplicable. Most true. That it does grow, however, no one doubts. *How* it grows, none pretends to explain. That there is a principle in nature called gravitation, I believe, because its operations are constantly and every where visible. *How* it acts, I no more venture even to guess, than to tell in what manner the effect is produced by its cause. But what has all this to do with the question under consideration? Observe, I deny the Trinity—not because it is a mystery, but because it does not exist. I deny it—not because I cannot comprehend it, but because the Scriptures have not revealed it; and so far as both reason and Scripture are concerned, it is a contradiction, an impossibility, and rank nonsense. Gravity and vegetation are not mysteries—it is only their *modus operandi* that is mysterious. Prove that there is a trinity of persons in the Godhead, and it will not be disputed on account of its being involved in mystery. I demand evidence of *the fact*. Before we lose labour in investigating the laws of a phenomenon, we should be well assured that it is a reality, and not an imagination. When the existence of a chimera is demonstrated, it will be time enough to consider its mode of existence. I repeat it then, *prove the fact;* shew either from Scripture or from reason, that there are three persons in the Deity; and that three are one, and one three, and I shall no more insist on being informed *how* such a paradox can be true, than to know by what secret influence the grass is made to spring, or the planets to gravitate. I shall rest contented with a knowledge of the fact, when it is demonstrated; but my ignorance of the means employed by nature in conducting her operations, shall never lead me to embrace a theological absurdity.

It was said long since, by one who was as wise, at least, as any of our modern controversialists, "Thou knowest not what is the way of the spirit, nor how the bones do grow in the womb of her that is with child." Eccles. xi. 5. But he did not make our ignorance of the manner in which a common physical phenomenon is conducted, an argument for the presumption of pretending to know what the Almighty has concealed, but simply an irrefragable proof that we know not the works of God, which maketh all;— he had no idea of making his observation the basis of a " tremendous doctrine."

There is no text in all Scripture half so strong in favour of the Trinity, as the words. "This is my body;" and some other expressions in the gospel of John, are in favour of the "real presence" of Christ in the Eucharist. Yet, Mr. Pope, it is presumed, rejects the doctrine of transubstantiation, because he deems it contrary to those principles of reason and common sense, which are so powerful in behalf of Unitarianism. But wherefore not adopt it, since it is taught in language so clear and unambiguous? " Verily, verily, I say unto you, except ye eat the flesh of the son of man, and drink his blood, ye have no life in you." John vi. 53. Mr. Pope shrinks with abhorrence from the literal interpretation of these words, " to avoid the idea of cannibalism being a tenet of Christianity,"* and adduces arguments against it from that very *reason*, which so many vilify as carnal, whenever it speaks against any favourite tenet. Mr. Maguire will, of course, think him as obstinately prejudiced, and as wilfully blind to the truth, as Mr. Pope thinks the Socinian, for not adopting his interpretation of the passages which he quotes in favour of the Trinity. Strange perversity ! may he exclaim. Here is a great advocate of the free use of Scripture, who refuses his assent to its plainest dictates ; one who, being alike ignorant how body and soul are united, and how a blade of grass springs, dares, notwithstanding, to controvert a doctrine, which the old, long-established mother-church has deemed essential to salvation; and all, forsooth, because it is beyond comprehension and irreconcileable to reason ! Does he not know that it is a mystery ?—a mystery too, much less profound than that of the *three in one ;* and which may be supported by Scriptural arguments, far more analogical than those derived from our ignorance of physical secrets in support of Trinitarianism. What greater difficulty in supposing bread to be converted into real flesh and blood, than water into wine, at the marriage-feast of Cana in Galilee ?

This, however, may be a point in which no great difference subsists between Mr. Pope and Mr. Maguire. The catechism which the former has been taught, most assuredly *expresses* itself as strongly in favour of transubstantiation, as any thing in the mass-book, when it affirms that the faithful do *verily and indeed* take the body and blood of Christ in the Eucharist. But transubstantiation, though a fine-sounding word, was rejected by Luther, and consubstantiation substituted in its place. What is the real and essential difference? The former doctrine is rejected with horror by the Church of England Episcopalians; and what can we thence infer, but that the catechism expresses one thing, and that they are taught another ? Would it not be wise to reform the language of the catechism, and make it, if possible, declare what is the real belief of the church, on so important a subject ?

It seems strange and paradoxical, that those who are so ready to adduce arguments from men's ignorance, should assume such superiority of knowledge and discernment, in speaking of doctrines avowedly inexplicable and incomprehensible. Strange, that he who cannot tell by what imperceptible ties his body and

* Rammohun Roy's Final Appeal, p. 380.

soul are united, shall yet speak, with perfect confidence, of the union of two natures in Christ, a subject of which the Scriptures say nothing! That he who knows not the essence of his own mind shall, notwithstanding, dogmatize about consubstantialities in the Godhead, and its composition of persons, contrary to the clearest deductions of reason, and the plainest declarations of Scripture that God is one! Strangest of all, that he should, with perfect complacency, solemnly declare, in his religious services, that whosoever does not believe his inexplicable creed, must perish everlastingly!

Mr. Pope accuses Unitarians of reasoning from *a priori* speculations on the character of the Deity. How justly might it be retorted on Mr. Pope, that he forms his ideas of God from creeds and theological systems, which are founded neither on reason nor Scripture; nay, that are contrary to all that the blessed Saviour has taught us of his paternal, gracious, and benignant nature?

The Unitarian cannot believe that any revelation from heaven contradicts reason and common sense. It is, from the exercise of reason, in the first place, that he admits the truth of revelation at all; and this being once admitted, he adopts from it those doctrines which it clearly teaches. He interprets its language by the aid of the understanding which God has given him; receives with gratitude and cheerfulness all the discoveries which it makes of the divine perfections, of the way to felicity, and the life to come. He rejoices to find its doctrines accord so much with the dictates of reason, though far beyond her own unassisted efforts to discover. But, if any tenet be proposed for his adoption, which contradicts all those natural principles of thought and judgment which God has bestowed, he must pause. The inspiration of the Almighty gives understanding as well as revelation, to man. Both are his gifts; and the one is not intended to supersede, but to enlighten, direct, and aid the exercise of the other. " *Nunquam aliud natura, aliud sapientia dicit*," is a good maxim in theology, as well as in other subjects. To the Unitarian the Scriptures appear in perfect harmony with all the conclusions of reason on religious topics; and to imagine otherwise, would be a reflection on the wisdom of the Creator. When, therefore, any article of faith is proposed for his adoption, irreconcileable to reason, he contends, that it has not Scripture for its basis. He admits that its incomprehensibility may be no just ground of rejection; but its self-contradiction, or opposition to some demonstrable tenet of true religion, may. Though an angel were to preach the doctrine of three in one, the Unitarian could not— durst not receive it, till such angel produced his commission from heaven—confirmed its truth by miracles—and so proved that he was authorised to abrogate the first commandment given by Moses, and corroborated by the Son of God himself, who came " not to destroy, but to fulfil."

SECTION FOURTEENTH.

General Reasons for Rejecting the Doctrine of the Trinity.

THE UNITARIAN REJECTS THE DOCTRINE OF THE TRINITY, not because it is beyond, but because it is contradictory to reason, as much as transubstantiation. The Apostle Paul tells us (Rom. i. 20,) That the invisible things of God from the creation of the world; even his eternal power and Godhead, are clearly seen, being understood by the things that are made. But the existence of three persons in one God was never clearly, nor even dimly seen in any of the works of creation. They all exhibit proofs that the supreme omnipotent contriver and fabricator is ONE.

The Unitarian REJECTS the doctrine of the Trinity, because as Priestley has justly observed, "There is no fact in nature, nor any one purpose in morals, which are the object and end of all religion, that requires it." He REJECTS it, because it subverts the fundamental principle of revealed, as well as of natural religion. "Hear, O Israel, the Lord our God is one Lord," a truth confirmed by the blessed Saviour, who, when solicited by the Tempter to worship him, replied, "Thou shalt worship the Lord thy God, and HIM ONLY shalt thou serve." In vain do the advocates of the Trinity contend, that the unity of design apparent in the creation, argues unity of *counsel* and not of cause. This is a sophism and a salvo for a plurality of persons in the Godhead, unworthy even of Paley, whose words are re-echoed by shallow critics, and whose principles, however closely they "symbolize" with those of orthodoxy, are not always consonant to gospel integrity and truth. Paley should have learned better of the honest Unitarian Lardner, to whom his "Evidences" are so much indebted; and in a chapter on the Divine Unity, he ought not to have introduced an observation calculated to mislead the unreflecting, without giving it a proper explanation. But to aim a blow at natural religion, seems preferable with many to the admission of a principle by which the doctrine of the Trinity must be overturned. Paley's observation is exactly such as would become a heathen, anxious to open the gates of heaven for the re-admission of the mythological councils of the *Dii majores et minores;* though even a heathen might be brought to allow there is ONE SUPREME, the Father of gods and men. Now for the argument:—the author affirms, that the unity of design apparent in the creation, declares the unity of the great first cause; nay, that the unity of all such designs, whether it be our own solar system, or any other in the expanse of the universe, which could be formed only by omnipotence, leads to the same conclusion. There may be millions of subordinate causes, but all must be under the controul of one directing mind, to which none can be equal, and from which all power must be derived. For suppose, with the Manichæans of old, and with such semi-Christians as invest the devil with the attributes of Deity, that there are two omnipotent beings, the one good, and the other evil; each might exhibit proofs of almighty power—the one in creating, the other in destroying; but we should behold no beauty and harmony, under the government of two such rival potentates. Suppose both of them, however, to be as good and wise as they are powerful, might they not act in perfect concert, and exhibit in their works all the order which we admire in the world around us? Granted. But is it not plain, even to a demonstration, that if one of two beings has as much power as the other, neither of them is omnipotent? The sum total of power is divided between them;—each is deficient by a half, and being so deficient cannot be the great first cause of all. The great first cause can have no rival—no equal—no counsellor. *"With whom took he counsel?"* asks the Prophet Isaiah, as if indignant at the thoughts of that plurality of persons, which it is the misfortune of so many to hear advocated in place of the plain Scriptural truth, that God is one. "Who hath stood in the *counsel* of the Lord?" asks Jeremiah, xxiii. 18.—"Who," reiterates Paul, "hath known the mind of the Lord, or who hath been *his counsellor?*" Rom. xi. 34. Instead, therefore, of making concessions, of which the Polytheist and Atheist may take an unhappy advantage, it would be more wise of such "examiners," as are really Christian, to symbolize with the Apostle Paul, and say, "To us there is but one God;" and leave it to the disciples of Vigilius Thapsitanus, the supposed author of the notorious creed ascribed to Athanasius, to expatiate on a plurality of persons.

It has been laid down by one, from whom few will have the hardihood to dissent, that in the investigation of nature, two causes are never to be admitted, where one will suffice. If one self-existent, all-powerful being, be a cause adequate to the creation of the universe, it is unnecessary and unphilosophical to admit two. Therefore, God is one; and thus does true philosophy*

---

* Not the "*insaniens sapientia*" condemned by Horace, nor the *ασοφος σοφια* of Greg. Naz. but that which is cultivated by such minds as Newton's and Milton's.

> How charming is divine Philosophy !
> Not harsh and crabbed as dull fools suppose,
> But musical as is Apollo's lute,
> And a perpetual feast of nectar'd sweets,
> Where no crude surfeit reigns.
>
> MILTON's COMUS.

This is that true philosophy, which "looks through nature up to nature's God," and through Scripture to the glorious perfection of the eternal ONE ;

symbolize with the Scriptures in proclaiming the unity of God, that philosophy which, like wisdom, cometh from above, though so much decried by the advocates of " old wives' fables," and of that spurious philosophy which the gospel condemns and classes with " vain deceit, the tradition of men, and the rudiments of the world." Col. ii. 8.

The Unitarian REJECTS the doctrine of the Trinity, because it contradicts all that we are taught, and all that we are capable of comprehending of the infinite perfections of Jehovah. It contradicts his

Self-Existence, by identifying him with Christ, whom it acknowledges to be begotten :

His *Immensity*, by confining in a human form, him whom the heaven of heavens cannot contain :

His *Simplicity*, by representing him as compounded of three persons :

His *Spirituality*, by making him incarnate :

His *Invisibility*, for he was seen :

His *Immutability*, for he was in the form of a slave :

His *Impassibility*, for he suffered :

His *Immortality*, for he died :

His *Omnipotence*, for there were things not his to give :

His *Omniscience*, for some things he did not know :

Consequently, it denies the infinite perfection of all' the other attributes of Deity. For, if any being falls short of infinitude in any one perfection, he falls short in all. Our Lord positively affirmed, that none is good but ONE, and that is God—if none supremely good, then none supremely wise—none supremely just. In vain do the defenders of the Trinity try to escape the force of this argument, by the clumsy invention of the " two natures ;" an invention which, like that of transubstantiation, seems designed to try the extent of human credulity, and which, as has been already shewn, would bring such impeachments on the character of our Lord as the Unitarian shudders to express.

He REJECTS it, because it confounds attributes with persons—qualities with substance—humanity with deity. It *materializes* our ideas of the eternal mind ; and by teaching, that it can be essentially connected with corporeal forms, yields an easy introduction to image-worship. Hence we need not be surprised, if the great majority of those who embrace the doctrine of the Tri-

the opposite of that wisdom which springs from below, which is characterised by an Apostle as " earthly, sensual, devilish ;" and which, instead of presenting to the mind " a perpetual feast of nectar'd sweets" set before it the everlasting *crambe repetitia*, the horny indigestible husks of the five Calvinistic points. How long will men suffer their understanding to be " mocked, insulted, and abused ?"

nity, have statues, waxen figures and pictures, not only of God the Son, but of God the Father, and of God the Holy Ghost.*

If we can once be persuaded, that the infinitely great and glorious Being, who fills immensity, appeared as a man to men, little farther persuasion can be wanting to induce a belief, that he may be represented by images of gold, of silver, and of stone, contrary to the Apostle Paul's declaration to the Athenians. The transition from the reality to the similitude is easy and natural; and that worship which is due to God only, may be transferred to the sculptured or painted representative. Wherefore the Israelites were forbidden to have any image : " Take ye, therefore, good heed unto yourselves, for ye saw no manner of similitude on the day that the Lord spake unto you in Horeb, out of the midst of the fire, lest ye corrupt yourselves, and make you a graven image, the similitude of any figure." Deut. iv. 15, 16. The Prophet Isaiah asks, " To whom will ye liken God?—or what likeness will ye compare unto him ?" xl. 18. Trinitarianism answers, I will compare the immortal, the eternal, the invisible, the intangible, and impassible Spirit, to him who, after his resurrection from the dead, said to Thomas, " Reach hither thy hand and thrust it into my side." John xx. 27 ; and to his disciples, " Behold my hands and my feet that it is I myself ; handle me and see ; for a spirit hath not flesh and bones, as ye see me have." Luke xxiv. 39.

He REJECTS it, because it is undefinable and incapable of explanation, as is clearly testified by those who have written upon it most learnedly. Their treatises and volumes, composed with the avowed object of proving and elucidating the doctrine, present us only with a chaos of unintelligibilities, insomuch that it requires some effort of faith to believe, that their authors understood themselves. In worshipping the Trinity, " they worship they know not what," even by their own confession.†

He REJECTS it, because, so far as the Scriptures are concerned, it is altogether a doctrine of *inference*. Were such a doctrine true, it is reasonable to suppose, that they would teach it clearly and distinctly ; and that whole pages would be occupied in its explanation. Instead of this, a number of texts is collected together from various quarters, distorted from the meaning which they convey in their proper situation, and are made, by their new location, to speak a language not their own. They are stitched together like the Sibyl's scattered leaves ; a process by which the most anti-scriptural doctrines have been often found and taught

---

* The author has read, that beggars go about the streets of Lisbon seeking alms, with a drum, a bagpipe, and *an image*, or *picture of the Holy Spirit !*

† " Every attempt that has been made to *explain* the doctrine of the Trinity, I scruple not to call an insult on the common sense of mankind."— PRIESTLEY.

in the language of the Bible.* But even this process fails, when applied to the doctrine of the Trinity. The language of Holy Writ, though flowing through the impure conduit of an orthodox translation, refuses to be further contaminated by being made a channel of conveyance, to a doctrine which can be spoken of only in the style of its inventors. New words and new ideas must be coined and added to mutilated texts, and dismembered fragments of Scripture. But there can be no amalgamation of such heterogenous elements. The gold of inspiration has no affinity to the earth and iron of orthodoxy. When subjected to the fiery test, it separates from the base alloy, and flows forth, pure and resplendent, and bearing the superscription originally stamped upon it by heaven—GOD IS ONE.

According to the mode in which Trinitarianism draws her conclusions, Moses may be proved to be God; nay, man may be proved to be omnipotent, omnipresent, and omniscient. Thus, says Paul, "I can do all things; therefore, he is almighty. Again, he says, "Though I am absent in the flesh, yet am I with you in the spirit." Col. ii. 5; therefore, he is possessed of ubiquity. "Ye have an unction from the holy One, and know all things," says John—1 Ep. ii. 20; therefore, they were omniscient! Q. E. D.†

* This is precisely the process which was followed by the Athanasians at the Council of Nice. "They collected together the passages which represent the divinity of the Son of God, and observed, that *taken together they amounted to a proof* of his being of the same substance with the Father."—MILNER's *History of the Church*, vol. ii. p. 59. It would be curious to know all the particular texts collected on this occasion, because it is thought that some texts have been pressed into the service since, which the good fathers either overlooked, or did not understand. It would also be interesting to know what portion of the proof, each of the texts supplied. They would be found on examination, *methinks*, like a collection of negatives to make an affirmative, or of fallibilities to form an infallibility.

† "John the Baptist is said to have gone before Jehovah, and to have gone before Christ, and this Mr. Wardlaw gravely offers as a proof that Christ is Jehovah;" in answer to which, Mr. Yates, in his Vindication of Unitarianism, p. 194, furnishes us with the following very apposite illustrations :—" It appears by Exod. xx. 2—Deut. v. 6 that he who brought the Israelites out of Egypt, was Jehovah ; and by Exod. xxxii. 7—xxxiii. 1, that he who brought the Israelites out of Egypt was Moses—therefore, Moses was Jehovah. It appears also by 1 Sam. ii. 12, that the same persons are called the sons of Eli, and the sons of Belial, therefore, Eli was Belial."
"Would not this be deemed most wretched reasoning, if employed for any other purpose than to prove the doctrine of the Trinity? What should we say to an astronomer, who should seriously argue in like manner :—the moon revolves round the sun, but the moon revolves round the earth ; therefore, the earth is the sun;—the sun turns upon its own axis—the earth turns upon its own axis; therefore, also the earth is the sun ;—Jupiter revolves round the sun, and the earth revolves round the sun ; therefore, the earth is Jupiter !"—*Letters to a Protestant Divine, in Defence of Unitarianism, by another Barrister*, pp. 138, 139.

He REJECTS it, because all the proofs of it, singly and collectively, have not the strength of the first commandment. Trinitarianism betrays the weakness of her cause, by having recourse to such auxiliaries as certain idiomatic phrases and grammatical constructions, which in the judgment of the most learned scholars, do not contain the meaning she would extract from them. For instance, she finds in a Hebrew plural,* the three persons of her Godhead, a discovery, which to this day has escaped the knowledge of the Hebrew people, who might be supposed to know the latent virtues of their own language as well as any modern theologian; and when she might as well find in it the thirty thousand gods of the heathen. If an epithet be twice or thrice repeated to mark the superlative degree, or intensity of thought, she grasps it with eagerness, as if it contained a demonstration of her doctrine. Moreover, she repeats her few favourite texts even to satiety, as if they were new arguments; and being wiser in her generation than the children of light, acts on the principle, that repetition and perseverance will supply the place of strength.

Gutta cavat lapidem, non vi, sed sæpe cadendo.

By frequent falls, not forceful shock,
The drop scoops hollows in the rock.

He REJECTS it, because it leads to the most fanciful perversions of the word of God, and gives the mind over to a " strong delusion to believe a lie." Under the influence of its imagination, even learned, and in other respects, rational divines are led into the most egregious errors in their interpretation of the Scriptures. Thus, they find the three persons of the Trinity in the command given by our Saviour to the disciples, to baptize, Mat. xxii. 19, though it says not a syllable of three persons, but simply enjoins to baptize into the name of the Father, i. e. to initiate them,

---

* " Were we even to disregard totally the idiom of the Hebrew, Arabic, and of almost all Asiatic languages in which the plural number is often used for the singular, to express the respect due to the person denoted by the noun ; and to understand the term " our image," and " our likeness," found in Gen. i. 26, as conveying a plural meaning, the quotation would by no means answer the Trinitarian's purpose; for the verse, in that case, would imply a plurality of Gods, without determining whether their number was three or three hundred without specifying their persons."

This was written by one, whose knowledge of Oriental languages gives him a right to speak with decision, RAMMOHUN ROY. He subjoins the following illustrations :—Exodus xxi. 4—in the original Hebrew, " If his masters (meaning his master) have given him a wife ;—6, " Then his masters (that is, his master) shall bring him to the judges ;"—29, " But if the ox were wont to push with his horn in time past, and it has been testified to his owners ;" (that is, his owner.)—Is. vi. 8, " To whom shall I send?—and who will go for us? (that is, for me.)

by the rite of baptism, into a profession of belief in the one supreme Being—in the Son, by whom he revealed his will—and in the Holy Ghost, or miraculous agency of the Spirit of God, by which the truth of the Gospel was established. It gives no more countenance to the doctrine of three persons in one God, than to that of three Gods in one person. The latter is as rational and Scriptural as the former; and it is surprising, that no one has maintained it, since nothing could be more easy than to find arguments in its support. Mr. Serle finds the three persons of the Trinity in the very commencement of Genesis:—"In the beginning God created the heavens and the earth, * * * * and the Spirit moved on the face of the waters." "Here," says he, "are three persons in one power, viz. the beginning, God and the Spirit." This is marvellously ingenious and convincing! He ought to have displayed a little more of his ingenuity, and found them in the earth, the form, and the void—and in the darkness, the face and the waters; and the three being thrice announced, who could withstand the force of the triple argument? Gregory Nyssen thought it typified by Adam, his Son, (which Son?) and Eve. One Rev. Gentleman finds it in the thrice repeated "holy" of Isaiah vi. 3; and another sees an *ocular* demonstration of it, in the three men whom Abraham entertained in his tent with "cakes of kneaded meal, and a calf, tender and good, of which they did eat." Gen. xviii. Why does he not find a duality in the two angels who befriended Lot, and a Trinity in the three radicals of the Hebrew verb? It has been detected, indeed, in the four letters of the Hebrew of Jehovah יהוה, in which the two *He's* represent the two natures of Christ! Horsley has discovered it in the "Watchers and holy ones" of Daniel, and identified Christ with the archangel Michael. But Hutchinson has shewn more ingenuity than all the rest, for he finds the divine and human natures of Christ in the prayer of the Psalmist, "*Make thy faces* (the divine and human united in Christ) *to shine upon thy servant.*" Ps. xxxi. 16. Should he not also find the mysterious union of two or three " somewhats," as Dr. Wallis denominated the three persons of the Trinity, in the 15th verse of the 104th Psalm, where it is said, "That God giveth oil to cause man's face (in the Hebrew, faces,) to shine?"—and in the countenance of Moses, for when Aaron and all the children of Israel saw him after his descent from Mount Sinai, behold, the skin of his face (Hebrew, faces) shone?" Exod. xxxiv. 29, 30. Nay, the deep itself (Gen. i. 2,) is represented as having more than one face, for in the original it is *panim*, faces, and not face, and, therefore, let the pluralist draw his conclusion; it will afford him as valid an argument for his Trinity as any other plural in the Hebrew language, with the exception of the Cherubim, in whose faces the same profound Hutchinson finds the whole Trinity, with the divine and human natures all congregated together, not, gentle reader, because their faces are *three,* but because they are *four.** He represents the Cherubim, with wings expanded over the mercy-seat, as a similitude of the ALEIM, and says, "it was fit there should be a type of man taken into the essence, * * * * that the lion and the man became one conjunct purifier, stand on the one side—the bull and the eagle (types of God and the Holy Spirit) stand on the other, giving their mutual assent to the transaction,"† by which divine justice is to be satisfied. This might appear to be the reverie of some wild enthusiastic imagination; but the learned Parkhurst thinks otherwise, for he says, that the Cherubim "in the holy of holies, were emblematical of the ever-blessed Trinity, in covenant, to redeem man, by uniting the human nature to the second person."‡ How profound are the arcana of theology! But both Hutchinson and Parkhurst must yield the palm to one, who is a still more profound diver into the bottomless abyss of these mysterious doctrines;—let Andronicus M'Cartan, M.D. be proclaimed victor. Should his infant work, entitled "The Christian Alphabet," reach the desired perfection, it is to become a " classical key of orthodoxy, and an *algebraical* confutation of heterodox writings." The obstinate Unitarian, who cannot be convinced either by Scripture or logic, must yield to algebra. We may judge what will be the potent effect of this novel application of the science of unknown quantities, from the admirable use which the author has made of his chymical and anatomical knowledge. He has instituted a comparison between oxygen gas and sanctifying grace; and in the "brain, the little brain, and the oblongated marrow," finds a parallel to Father, Son, and Holy Ghost! This is all done in sober seriousness, and with the most devoted attachment to the cause of the Roman Catholic Church.

He REJECTS it, because it leads to the adoption of notions respecting the nature of God which expose Christianity to the scorn and contempt, not only of unbelievers at home, but of Indians, Turks, and Jews abroad. For instance, Trinitarianism does all this by the false meaning which she affixes to the text, Acts xx. 28, "Take heed, therefore, unto yourselves, and to all the flock, over which the Holy Ghost hath made you overseers, to feed the Church of God, which he hath purchased with his own blood." Every reader, whose ideas of the eternal mind are not *carnalized,* must know that God being a spirit, and, as is truly stated in the first Article of the Church of England, without *body, parts, or passions,* he can have no blood. This the Apostle Paul knew well; and it is utterly incredible and impossible, that he could be guilty of the

* Abstract from the works of John Hutchinson, Esq. p. 132.
† Id. p. 185.
‡ Lexicon, Cherub.

blasphemy of ascribing an animal nature to Jehovah; or supposing the eternal God to be clothed with a mortal, sanguiferous body. But how ward off the imputation in the present instance? Nothing more easy. Simply by understanding the words just quoted in the rational sense in which they were written, if, indeed, those are the very words which fell from the mouth or the pen of the inspired author. The strongest reasons, and by the ablest critics, have been adduced for reading " Lord," instead of God ;* and all objections to the change answered by Griesbach, Nov. Test. vol. ii. p. 112. But the author, so far as his Unitarian doctrine is concerned, has not the smallest objection to the text as it stands; he meets orthodoxy on her own ground. It is stated in the text, that *God purchased*;—to this expression there can be no objection, because it harmonizes well with similar expressions in Jewish phraseology. Thus, in texts already quoted, Jehovah is said to have *bought, purchased, redeemed,* his people Israel.†

---

* Grotius says, that in transcribing the Greek MSS. the contracted word Θυ (for Θεου,) might be easily substituted for χυ (χριστου;) that the Apostles commonly denominated Christ, Lord, and the Father, God; and that many MSS. read Lord in place of God—" et Syrus sic legit qui vertit Christi." On the other hand, Whitby says, the common reading is confirmed by the vulgar, Arabic, Æthiopic, by St. Chrysostom and Oecumenius. But in Irenæus, lib. 3, 14, in the Alexandrian MS. and *in the Syriac*, we read the Church of the Lord; viz. the Church of our Lord Jesus Christ. Wakefield says, " the Syriac, that *most ancient*, and, indeed, inestimable version, which would be ill exchanged for all the MSS. of the Greek Testament in the universe, renders it the Congregation, or Church of the Messiah, or of Christ." Griesbach refers to a great variety of MSS. gives the most decided opinion against the common reading, and declares that it is not supported by any MS. that is rendered respectable by its antiquity, its internal excellence, or the commendation of a competent, uncorrupted judge. He adds, that he is ignorant how it can be defended without a violation of all the rules of criticism. " Quo modo igitur, salvis criticæ artis legibus, lectio Θυ, ut pote *omni auctoritate justa destituta* defendi queat, equidem haud intelligo." Nov. Test. vol. ii. p. 115. The orthodox Eclectic Review also, for 1809, says, " On seriously weighing all the evidence, every impartial mind, we conceive, will admit, that the last (viz. Lord) has the fairest claim to acceptance, as the genuine reading." The Vatican MS. however, which is of high authority, having been carefully examined *for a Unitarian critic*, is found to have Θεου, and instead of του ιδιου αιματος, it has του αιματος του ιδιου. *The blood of his own*, viz. Son.—See *Monitum* to the beautiful edition of Griesbach, by Richard and Arthur Taylor, London, 1818.

† " The metaphorical expressions and symbolical allusions applied to the death of Christ are numerous. The world is said to have been ransomed, redeemed, purchased, and bought. These are terms borrowed from the Old Testament, where they are applied to the deliverance of the Jews from Egyptian bondage. The Apostles adopted these forms of speech from habit, from a wish to accommodate themselves to the usages of their correspondents and disciples; and from the resemblance that subsisted between the emancipation of the Hebrews, by Moses, and the redemption of the world

These are metaphorical expressions, borrowed from one of the most common transactions of life. But let us take care not to pursue the metaphor too far, for such pursuit has led to some of the most monstrous errors connected with religion. Literally speaking, there can be nothing of the nature of a commercial transaction between Jehovah and any other being whatsoever. He can neither give nor receive a price or ransom; for, all things are his, and he giveth us all things freely and gratuitously to enjoy. How then did he *buy, redeem, ransom*, his people Israel? Not by silver and gold, but by a mighty hand and an outstretched arm— by signs and wonders which he wrought by the hand of Moses, he rescued them from the tyranny of Pharaoh, and freed them from the house of bondage. Thence they became his people, and were bound by the strongest ties of gratitude to serve and obey him, as their Saviour and Redeemer. Thus, also, in a similar way, is God said to have *purchased* his Church. What was the price paid here? Blood. What!—*his own blood?* Yes, un- questionably, HIS OWN; for it is written, Rom. viii 32, "that he spared not *his own Son*, but *delivered him up* for us all." If Christ be denominated God's own Son, then was the blood of Christ God's own—his own peculiar property. The Apostle tells us that *we* also are God's.—"Ye are not *your own*," says he, Whose then? God's. How? Because ye are his by the right of purchase. "Ye are bought with a price;"—God, the ETERNAL FATHER hath *purchased, ransomed, redeemed* you, from ignorance and sin, from misery and death, by the precious blood of his Son, as he purchased, ransomed, redeemed Israel from the bondage of Egypt, by the rod of Moses. "Therefore glorify God in your body, and in your spirit, which are God's." 1 Cor. vi. 20. "Blessed is the nation whose God is the Lord, and the people whom he hath chosen for *his own* inheritance." Ps. xxxiii. 12. Isaiah lviii. 7, says, "Hide not thyself from thine own flesh." The expression our *own flesh and blood*, as applied to relatives and friends, is not unusual.* But who could think or speak so abhorrently from common sense, as to identify the persons of two kinsmen? Erasmus paraphrases the passage well, " Goddes own Congregation * * * which God did sette so much store by, that

---

from sin, by Jesus Christ; but literally, these words had no more relation to the one than the other; for the Israelites were not ransomed nor redeemed. They were rescued by the power of the Almighty, and by the most awful displays of his providence, by the plagues of Egypt, the death of the first- born of the Egyptians, and the overthrow of Pharaoh and his host in the Red Sea. The phrases, however, are not to be taken literally in either case." *Bruce's Sermons.*

* Thus, in Virgil, the *bloodless shade* of Anchises, apostrophizes Cæsar :—

Projice tela manu, *sanguis meus.*—ÆN. VI. 835.

he purchased it by the blood-shedding of hys onely begotten, Sonne." Here Scripture and reason beautifully blend, and guard us against the hideous fiction of a suffering, incarnate, wounded, blood-streaming Deity, expiring as a sacrifice to the wrath, or the justice of a vindictive God, which God was his father, nay, his own essential self! Such an appalling and incredible imagination never entered the mind of an Apostle;—it surpasses the most extravagant fictions of the heathen poets,* is an indelible stigma to the Christianity that does not repel it, and, in more senses than one, puts to open shame, and crucifies the Son of God afresh.

He REJECTS it, because he can find no vestige of it in all the preaching of the Apostles. It is not only reasonable to suppose, but very unreasonable not to suppose, that the topics on which

---

* Homer has been censured *for making gods of his heroes, and mortals of his gods;* for which heinous impiety he is banished by Plato from his republic, and by Pythagoras doomed to the infernal regions. What would those philosophers have thought, had the poet, though privileged to indulge invention, represented Jupiter, his father of gods and men, as not only wounded, like some of his inferior divinities, but crucified, dead and buried? Every reader of such an impious figment, would have instantly exclaimed, *incredulus odi!* But Homer had too much judgment to impose such a tax even on heathen credulity. Aware that he is trespassing on poetic licence, when he wounds Pallas, he tries to reconcile the reader to his improbable fiction, and preserve his divinity from the degradation of being regarded as a mortal, by informing us, that it was not blood but *ichor*, which flowed from the wound:—

> "Pure emanation! uncorrupted flood!
> Unlike our gross, diseased, terrestrial blood;
> For not the bread of man their life sustains,
> Nor wine's inflaming juice supplies their veins."

The Grecian bard puts to shame those *orthodox* poets, who outrage all judgment and taste, *all sense of moral rectitude,* and all just notions of religion, by such blundering imaginations as the following:—

> " ———— Omnipotence *oppressed*
> Did travel in the greatness of its strength;
> And everlasting *justice* lifted up
> The sword to *smite the guiltless* Son of God."

In the same delectable chaos of Calvinistic monstrosities, "Pollock's Course of Time," we hear of one who

> "Quenched eternal fire with blood divine."

And of others, who

> "Enacted creeds of wondrous texture—creeds
> The Bible never owned, unsanctioned too,
> And reprobate in heaven."

Of all which creeds, that of the poem just quoted, may claim due precedence.

they insisted most strongly, and thought of the most importance, are to be found in the record of their "Acts," and in their Epistles. And yet we find in them nothing of those doctrines, which are the everlasting burden of modern evangelical song. Not a syllable of three persons in one God—not a syllable of an infinite satisfaction made to divine justice. Peter, immediately after the effusion of the Holy Spirit, while he was yet glowing under its influence, opened his mouth and taught the Jews those doctrines which he was commissioned to reveal. And what did he teach them?—Any thing like the doctrines just noticed? Nothing. Instead of astounding them with a declaration, which would have stamped him as a lunatic, that they had put to death the second of the immortal three, he stated, that Jesus of Nazareth was " a man approved of God among them, by miracles, and wonders, and signs, which God did by him in the midst of them;" that him they had taken, and by wicked hands had crucified and slain ; but God had raised him from the dead, and had made him Lord and Christ. This was the sum of his doctrine. No Trinity —no two natures—no crucified Jehovah—not a word on which his bitterest enemies could place so impious a misconstruction. For when the high priest reprimanded the Apostles, after their miraculous release from prison, he says, " Behold, ye have filled Jerusalem with your doctrine, and intend to bring this man's (not this God's) blood upon us." Acts v. 21. How much more heinous, and how much better adapted to serve the high priest's purpose, would have been the accusation that they intended to subvert the fundamental principle of the established religion, and introduce a new object of divine worship ? Let us not be told, that the Apostles did not divulge the whole extent of their commission, and that they had truths in store which they found it inexpedient openly to proclaim. This argument is not for Protestants. The Apostles knew little of the art of expediency. Paul declared to the elders of Ephesus, that he "*kept back nothing which was profitable unto them ;*" and that he had " not shunned to declare unto them *all the counsel* of God." He never taught the doctrine of the Trinity, therefore he did not think it *profitable*; he never noticed it in declaring unto them all the counsel of God, therefore it formed no part of what he was commissioned to reveal— he knew nothing of it—how should he, having never heard of such a thing, except, perhaps, in Greek mythology ?

When he was converted, the voice from the glory which surrounded him, said, not that I am God the Son—the second person in the Godhead—equal and consubstantial with God, but " I am Jesus of Nazareth whom thou persecutest." When pleading before Agrippa, he said, that he " taught the people *none other things* but those which the prophets and Moses did say should come ; that Christ should suffer, and that he should be the first that should rise from the dead, and should shew light unto the people, and to the Gentiles." Acts xxvi. 22, 23. How would the good

P

Apostle have been amazed and confounded, had any Jew spoken
to him of the mysterious *three-in-one*, as an article of Christian
faith, or accused him of propagating a doctrine, of which he was
profoundly ignorant, and which would have peremptorily contra-
dicted his declaration, that he taught nothing which was not
sanctioned by Moses and the prophets? This argument prostrates
the Trinitarian hypothesis, and shews that it must be classed
among those inventions with which fathers and councils, in after
ages, according to Monsieur Jurieu, *immensely improved* and
beautified the Gospel of Christ.

He REJECTS it, because, instead of depicting religion as an
angel of light to be admired for beauty and symmetry, it presents a monstrous and confused image to the mind—*forma tri-
corporis umbræ*, shadowy and visionary. Simplicity and uniformity contribute essentially to the beauty and perfection of all
the works of nature; but Trinitarianism resembles the composition of a bad artist, an incongruous assemblage of disjointed
members, whose junction bears no similitude to any thing in nature. Trinitarianism also employs a language singularly gross,
indecorous, and unscriptural. Even Calvin condemned her style
of devotional address, when he said that the words "holy, blessed, and glorious Trinity, savoured of barbarism." She sets up
her own standard of doctrine, and asserts that all who do not
conform to it are heretics and infidels; nay, that the Son of
God himself, if he were not the supreme Deity, must have been
an egregious impostor. Romaine accuses the Jews of Atheism,
and says, "They are without a God, because they have rejected
the blessed Trinity of their fathers." He farther alleges, that
"If you deny that Jesus Christ is self-existent and equal with the
Father in every perfection and attribute, you take away the foundation of Christianity; and that it is the most stupid and idolatrous
religion, if the author of it (Christ) be not the true God." Dr.
Tucker says, "If Christ be not the great I AM, he must have
been one of the *falsest and vilest* of the human race;" and that if
the system opposed to Dr. Tucker's "be really true, the Scriptures, of course, must be false, and Christ and his Apostles be
ranked among the greatest hypocrites and impostors that ever appeared on the face of the earth." It is much to be wished that
such language had died with its authors, or been confined to the
bitter controversies of days gone by. But refusing to yield to the
growing influence of taste and refinement, to say nothing of higher
and nobler influences, it still preserves its place in the schools of
orthodox polemics; and writers of our own days evince that they
can be as successful, as they are ambitious, in improving the
satanic style of their precursors. We may judge of Mr. Pope's
proficiency, from a specimen already quoted in the thirtieth page.
Another, with whom Mr. Pope will probably agree, declares that
unless his intrepretation of Scripture be true, Jesus Christ himself
employed "the language of unexampled presumption, and out-

raged every feeling of fitness and propriety."* But all must yield the palm to the antagonist of our excellent Brahmin. Not contented with accusing Jesus of prevarication, and of retracting his doctrines for fear of death, he declares that "If Jesus were not God, the Apostles, the primitive saints, and the angels of heaven, would be guilty of idolatry, and the eternal Father of encouraging it!".† The Unitarian shudders as he writes these words—presumptuous as they are unhallowed—false in argument, as impious in assertion. They expose the desperation and folly of an untenable cause. Coming, as they do, from those, who are obliged to employ the unscriptural invention of two natures in Christ, to reconcile the manifest contradictions of their system, what must be thought of them, by every reader of good moral taste and feeling? The spirit of Unitarianism, it is hoped, is widely different from this ;—it says, "Let God be true, but every man a liar." Rom. iii. 4. What! shall we, with all our passions, prejudices, ignorances, and theological hatreds, form a system of opinions, and dare to assert, that if we are not right, the omniscient mind must be wrong? "Oh! madness, pride, impiety!" No; though all human interpretations of Scripture, and all our ideas of Christ, should be glaringly false, the perfections of God must be unblemished and unimpeached. God forbid! that, under any circumstances, we should admit the possibility that Christianity is "a stupid and idolatrous religion, and its author an impostor," and "one of the falsest and vilest of the human race." God forbid! though we should lose our belief in its divine origin, that we should ever become so blind in understanding, and so hard in heart, as not to see and feel the matchless excellence of its precepts. The spotless purity, the unrivalled benevolence, the captivating wisdom of the Redeemer's character, must challenge the admiration of infidelity herself. Though stripped of the divinity in which it glistens, its superior brilliancy throws every other character into shade.

He REJECTS it on a principle of science :—the first lesson we learn in arithmetic, is to call one and one, two; and two and one, three. Theology alone contends that three persons make but one God, as if God alone were not a person, i. e. an intelligent being, by himself. Three units constitute the number three, call it by what name you please ; and the number three being resolved into its component parts, forms three units. Three persons are no more necessary to the constitution of one God, than to the constitution of one man. The word person occurs very frequently in the sacred volume, and always, the author presumes, in the popular

---

* See Yeates's Answer to Wardlaw, p. 241, a work well deserving the perusal of all who are interested in the controversy.
† Rammohun Roy.

is the same as Tritheism. It sets up three objects of adoration, and worships each by peculiar titles and epithets; and though its advocates endeavour, by the most miserable sophistry, to maintain that the three are in essence one, they cannot speak of them but as of three separate existences. Their own language and their own practice confute their theory:—they neither honour the " persons" alike, nor pray to them alike. When more than one object of worship is admitted, it commonly happens that the inferior usurps the homage which is due to the supreme only. Do not the great majority of Trinitarians honour the Son more than the Father; and Roman Catholics the Virgin Mary, more than either; while the Holy Ghost, whose claims are equal, is almost, if not altogether, forgotten, or disregarded? When a saint happens to be a favourite and the fashion, as Thomas-a-Becket of old, he becomes the primary object of devotion. Such is the danger of a divided allegiance, that it may lead from the worship of the true God altogether, and precipitate us into the gulf of superstition and idolatry.

He REJECTS it on a principle of benevolence to his fellow-creatures. He wishes, as a believer in the true God, and as a Christian, that the glad tidings of the Gospel may be resounded through the world. Had the true doctrine of the divine unity, taught in the Scriptures, been as zealously advocated as Trinitarianism has been, we should, at this day, see Christianity more extensively diffused abroad, and its influences more sensibly felt at home. When it was first preached to the heathen nations, as we find in the Acts of the Apostles, that doctrine which is so easy of comprehension, and so admissible by its simplicity into the mind of man, was readily embraced, and conversions rapidly followed. But Trinitarianism has never found a welcome reception among enlightened and reflecting heathens;—they think their own system of Polytheism as good as any other.* It is absurd to speak to them of a distinction of persons in the Godhead—of subsistences and hypostatic unions. If the most learned polemics, who are

---

* " The incarnation of the Deity, is an idea extremely familiar to the native mind (of the Hindoos ;) but idolators, instead of being conciliated and won over by a doctrine so consonant with their own, are rather flattered by the close resemblance which they suppose can, in this respect be traced between Christianity and Hindooism, and are thus confirmed in their ancient superstitions."

" Connected with the doctrine of the incarnation is that of the Trinity, both of which, while they are retained, will prove insuperable obstacles to the propagation of the Gospel in this country. It is to these that Mussulmans constantly recur in their reasonings against Christianity, and it is upon these that Unitarian Hindoos, or those who have relinquished idolatry on the authority of the Vedas, have hitherto grounded all their objections"—*Correspondence relative to the prospects of Christianity, and the means of promoting its reception in India.*" pp. 81, 82.

familiar with the terms, have no clear ideas attached to them; how is it to be expected, that any thinking heathen will be converted by them? The learned Brahmin has shewn the vanity of such an expectation with regard to his countrymen. "If Christianity," says he, "inculcated a doctrine which represents God as consisting of three persons, and appearing sometimes in the human form, at other times in a bodily shape like a dove, no Hindoo, in my humble opinion, who searches after truth, can conscientiously profess it in preference to Hindooism; for that which renders the modern Hindoo system of religion absurd and detestable, is, that it represents the divine nature, though one, as consisting of many persons, capable of assuming different forms for the discharge of different offices." Even to his mind "the doctrine of the Trinity appeared quite as objectionable as the Polytheism of the Hindoos, and presented an insuperable obstacle to his conversion to Christianity, as he found it professed by those with whom he conversed." Happily, however, he determined to study the Scriptures for himself, and after a long and diligent perusal, he rose with the conviction, that the objectionable doctrine formed no part of their contents, and that the Christian religion was true and divine.* What is the Jew's first and most invincible objection to Christianity? The doctrine of the "three in one." Were he taught the theology of the Gospel, and shewn that the God and Father of our Lord Jesus Christ is the same individual being, whom his ancestors worshipped as the God of Abraham, of Isaac, and of Jacob, his prejudices might be overcome. Until he be thus instructed, in vain shall we hope for his conversion.

He REJECTS it, because in all ecclesiastical bodies in which it is adopted, it is accompanied with a determined spirit of hostility to the rights and liberties of man. Such bodies, not contented with the quiet enjoyment of their own opinions individually, are restless and indefatigable in forcing them on others, usurping a right of dictation, and like the Pharisees of old, "they bind heavy burdens and grievous to be borne, and lay them on men's shoulders," never remaining satisfied till they have caused them to pass under the yoke, and clothed them in the *uniform* of slaves or hypocrites. The Synod of Ulster presents us with the most recent illustration of this melancholy fact. Will posterity believe, that in the 27th year of the 19th century, it was moved and carried in said Synod, that "it is absolutely incumbent on them, for the *purpose of vindicating their religious character*, as individuals, to declare that they do most firmly hold and believe the doctrine concerning the *nature of God*, contained in these words of the Westminister Shorter Catechism, *that there are three persons in the Godhead, the Father, the Son, and the Holy*

---

* Preface to the "Precepts of Jesus."

*Ghost ; and these three are one God, the same in substance,
equal in power and glory ?"* Will it be believed, that 117 ministers and 18 elders, to *vindicate their religious character !* said
they believed this portentous proposition ? If either minister or
elder among them *understood* it, it is " absolutely incumbent" on
him for a farther vindication of his religious character, to come
forth and explain it clearly and satisfactorily, that Unitarian
Christians may understand it also. As it is wise in all inquiries
to begin with simple ideas, before we proceed to combine and
make them complex, the first thing required will be accurate de-
finitions of the terms, *nature, Godhead, person, substance, God.*
These being clearly defined and made perfectly intelligible even
to a Unitarian's understanding, we may be told, that there are
three persons in the Godhead, the Godhead being the container,
and the persons the contained. But says the Unitarian, who is
always thrusting forward his teazing common-sense objections,
the container and the contained cannot be the same, more than
the earth, the sea, and air, are the same as the ethereal vault
which surrounds them. Again ; the three persons in the Godhead are the same in substance ;—supposing our ideas of substance to be quite clear, how is this part of the proposition to be
proved ? How many kinds of substance are there ?—for this
also must be known before he can conscientiously subscribe the
proposition. How is it ascertained that the three persons are of
one, and not of two or three different substances ? What was
made of this subject by the old Homoousians, Homoiousians, and
Heteroousians, whose souls, were it not for their superior knowledge of Greek, we might almost suppose to have transmigrated
into the venerable Fathers of the Synod ?

Sir Isaac Newton, no mean authority, has affirmed, that we
know but the superficial qualities even of the bodies with which we
are most conversant. Neither by the senses, nor by any reflex act
of the mind, can we acquire a knowledge of their substance, *much
less can we have any idea of the substance of God.* But we
live now in the 19th century, and understand metaphysics as
well as the old Homoousians, and better than Sir Isaac. The
members of the Synod have kept full pace with the "march of
mind," and even preceded it, so that we shall suppose they can
give a satisfactory solution of the difficulty. We proceed, then,

---

* " Corpore omni et figura corporea (Deus) prorsus destituitur ; ideoque
videri non potest, nec audiri, nec tangi, nec sub specie rei alicujus corporeæ
coli debet. Ideas habemus attributorum ejus, sed quid sit rei alicujus sub-
stantia minime cognoscimus. Videmus tantum corporum figuras et colores,
audimus tantum sonos, tangimus tantum superficies externas, olfacimus odores
solos, et gustamus sapores ; intimas substantias nullo sensu, nulla actione
reflexa, cognoscimus ; et *multo minus ideam habemus substantiæ Dei.*"—Newt.
Prin. Math. Lon. 1726, p. 529.

to inquire, how can the three persons, who are of one substance, be equal, and yet the same, for equality and identity, as has been elsewhere remarked, are two different things? We can comprehend how three persons may be equal in power and glory, and form a triumvirate, or a tri-theocracy, but we cannot comprehend how they can either be the same, or how each of them can be omnipotent. It has already been demonstrated, that there cannot be two omnipotent beings, much less can there be three. Again, it is stated, that there are three persons in one God, consequently, one person cannot make one God; and so neither Father, Son, nor Holy Ghost, is God by himself, but each forms a third part of the being so denominated. Notwithstanding, we are told, that each person is God himself, and then there must be three Gods; but this supposition contradicts all that was previously stated, respecting three persons in one God, and this the venerable Fathers of the Synod would brand as a damnable polytheistic heresy.

Reverend Fathers of the Synod of Ulster, what are we to believe? Do, in compassion to your weaker brethren, whose consciences are tender, explain in intelligible language, the proposition which you think necessary to be adopted for the vindication of your character.* You have given the subject all the mature deliberation which its gravity requires. You can enlighten what is is dark, and simplify what is complex; gifted as you are with genius of no ordinary description, and illumined by that " wisdom which is from above, which is first *pure*, and then *peaceable*, *gentle*, and easy to be entreated, full of mercy, and of *good fruits*, without *partiality*, and without HYPOCRISY." Most reverend, and most sapient fathers, when you give the explanation required, you will vindicate your character——and not till then.

He REJECTS it, because he thinks it the greatest of Antichristian heresies. From its adoption have sprung the grossest superstitions, the most erroneous notions of providence, and infidelity itself. Mr. Pope and Mr. Maguire accuse each other of opening a door to unbelievers; and each, no doubt, could prove the

---

* Mr. Francis Cheynel, in his Book of the Divine Trinity, says, " We may best resemble all that difference which is between the essence of God, and the divine subsistencies, by considering the transcendent affections of the *Ens simpliciter*, and the attributes of God, who doth infinitely transcend, not only a predicamental substance, but a metaphysical entity; as the most metaphysical men, who are sound in the faith, do honestly confess. Concerning the transcendental affections of *Ens* which are *unum verum bonum*, we say, these three affections, and *Ens in latitudine*, do not make four things really distinct, and yet we say, they are real and positive affections."

This explanation of the mysterious doctrine which the Rev. Synod are desirous of having subscribed, is respectfully submitted to the consideration of their *heart-probing* Committee; and, if approved, it may be adopted and enforced, under pain of excommunication from their learned body.

accusation well-founded. It is a fact, indeed, too notorious to be denied, that many have been led, by the corruptions of Christianity, to renounce it altogether, as the invention of priest-craft, and a system of fraud and delusion. Whereas, had it been presented to their view, not through the distorting medium of creeds, articles, and confessions of faith, but in its genuine beauty, they would have seen and felt its superior excellence, and become its zealous advocates. Did not Unitarianism furnish a sanctuary for conscientious inquirers of other denominations, the votaries of infidelity would be far more numerous, as can be proved by the most incontestible facts. Many who have been disgusted, repelled, and driven to the verge of Deism, by the unscriptural doctrines of some popular systems of belief, will own, with gratitude to God, that they first found out the right way to happiness, to evangelical truth, and the life to come, when they joined in Unitarian worship. Then first the simple majesty of the religion of Christ won their devotion, and established its dominion in their hearts;—then, for the first time, they saw its celestial beauty revealed, and heard its life-imparting dictates spoken. The hour of their regeneration was come—their darkness was dispelled—the clouds of false doctrine, which had obstructed their mental vision, rolled away, and left them surrounded with a sudden light from heaven. Then could they contemplate God, not through the spectral gloom of Calvinism, as clothed with vengeance, seated on a burning throne, his face in wrath, and sprinkled with blood; but in the pure radiance of gospel truth, clothed with salvation, seated on a throne of grace, and smiling with infinite benignity, as their friend and father, on all the generations of men;—their souls felt relieved from an oppressive load—they heard freedom proclaimed to the captive—their chains had dissolved away—their spirits felt light and buoyant—they were emancipated and redeemed—and they exulted in their " deliverance from the bondage of corruption into the glorious liberty of the children of God."

He REJECTS it, because it was unknown to the primitive Christians; and, as far as he has been able to ascertain, had its origin in Paganism, which early began to incorporate its rites and doctrines with Christianity. Of all numbers, the number three delighted the heathen most, as the whole mythological creeds of Greece and Rome testify.* Horsley says, "The notion of a

---

* " Omnium prope Deorum potestas triplici signo ostendatur ; ut, Jovis trifidum fulmen, Neptuni tridens, Plutonis canis triceps : vel quod omnia ternario continentur."—*Servius in Virg.*

The government of the universe was divided among three of the *Dii majores*, but Jupiter was the greatest and best; and were not the minor deities, both of the supernal and infernal worlds, generally grouped in *three*, as the Graces above, and the Fates and the Furies below?—Did not three female divinities contend for the prize of beauty ?—Were not the Muses three times three ?—And was it not from a three-footed stool that the Sibyl gave her oracular responses ?—But the heathen was never guilty of such foolery as to say that *three* are *one*.

Trinity, is found to be a leading principle of all the ancient
schools of philosophy." He speaks of the joint worship of Jupiter,
Juno, and Minerva, in the Capitol, and of the *three* mighty
Ones in Samothrace, to which they may be traced. The doctrine
of the Trinity, he thinks, rather confirmed than discredited by
the suffrage of the heathen sages. He did well to seek it in any
source, rather than the Bible; though we are not convinced that
Samothrace and the Roman Capitol would not have felt dishonoured by having it imputed to them. Sure we are, that for any
figment so monstrous as the Athanasian *Three-in-One*, heathenism
is explored in vain. We are of opinion, that the doctrine of the
divine unity, and of the *unrivalled supremacy of the Father,* is
" rather confirmed than discredited by the suffrage of the heathen
sages," and of all who gave to Jupiter the epithets *Optimus* and
Maximus, best and greatest. A Roman poet, who knew as
much of the Capitol as Horsley, could have taught the orthodox
divine a lesson on this subject, and put his false theology to
shame :—

> Quid prius dicam solitis *Parentis*
> Laudibus; qui res hominum ac Deorum,
> Qui mare et terras, variisque mundum
> Temperat horis?
> Unde nil majus generatur ipso ;
> *Nec viget quicquam simile, aut secundum ;*
> Proximos* illi tamen occupavit
> Pallas honores.
>
> Hor.

> What nobler than my wonted theme,
> The praise of FATHER Jove—supreme
> O'er gods and men—o'er sea and land ;
> Who guides the various seasons bland ;
> From whom no power more high
> Than Jove's great self, e'er springs to light ;
> None *like* to him in glory bright,
> No *second* rules the sky.
> Yet Wisdom, offspring of his love,
> Next honours holds to sovereign Jove.

We shall, probably, be told, with a sneer, that this is poetry.
Well—what then? We say, so much the better. The Psalms
of David are poetry ; so is the Book of Job, and the greater part
of the Prophecies, and some parts of the Pentateuch, and of the
historical books of the Old Testament—and in the New Testament may be found quotations from heathen poets, and fragments
of hymns in Anacreontic verse. The heathen poetry which we
have quoted, is more worthy of Christianity, than the orthodox
prose, which it confutes. It shews, that a great fundamental
truth of religion was better understood by a heathen poet, than

---

* Sed longo tamen intervallo proximos.

by a vaunted champion of Athanasianism; and that it is doing
foul wrong to "the Capitol" to impute to it "the tremendous
doctrine." Athanasius and his followers have an exclusive right
to it, and let them enjoy it. It is not, however, denied that the
first rudiments of a Trinity may be found among the heathen; but
it is not the author's design to trace it through the dark labyrinths
of tradition, contented as he is with knowing that it is not in the
Scriptures. He may observe, however, *en passant*, that its most
credible source is the philosophy of Plato, though, as Priestley has
justly remarked, "It was never imagined that the three component members of his Trinity were *equal* to each other, or,
strictly speaking, *one*." Many of the early philosophising Christians were greatly attached to the doctrines of that sage. Irenæus,
Justin Martyr, Clemens Alexandrinus, and Origen, all contributed
to corrupt the simplicity of the Gospel, by amalgamating it with
their Platonic reveries. Some of them imagined they could discover a similarity between certain expressions of the Scripture,
and the Trinity of their philosopher. The idea being once suggested, was readily embraced, enlarged, moulded into proper form,
and, in evil hour, adopted into the household of faith. *Hinc
prima mali labes*. Pious frauds were practised to give plausibility
to the figment—the meaning of Scripture was perverted—the
genuine text corrupted by false readings, and by the introduction
of new passages; among which is that famous one in 1 John v. 7,
now admitted by the most sturdy Trinitarians to be an interpolation. Much ingenuity, false reasoning, misapplied talents, mys-
tification, and terrorism, have been employed to prove it to be the
legitimate offspring of truth—but in vain;—it is a corrupt branch
of an evil weed, "graffed contrary to nature" on that heaven-
planted tree, "whose leaves are for the healing of the nations,"
and its fruit has been as the apple of discord to the religion of
Jesus.

He REJECTS it, because the whole of its history, as far as he
has been able to trace it, betrays its earthly and corrupt nature.
It did not spring into existence like a being of celestial birth, full-
grown and full-armed; but like a certain heathen personage, of
far different origin, it was at first small through fear, and did not
attain its full growth and proper proportions for many centuries.*

"First small with fear—she swells to wondrous size,
And stalks on earth, and towers above the skies."

Those who had any knowledge at all of Christianity were, at

* It has been truly observed in a recent number of the Monthly Repository,
that the three creeds of the law-established Church, mark *the progress* of the
Trinity. The first and most ancient, which is UNITARIAN, speaks of God
the Father Almighty, maker of heaven and earth; and Jesus Christ our
Lord, his only Son. The second makes Christ, God *of* God; the third, Jesus
Christ, God *with* God, equal in power and eternity to the Father.

first, startled at the idea of ascribing to any being but Jehovah, those attributes which are peculiarly his own, and were still for maintaining his supreme "monarchy." The title of "the only true God," which our Lord appropriates to the Father, is never once given to Christ, even by the Post-Nicene Fathers, and the reason must be, that their understanding revolted at so strong and unwarranted an expression."* Novatus A. D. 250, is said to be the first who wrote expressly on the Trinity, and his views of it appear similar to those of Origen, and very different from the modern doctrine. Sabellius, an African Bishop, about the middle of the third century, taught that the Father, Son, and Holy Spirit, are only names and offices of the same person. Then arose various interminable disputes about the words *substance* and *hypostasis.* In a council held at Antioch, A. D. 270, it was proposed and rejected by a large majority, that Jesus should be decreed to be *homoousios*, of the same essence with God. Instead of that term, the Semiarians adopted another, which differed from it in a single letter, and said, that Jesus was not *homoousios*, but *homoiousios*, i. e. of a like substance. The Eunomians, in opposition to both, alleged that Christ was *heteroousios*, or of a substance neither identical nor similar to that of the Father. Each party anathematized the other, of course, and the less they understood their own and their opponents dogmas, the more violently did their hostility rage, and in louder and more incessant volleys were their spiritual thunders rolled.

The Nicene Fathers, in the first general council held at Nice, A. D. 325, adopted the creed which bears their name; but in its original form it said nothing of the *personality* of the Holy Spirit.† Ten years only had elapsed, when a council, assembled at Jerusalem, decreed in opposition to one of the principal declarations of the Nicene Creed, that Christ is not of the same essence with the Father. The word *ousia*, or essence, soon became heretical, and *hypostasis* was substituted. A great dispute sprang up between the Eastern and Western Bishops, the latter contending that there should be three hypostases—the former only one. A council held at Sardica, A. D. 347, resolved that there should be only one both in the East and in the West; but a council at Alexandria, twenty-five years afterwards, decreed, that there should be three. In 364, Apollinaris becoming the leader of a new sect against the Arians, denied that Christ had any occasion for a human soul, and hence he was charged with maintaining that God suffered on the cross. Prior to this, indeed, Noetus of Smyrna, in the third century, had maintained that the Father united himself to the man Christ, and was born and crucified with him;—hence, the Patripassians, a sect not yet extinct. Half a century has not elapsed since

* Ben Mordecai, vol. 1, p. 393.
† See its original form in " Bulli Opp."

Whitaker alleged, that the Jews crucified the God of the Patriarchs on Mount Calvary; and since his day, some have been heard to assert, that when Christ hung on the Cross, there was no God in heaven!

Basil in 370, is said to be the first who taught the *full* equality of the Son to the Father—the equal deity of the Holy Ghost with the Father and Son had not yet been asserted; but it was decreed in the second general council held at Constantinople, A.D. 381. This new discovery was added to the Nicene Creed—and thus, says Mosheim, "This council gave the *finishing touch* to what the Council of Nice had left imperfect; and fixed, in a full and determinate manner, the doctrine of three persons in one God." He appears, however, to have forgotten, says the Rev. Mr. Scott, of Portsmouth, "That neither the hypostatic union, nor the procession of the Holy Ghost from the Son, as well as from the Father, had not yet been discovered." Pope Nicholas the First, A. D. 863, added the words, *and the Son* (filioque*) to the Nicene Creed. The Eastern Church would not receive this addition, and hence the Greek Trinity is *less complete* than that of the Roman and Lutheran."

He REJECTS it, because it degrades the Father,† and dishonours the Son. It degrades the Father, by imputing to him such conduct as is in opposition to all the sentiments and principles of right and wrong, which he has himself implanted in the heart of man. It makes the Son his rival, and in generosity of of character, his superior. It dishonours the Son by giving him titles and epithets which he disclaims—representing him as a being which he never affirmed himself to be—and by frequently contradicting his own plain and most positive declarations:—"The Son," said he, "can do nothing of himself." Nay, says Trinitarianism, he can do all things by his own sovereign underived power. "Of that day and of that hour," says Christ, "knoweth no man; no, not the angels which are in heaven, neither the Son, but the Father." Notwithstanding, replies Trinitarianism, he knows it as well as the Father himself; for he and the Father are one in essence. "My Father," says Christ, "is greater than I." Here,

* "The addition to the Nicene Creed of *filioque* was projected in the seventh century, and not received by the Latin Church before the ninth." *Jortin's Remarks on Ecclesiastical History*, vol. iii. p. 62.

† "All the indignities offered to the person of Christ were done to Jehovah, who was joined to that person, and his final sufferings on the cross denominated him by the sentence of the law, *cursed. It is false* to say this is only applicable to the humanity of Christ, for none but Jehovah could sustain our execration!"—*Abstract of Hutchinson's Works*, p. 198.

This incomparable Trinitarian says, that "the self-contradicting notion of eternal generation, has confounded the Christian faith more than any other position."—*Id.* 223.

says Trinitarianism, he speaks not as a "whole and entire," but only as a part of himself; and when he says " I," we must not understand an individual being, as the singular pronoun I, in all other cases, signifies; but two beings, of one of which only, what he utters, can be true; for the other being is equal to the Father in all his attributes; and to deny it is an Arian and Socinian leprosy, and a soul-destroying heresy!

SECTION FIFTEENTH.

The Superior Excellence, and cheering Prospects of Unitarianism.

THE Unitarian turns with delight from the Trinitarian hypothesis, to the contemplation of his own simple and sublime faith. He pants to escape from the dank fogs of a dungeon, from the sepulchral lamp-light, and the sorcerer's spell, to view the ethereal vault, to respire the pure breeze, to hear the voice of nature, and enjoy the warm and cheering light of heaven. His soul feels emancipated from bondage; and he comes forth rejoicing in the benignant smile of the Father of all. His heart expands and thrills with emotions of love, to the Almighty ONE, his everlasting benefactor and friend. In the scheme of man's redemption, he beholds a scheme of ineffable love, planned by the great Author of good, and executed by the ministry of his divine Son. He drinks of the waters of salvation, flowing from the living rock, as an emanation from the free grace of God, unmerited and unbought; not as the purchase of a bloody sacrifice, or as a right extorted, by an infinite price, from inexorable wrath. The supreme exaltation of the Father, does not diminish the honour and glory which are gratefully acknowledged to be due to the Son. But he believes that he loves and honours the Son most, when he acts most conformably to his precepts. He honours the Son, even as he honours the Father, in receiving his dictates as the dictates of God himself.

Unitarianism recommends itself by its simplicity. It needs no tedious ratiocination to explain or support it. It does not begin with incomprehensibility, and end with mystery. It can be comprehended by babes, and understood by the illiterate. It is among religious creeds, what Newton's system of the universe is among the systems of other philosophers. The astronomer, who had not read nature truly, was obliged

" To build, rebuild, contrive
To save appearances, and gird the sphere
With centric and eccentric scribbled o'er,
Cycle and epicycle, orb in orb!"

And for the purposes of astrology, to prescribe

> " The planetary motions and aspects
> In sextile, square and trine, and opposit
> Of noxious efficacy, and when to join
> In synod unbenign ! "

But when the true astronomer, the great hierophant of nature, comes forth to exhibit her temple from a point of view whence it can be fully contemplated, all confusion and irregularity disappear. Unitarianism has no phenomena, for the explanation of which she is obliged to have recourse to invention. She requires no contrivance *to save appearances.* But true to the principles of sound philosophy, she does not admit two causes where one will suffice. Her system is consentaneous to the laws of nature and revelation—simple, as it is grand—harmonious, as it is magnificent. God is the centre from which all beauty and order emanate; around which, all lights revolve; the great prime mover; the unwearied dispenser of life and happiness to men, to angels, and every order of animated being.

The Unitarian is more strongly armed by a single shaft from the armoury of divine truth, than Trinitarianism with all the weapons she can collect from the same store; for in her hands they are powerless, refuse to be wielded in her cause, and turn their edge against her own bosom. As to the triple mail of fathers, councils, and human legislatures, in which she chooses to array herself, it shivers like glass beneath a single stroke of the sword of the spirit, which is the word of God. A single text, " There is ONE God, and there is none other but he," Mark xii. 32, is fatal to her system. It subverts her councils, and turns her gravest deliberations to folly. Powerful as the pebble from the sling of David, it smites through her forehead, and penetrates her sensorium.

Unitarianism " has a superior tendency to form an elevated religious character." This has been demonstrated by Channing in a sermon of superlative excellence ;—he observes truly,

" That it promotes piety by presenting to the mind one supreme spirit, to whom all religious homage must be paid—by admitting no divided worship—by opening the mind to new and ever-enlarging views of God—and especially by the high place it assigns to piety in the character and work of Jesus Christ," * * * * " We deem our views of Jesus Christ *more interesting* than those of Trinitarianism. We feel that we should lose much by exchanging the distinct character and mild radiance, with which he offers himself to our minds, for the confused and irreconcileable glories with which that system labours to invest him. According to Unitarianism, he is a being who may be understood—he is one mind—one conscious nature. According to the opposite faith, he is an inconceivable compound of two dissimilar minds—joining in one person a finite and infinite nature—a soul weak and ignorant, and a soul almighty and omniscient ; and is such a being a proper object for human thought and affection ? "

burn for ages with increasing splendour. It has flashed upon Greenock, and we do not despair of its piercing even the dense cloud that hangs over Paisley, and imparting light and joy to those "who are sitting in darkness, and the shadow of death." Ireland has felt and owned its influence from north to south;—intolerance and persecution have promoted the cause which they conspired, with the Synod of Ulster, to crush. We owe them much for having roused to vigorous exertion, the spirit of a Montgomery, a Porter, a Mitchel, an Alexander, a Blakely, and a Glendy. Those pure-minded Christian men, with the other " Remonstrants," must feel happy in their separation from the hypocritical cant, the Pharisaical grimace, and the Presbyterian Popery, which they had so long to endure, while in connexion with the venerable Synod. Long may they enjoy the approbation which they have merited and won from the wise and good ; with the proud consciousness of having acted as became the disciples of him, who is " the way, the truth, and the life ;" and widely may they extend the hallowed power of those Christian principles, in defence of which they have so heroically stood ! Dr. Bruce, of Belfast, has spoken with a force of argument, an elegance of style, and knowledge of Scripture, worthy the reprobation of Calvinism. Why is Vindex so long silent ? He has given us only enough of his racy letters* to stimulate our relish for more. The Rev. W. Porter has served the cause of truth, by strangling the viperous calumnies which followed him into his quiet retreat, and by exposing Pharisaical malignity and falsehood, to the merited indignation of every honest man. The Pastor, of Moneyrea, who has long taken his post in the van of Bible Christianity, still continues to present an invincible front to its enemies. The Rev. Mr. Hunter, of Bandon, "on evil times, though fallen," maintains his post with cheerfulness and intrepidity : and in Cork, a Unitarian Christian Society has been formed under the auspices of a number of ladies and lay gentlemen of high respectability by their rank in society, but still higher by their moral and intellectual attainments, by a more generous zeal, and a far more intimate knowledge of Scripture, than are to be often found in a sacerdotal stole. Long may they flourish, happy, *free, and independent !* Dublin could boast of an Emlyn once ; an Emlyn who, with a courage like that of the ancient martyrs, dared to stand alone and assert his faith, in defiance of cruel persecution, the fine, and the gaol. She could also boast of some illustrious examples of men, who " counted all things but loss for the excellency of the knowledge of Jesus Christ our Lord," a Mather, a Veal, and a Norbury, Fellows of Trinity College, who, with Winter, the Provost, resigned their situations, rather than suffer their consciences to be either

* Published in the Christian Pioneer.

so successfully employed in rendering the commandments of God ineffectual? And why do those who exalt the supremacy of Scripture, belie their professions by the substitution of unhallowed creeds of human invention? The Reformation was long in making its appearance, and since it has appeared, why did it ever become stationary or retrograde? In the Synod of Ulster, at this day, its principles are neither acted on, nor understood. "This is the condemnation, that light has come into the world, and men love darkness rather than light, because their deeds are evil" As to Unitarianism, the marvel is, not that it is so confined, but so extended, maugre the multifarious obstacles by which its progress has been obstructed. It is among the ordinances of a probationary state, that virtue shall be opposed by vice, and truth by falsehood. Unitarianism must expect, and should always be prepared to meet the hostilities of Polytheistic creeds. The gods of the Ammonites, Moabites, and Zidonians; Moloch, Mammon, and Belial; Ashtaroth, Chemosh, and Milcom, arrayed themselves against it, among the Jews; and the passions which those idols represented, have been equally hostile to it among Christians; the worship of groves and images, under the old dispensation; pride, avarice, ambition, and spiritual wickedness in high places, under the new. It has been obscured—almost buried and lost, beneath a mass of superstition; argued against by the subtle, crushed by the strong, and anathematized by the bigoted; reviled, tortured, and robbed. It is passed by with contempt by the sanctimonious Pharisee, excluded from the wealthy synagogue of the lordly Sadducee, and branded with the names of leprosy, infidelity, deism, and enmity to God.* But it has always possessed a mind conscious of its own rectitude, and a holy reliance on the eternal One, whose name it delighteth to honour. Its spirit is immortal;—it may be repressed, but never extinguished—" persecuted, but not forsaken—

---

* Every man who writes in support of it, may be almost certain of having not only his literary and religious, but his moral character assailed and calumniated by Calvinism. If he escape with being accused simply of want of candour, and not of downright forgery and falsehood, he may deem himself fortunate. An *honest* review of *any* composition of an Unitarian author, by an orthodox critic, would be a strange anomaly in the history of criticism.

Let the Eclectic Reviewer, *if he dares,* answer the challenge of " the Watchman," in the Monthly Repository, for November 1830, to discuss the question of the unity and supremacy of the Father. The pages of the Repository offer him a fair field for the contest. But will he accept it? We venture to answer, no. And from what cause? Conscious imbecility.

Tutius est, igitur, *fictis* contendere *verbis*
Quam pugnare manu

Safer for him to shoot poisoned arrows from his secret den, than to come manfully into the field with the honest weapons of war.

cast down, but not destroyed." It may be silenced by clamour, never overcome by argument—harassed by Test and Corporation Acts, never deprived of communion with God,—it is driven from courts, and finds an asylum in heaven.

Unitarians are charged with blindness, obstinacy, leprosy, and soul-destroying heresy, because they do not follow some of the more popular forms of religion. With equal reason should they be censured for being able "to afford to keep a conscience." There are Unitarians who, in learning and piety, are not behind the very chiefest of the apostles of Trinitarianism. Their intellects are not less acute, nor is their love of truth less sincere. Wherefore should *they* be attached to error? What system have *they* to support at the expense of the smallest tittle of their integrity? Unitarianism has no patronage ; she is no favourite with the titled few, or the fame-bestowing many ; the world, and the world's law are against her; if she were of the world, and could fashion her doctrines to the depraved public taste—did she excite sensations, instead of inculcating principles, she would be less calumniated, and more kindly received. She has not even a church, or any thing which the mitred hierarchs of the land could properly condescend to call a church; she has only the pure religion of the Gospel. From this she learns, or should learn, to bear the slights and discourtesies to which she is often exposed, and the bitterness, clamour, and wrath, with which she is constantly pursued. In this she may read of one, " who esteemed the reproach of Christ greater riches than the treasures of Egypt." Herein also she may remember to have read of one, who taught the people standing on the shore, from a fisherman's boat ; and who, as he sat on the green sward of a mountain-top, beneath the clear blue sky, with the people congregated around him, delivered a discourse not inferior in beauty, pathos, and sound divinity (in the opinion of some* judges at least) to the most elaborate, episcopal composition of modern times. The instructions of that teacher, she doubts not, were as efficacious as if they had been delivered from the Papal Throne, in full convocation of the clergy; and the devotions of the people as acceptable to the Father of all, as if they had risen from beneath the fretted vault, or been re-echoed through the long-drawn aisles of the most magnificent cathedral. She may remember farther, to have seen it written, that all the disciples of Jesus were once assembled at Jerusalem in an upper-room ; and may wish to be informed what, at that time, constituted the church of Christ; or if the disciples, having nothing which their

* *Some*, not all—for the Saviour's Sermon on the Mount, appears to others of more sublimated taste, a piece of good morality, indeed, but destitute of what they can *properly* call religion ; nothing to be compared to their own empyrean rhapsodies !

sacerdotal Mightinesses of the Jewish temple, could properly denominate a church, were in the same condition then, as their
Unitarian brethren are now.

Unitarians lay no claim to infallibility; but they do with the
greatest confidence deny that they are under any temptation
whatsoever to tamper with the conscientious dictates of their own
minds; unless it be to forsake the principles of their profession,
for others which are more popular and fashionable, and which
may prove more lucrative. There are temptations enough to
induce such of them as would aspire to power and place, to
abandon their faith; none which the worldly-wise will applaud,
to attach them to it. Those who would proselyte Unitarians have
every thing to assist them, except truth and the Gospel.

What but the strongest conviction can bind them to their un-
popular belief? Overcome that conviction—prove to their satisfaction that they are in a wrong path, and they will join the many
who have entered by the broad gate, and are crowding along the
royal high-way. Shew them a religion, with credentials from
heaven, more beautiful and more easily comprehended than their
own, more influential on human conduct, and more adapted to the
wants, the hopes, the wishes, and all the lofty and holy aspirings
of the immortal soul, and be assured, they are not such enemies
to their own good, as to refuse its adoption. They stand on the
right of private judgment, and this right with them is not a name,
but a reality.

Much is said and written now-a-days in behalf of this right,
particularly by some of those who are endeavouring to proselyte
the Church of Rome. Mr. Maguire seems to contemplate many
of their declarations respecting it as a complete fallacy; for they
allow the right to be exercised only till it leads to the rejection of
the Papal authority, and then it must cease. The Church of
Rome herself allows a similar right until you have adopted her
as your spiritual guide, but from that instant your right is no
more. Your understanding has performed its office, and is thence-
forth, as some worn-out or hurtful instrument, to be thrown away.
You have seen enough, and must quietly submit to have your
eyes put out. The process of some of our Reformers is not very
dissimilar. They not only allow—they imperatively insist on the
frequent perusal of the Scriptures; but then you must read them
with the spectacles of Athanasius or Calvin; or should you happen to take a glance with your own eyes, and get more expanded
views of the perfections of God and his divine dispensations, you
are immediately stigmatized as a leper and a heretic;—you must
be cut off from " the covenanted mercies of God,"* and doomed

---

* Will it be believed, in an age to come, that there are orators in this our
day, who class invincible error with presumptuous transgression; and mo-

to dwell for ever in that dire abode, over whose gate is written,

Lasciate ogni speranza, voi, che 'ntrate.
" All hope abandon ye who enter here."

Mankind, however, are beginning to shew some symptoms of uneasiness, even under the mitigated yokes of Popery reformed. Having once learned to exercise the rights of free-born men, they will not suffer their minds to be enslaved by the usurped authority of predestinating liberators and Jesuitical saints. Mr. Pope himself exhibits some restiveness, and in his curvetings has shaken off a few of the " Articles" that were too oppressive to be borne. Let him fearlessly dash all his fardels to the ground, and asserting the liberty wherewith Christ has made him free, resolve to be under spiritual servitude to none but to one who said, " that his yoke was easy, and his burden light."

There is some hope that this admonition will be followed; for Mr. Pope says, " he trusts that the result of his discussion with Mr. Maguire may be, that we shall throw the Fathers overboard, and sailing in the ark of the living God, the holy Scriptures, launch out upon the great ocean of religious truth."* In this wish, the Unitarian most heartily joins; and along with the Fathers, in order to render the bark light and buoyant, he would throw out their whole offspring, both spurious and legitimate—the Westminster Confession of Faith—the Nicene and Athanasian Creeds—a thousand folios of Scholastic Divinity and dogmatic Theology,—huge bales of Magazines, falsely entitled Evangelical—all war-denouncing ecclesiastical "Charges"—reams of declamations against good works—the sanctimonious cant by which fortunes and titles, with the "silly women" appended to them, are led captive—the impious declarations of fanatics, that nature is under the curse of God ; and the uncharitable invectives against their neighbours, misnamed sermons, and headed with the appropriate text, "Curse ye Meroz—curse ye bitterly the inhabitants thereof." Let all such trumpery be "shouldered" and shovelled out ;—down let it sink, ten thousand fathoms deep !—as long as

---

dly affirm, that if after the most painful and sincere investigation of the truth, we have the misfortune to adopt an erroneous belief; i. e. a belief different from that which they advocate, we have nothing to expect but headlong precipitation into the fiery gulf,

" There to converse with everlasting groans,
Unrespited, unpitied, unreprieved,
Ages of hopeless end ? "

Hard fate of involuntary ignorance ! Such was not the spirit of him who prayed, " Father, forgive them, for they know not what they do."
* Discussion, p. 45.

it remains on board, it will impede the motion of the vessel, embarrass the movements of those who should work her, and keep up the continued cry of danger.

Mr. Maguire boasts of an infallible remedy for putting the Unitarian to silence; does he also intimate his mode of applying it, when he says, " he would take him by the throat?" If he has sufficient energy in his grasp, this mode would, no doubt, succeed, when the senile babblings of tradition, and the arrogant pretensions of church authority, would only provoke laughter and contempt. But the Unitarian has no apprehension of being so roughly handled, defended as he is, on one side, by reason, Scripture, and common sense; and on the other, by the shield of the British Constitution." With these allies in the fair field of argument, he dreads not the grasp of any Tritheistic man of Gath, nor the gauntlets of a hundred-handed Briareus of Polytheism.

Let Unitarianism profit by the concessions which have been granted to her, and come forth in her panoply of truth, conquering and to conquer. A new and a brighter era in her history has arrived. Men of learning, piety, and first-rate talents, are beginning to exalt their voice most audibly in her behalf. Many erudite divines, who, like Lindsey, Priestley, and Belsham, were early imbued with Trinitarian principles, have also, like them, overcome the prejudices of education, and had the magnanimity to turn from lying vanities, to worship and serve the one only living and true God. Her doctrine is making rapid progress in England; and, without boasting of a prophetic spirit, we venture to predict, that it will go on with accelerating speed;—let its tacit converts only assume courage to brave the scowl of orthodoxy, and stand up manfully as its advocates. It has passed the Tweed, and in Scotland is proceeding with firm and steady pace. In Edinburgh it has found a permanent asylum; and in due time, we doubt not, that city will add to her renown, by the adoption of a faith more worthy of her intellectual character, and more accordant to the soul-enlarging truths of inspiration, than the dark and illiberal metaphysics of her popular creed. Glasgow, one of the darkest dens of Calvinism, has been cheered by the celestial light of Unitarian Christianity. There the Rev. J. Yates has had the glory of proclaiming its truth—of combating successfully, in its behalf, and causing its enemies to quail. There the Rev. G. Harris is fighting " the good fight of faith"—foiling the insolence of rampant bigotry, and sending forth his able "Christian Pioneers" to prepare the way of truth, and lay a bright and trenchant axe to the roots of the tree of corruption. The sour and melancholy gloom, which a misanthropic creed had spread over the countenances of the good people of Glasgow, and which excited the wonder of the celebrated philosopher Reid, when he first commenced his academical labours in that city, is beginning to be dispelled before the beams of a cheering evangelical faith. The holy flame has been kindled in Dundee, and there, we trust, it will

stretched or curtailed on the Procrustean bed of conformity. She had an Abernethy, a Duchal, a Mears, and a Leland, who were "as the sons of God without rebuke, in the midst of a crooked and perverse nation, amongst whom they shone as lights in the world." In our own time, CATHOLICUS VERUS has spoken with a voice most sweet and eloquent. Would that it were raised again to a higher note, and like a trumpet make the welkin ring! Here, as in Cork, a Unitarian Christian Society has been formed, by the exertion of some individuals, who stand high in the scale of civic respectability, and mental cultivation. They have opened a friendly correspondence with their brethren in England, and established a Repository for such publications as they deem best calculated to promote evangelical truth. They have among them wealth, influence, talent, learning, and high moral integrity; and these, if liberally and energetically employed in the best and noblest of causes, must eventually succeed in promoting their desired object. Let them be only constant and zealous in their endeavours, by frequent meetings, by mutual exhortation, by circulating tracts, and encouraging every effort in their behalf, both of the pulpit and the press; and fear not, that under a gracious Providence, they will be mainly instrumental in advancing the interests of true religion. In proportion as the Scriptures are read and understood, and as men learn to think and judge for themselves, must the reign of superstition and idolatry be brought nearer and nearer to a close.

Abroad, Unitarianism is spreading like the light of heaven. The mountains and vallies of Switzerland are re-echoing her hallelujahs, while Malan and his fanatics are howling a funeral dirge over the "lifeless carcass" of Calvinism.* The erudite Brahmin in the East has commenced her hosanna to the Son of David, and proclaimed that Jehovah is One. But we must turn to the land beyond the western ocean, to the land of the learned and pious Channing, to see how she can triumph when she has an open arena, and is not opposed by fashion, worldly interests, and those inveterate prepossessions of custom and education, which chain men to Popery and Calvinism in Europe. Half a century has not elapsed, since she could not boast of more than one congregation in that great division of the globe—now she has many;† may it soon be all her own! She is rapidly progressing, and scattering wide the good seed of the Word, which, in due season,

---

*—"The priestlings of Moloch are loud in their wail,
  And the idols are broke in the temple of Baal;
  And the might of *grim Calvin* smote down by the *word*,
  Hath melted as snow at the glance of the Lord."

† A gentleman, just arrived from America, has informed the author, that in Boston alone, there are fourteen congregations of Unitarian Christians—1827.

s

will shoot above all the noxious tares that would impede its growth. In that new world, the prejudices of Europe find no appropriate soil. There the religious mind has room to expand, unchecked by the blighting influences of established error. There Calvinism will cease to cast its heart-withering shade, to exhale its azotic effluvia, or encumber the ground with its jagged and poisonous roots. Trinitarianism will be cleared away by the sickle and the hoe of true labourers in the vineyard of the Lord; for " every plant," saith our blessed Saviour, " which my heavenly Father hath not planted, shall be rooted up." It must, therefore, be extirpated from all Christian ground, and the religion of the Redeemer produce its genuine fruits—"love, joy, peace, long-suffering, gentleness, goodness, faith, meekness, temperance." These are the true fruits of Christian principles; and it is written, " by their fruits ye shall know them." There it has been calculated, that seven-eighths of the Society of *Friends* have renounced the doctrine of the Trinity.* The "Christians,"† the Universalists, and the Congregational Unitarians are, every day, becoming more and more numerous; and besides these, there are many who are well known " to cherish our opinions, having drawn them from Scripture, and matured them in their own thoughts, without knowing that they harboured the heresy of Unitarianism." All North America is turning to the worship of the only living and true God;—soon may the universal conversion be complete! Then shall " the wilderness and solitary place be glad; and the desert shall rejoice and blossom as the rose;—it shall blossom abundantly, and rejoice even with joy and singing * * * * they shall see the glory of the Lord, and the excellency of our God."

---

* " It may not be generally known, that since the beginning of the present century, there has sprung up in this country a very numerous sect, who, abjuring all distinctive names, call themselves the Christian Denomination. Originally they were Seceders from the Presbyterian, the Baptist, the Methodist bodies ;—of course, they were all nominally Trinitarians, having been educated in that doctrine. The doctrine, however, was soon canvassed, brought to the test of revelation, and universally rejected, with all its concomitant doctrines, as unscriptural. Within 25 years, their growth has been wonderful, particularly in the Western States of the Union, and chiefly *among the common people.* They have now 500 ministers, from 700 to 1,000 churches, and they number about 200,000 persons, who have embraced their principles and doctrines. One of their principal preachers says, ' We are evangelical Unitarians in preaching, and applying the Unitarian doctrine; and it is this mode of preaching and applying it, which has crowned our labours, with such a rich harvest; it is this which gives us access to the *common people*, who constitute the greatest part of our congregations.' "—See an American Tract, entitled " Evangelical Unitarianism adapted to the Poor and Unlearned." Mon. Rep. Oct. 1830, p. 700.

† This is stated on the authority of one of their own body, a gentleman of Philadelphia, of known veracity and candour, now on a visit to Dublin. Nov. 1830.

Such intelligence is exhilarating to the friends of true religion at home. Let them not despair;—the great Reformation has commenced, and if they will lend their aid, it will go prosperously forward. The authors of the last Reformation only half executed their task. They did much, but more remains to be done. They did all that could reasonably be expected of men emerging from midnight shades, and awakening from a profound slumber: but their vision, long habituated to darkness, could not bear the full radiance of Gospel truth. They still hovered on the confines of their ancient haunts. They wanted the eagle eye and the eagle pinion that could sustain and direct them, in more elevated flights towards the Sun of Righteousness. It is left to men of the present and coming age to complete the task which they began; to establish the doctrine of the divine unity; and make the religion of the Bible the only religion in the world.* Let Mr. Pope employ his talents in promoting this design—disenthral his mind from the spiritual chains by which it has been confined—take more enlarged views of nature—(how can a mind like his admit the monstrous idea that nature is under the curse of her Creator?) and adopt more expanded sentiments of Providence, and Revelation, and more worthy of the name and profession of him, who has taught such heart-touching lessons of the inexhaustible benevolence of his and our heavenly Father, who feeds the fowls of the air, and clothes the lilies of the field; who causes his sun to shine, and his rain to fall, on the unthankful and the evil. Instead of persisting in a fruitless advocacy of the unscriptural doctrine which he has espoused, let him dare to become a champion in the cause of truth. Whitby, Watts,† Lindsey, Robinson of Cam-

---

* " We have been told by the acutest champion of Popery in our own times, that Unitarians are of all Protestants the most consistent, and carry the principles of the Reformation to the fullest extent ;‡ and in this declaration, though intended by its author as the bitterest taunt, we acknowledge a truth, while we despise a sneer. The orthodox Protestant, who has come to the contest, expecting an easy triumph over the Catholic, by proving to him how little of his creed is found in Scripture, will be staggered when the Catholic proves to him in his turn, how little of his own can be derived from it. He will find that he can escape from the admission of transubstantiation, only by that plea of figurative language which the Unitarian takes up to prove, that a great deal of the popular theology is built on figures of speech, never designed by those who used them to be taken in a literal sense."
Obstacles to the Diffusion of Unitarianism. A Sermon, by John Kenrick, M. A. London, 1827. The author recommends this Sermon to the serious perusal of his readers, as pious, learned, eloquent—and to the friends of Gospel truth, cheering and consolatory.
† The Unitarianism of Watts is disputed. No wonder. The hymns written by him when a young poet, are too full of Calvinism for their author to be easily given up by the advocates of that heart-withering system. Watts would have purged them of their unchristian sentiments; but they had become the property of booksellers, who would not suffer their popularity to be

---

‡ Lingard's Tracts, (1826) pp. 42—132.

bridge, and a host of others, who have written, and written as well as men could write in support of false principles, have at last discovered their error, and with magnanimity to avow it, turned to the worship of the One God. If Mr. Pope and Mr. Maguir would follow their great example, each would win a more permanent, and more glorious wreath of triumph, than will ever be gained by the victory of one corruption of Christianity over another.

---

injured by such a purgation. A letter, quoted by the late Rev. and learned Samuel Merivale, of Exeter, to Dr. Priestley at Leeds, exhibits the most authentic account of Dr. Watts's last sentiments concerning the person of Christ; from which it appears, that in Dr. LARDNER's estimation, Dr. Watts became, in the strict and proper sense of the word " an Unitarian." The reader who wishes for further satisfaction, may see a letter of Lardner's on the subject, in Belsham's Life of Lindsey, pp. 220, 221. In this letter he states, that " *Dr. Watts's last thoughts were completely Unitarian.*"

It is much to be lamented that Dr. Watts's papers were not preserved and published, that they might have shewn how the light of Unitarian Christianity first dawned upon his soul, and dissipated the dark clouds of Trinitarian prejudice, by which it had been so long and so darkly enveloped. "The feelings of his humble, pious, and inquisitive mind are beautifully exhibited in that devout address to the Deity, from which Mr. Lindsey has made copious extracts, of which the following are an interesting specimen :"—

" Hadst thou informed me, gracious Father, in any place of thy word, that this divine doctrine is not to be understood by men, and yet they are required to believe it, I would have subdued all my curiosity to faith. But I cannot find that thou hast any where forbid me to understand it, or make these inquiries. I have, therefore, been long searching into this divine doctrine, that I may pay thee due honour with understanding. Surely, I ought to know the God whom I worship, whether he be one pure and simple being, or whether thou art a threefold Deity, consisting of the Father, the Son, and the Holy Spirit.

" Thou hast called the poor and the ignorant, the mean and the foolish things of this world, to the knowledge of thyself and thy Son. But how can such weak creatures ever take in so strange, so difficult, and so abstruse a doctrine as this, in explication and defence whereof multitudes of men, even men of learning and piety, have lost themselves in infinite subtilties of disputes, and endless mazes of darkness ? And can this strange and perplexing notion of three real persons going to make up one true God, be so necessary and so important a part of Christian doctrine, which in the Old Testament and the New, is represented as so plain and easy even to the meanest understanding ?"—The Life of the Rev. Isaac Watts, D. D. by Samuel Johnson, L.L.D., with Notes, containing Animadversions and Additions, 1785. Quoted from Belsham's Life of Lindsey, p. 218.

END OF THE ESSAY.

REVIEW

OF THE

REV. JAMES CARLILE'S BOOK,

ENTITLED

"JESUS CHRIST, THE GREAT GOD OUR SAVIOUR."

THE first edition of the preceding Essay had scarcely appeared
before the public, when it was attacked by a host of polemics, as
by a simultaneous impulse, and almost every pulpit in Dublin
rang with declamations against the soul-destroying heresy.   In
the van stood the Rev. James Carlile, one of the Ministers of
Mary's Abbey Meeting-house.   Not contented with hurling his
oral fulminations against it week after week—he determined to
give the fruit of his oratorical labours to the world in the permanent form of paper, ink, and type.   Great expectation was excited—mighty efforts were made among the orthodox, so called,
of his own persuasion, to encourage him in the task—subscrip-
tions were received—the work proceeded—the hour of parturition
at length arrived—

> " The mountain laboured——and a mouse was born?"

No—but an overgrown semi-animate nondescript *lusus theologiæ*,
which expired a few days after its birth, and which it is our busi-
ness to dissect for the instruction of students in theological
anatomy.

This new birth came out, branded with its dogmatical and idolatrous title, in the shape of a heavy volume, swollen with verbiage
and tautology, containing 471 pages, with a preface of xv.   In this,
our author acknowledges his obligations to Dr. Wardlaw, whose
old panoply, dinted and shattered as it was in the conflict with
the Unitarian Yates, he is contented to stitch clumsily together,
and to buckle on.   He acknowledges his obligations to old An-
drew Fuller, in whose putrid relics he had been raking in search
of *materiel* to be employed in his *sortie* against the Unitarians.   He
"damns with faint praise" the Synod of Ulster, and evinces what
spirit he is of, by treating as a Unitarian forgery that prayer of

Dr. Watts, which the reader may see in the note of our 140th
page, and affirming of the virtuous, the learned, and scientific
Priestley, that in his history of the Corruptions of Christianity,
" he exposed his learning to utter contempt," and " forfeited all
just claim to the character of an honest man ! ! ! "

In order to prepossess his readers with a high idea of his veneration for Holy Writ, he informs them, in the commencement of
his *opus magnum*, that he " reasons on the principle of the plenary
inspiration of the Scriptures—of the *ipsissima verba* as they
originally stood in the sacred canon." Now, it would have been
benevolent of him to have informed us where those *ipsissima verba*
are to be found. Where has the original canon been deposited
for so many centuries?—and by what happy providential discovery, has it been placed under the scrutinizing eye of the Minister
of Mary's Abbey? Notwithstanding his pious tenacity of the
very words of the inspired Volume, he leaves " the original reading
to be ascertained by the ordinary rules of evidence in such cases ;"
and has no objection to yield to a preponderance of authority for the
expulsion of a word, (what if it should be the *verbum ipsissimum?*)
when it is unfavourable to orthodoxy. Accordingly, he tells us
of one Ambrose, who lived prior to the age of any MSS. now extant, who affirmed that part of a certain heretical text was an interpolation ! So much for his *ipsissima verba*, and the principle
on which he *reasons*.

Mr. C. seems to be one of that class of theologians, who think
that the more they vilify the works of creation, the more they
exalt Revelation, and better prepare a way for their own peculiar
tenets. They not only shut their eyes against the clearest displays of divine wisdom and power in the great volume of nature,
but they make the most preposterous assertions in direct contradiction to the volume of inspiration. Thus, Mr. C. asserts, that
" of the manifestation of God to his creatures, and the *internal constitution of the divine mind* the book of nature says absolutely
nothing." What does any book say of the internal constitution of
the divine mind, unless, perchance, some audacious work on the
Trinity, which speaks of the substance or essence of God, and
pretends to reveal what is communicable to none in earth or
heaven ? But as for the manifestation of God to his creatures,
this is apparent in every region of the universe.

> " Lo! the poor Indian——his untutored mind
> Sees God in clouds, or hears him in the wind."

David affirmed, that the heavens declare the glory of God;
and the Apostle Paul, that his eternal power and deity are clearly
seen, being understood by the things that are made; and yet with
these, and a multitude of other passages of Scripture, equally explicit, shall we be told by a Christian divine, in the 19th century—
a star of the first magnitude in the Synod of Ulster, that of the

manifestation of God to his creatures the book of nature says absolutely nothing?

After such an egregious declaration, we cannot be much surprised to find our author attributing to reason and common sense, the very errors which they detect and expose. " Reason and common sense," he says, " discovered that the world was a vast plain, sustained on the back of an elephant, and that elephant supported on the back of an enormous *crab?*" We thought it had been a tortoise—but *n'importe.* What principles have discovered that this was an error? Do the Scriptures teach the true system of the universe?

He asks—" Was it not reason and common sense, that converted the worship of the Creator into orgies of the most detestable pollution, and the most revolting cruelty?" * * * * " Common sense and reason are employed to support the Church of Rome"—*(indeed!)* " On the Continent of Europe they have divested Christianity of all its peculiarities"—*(marvellous!)* " They taught Socrates to sacrifice a cock to Esculapius" (*poor Chanticleer!*) They taught Dr. Geddes " that the sacred historians wrote like other historians, from such documents as they could find, *(did they write from such documents as they could not find?)* and consequently were liable to make mistakes."

All *mistakes, it seems, have been avoided, by their having compiled their histories from unfound documents!* and left reason and common sense to Socrates and Dr. Geddes—to the Church of Rome, and the disciples of infidelity—to the orgies of the heathen, and the cosmogonists with the " enormous crab!"

But, notwithstanding the mischievous effects of reason and common sense, our author would not discard them. He allows, that they must be admitted, but then he would confine them strictly to an investigation and arrangement of facts. Facts are always of importance; but when they are collected and arranged, should we not be permitted to reason on them, and from particular facts ascend to general principles; from the effect to the cause—from the creature to the Creator? What is the province of reason? To combine—to compare—to draw conclusions. Any person of common observation and industry, may collect facts: but it is only he who can reason upon them justly, that knows their value, and applies them to their proper object.

After his long tirade against reason and common sense, we are surprised to hear him chanting a palinode in the following strain :—

" We must, I think, concede *something like common sense* principles to the construction of the Bible!" And again, " My readers will find, that I shall have continual occasion to appeal to their reason and common sense."

What! to those exploded principles which support the lady in scarlet—that make the earth a plain—fix it on an " enormous crab," and sacrifice chanticleer?

We agree with our author when he states, that theologians

" Have not sat down to the study of the Bible, for the mere purpose of ascertaining what it contains, as philosophers have sat down to the study of nature, for the mere purpose of eliciting facts. Like the ancient philosophers, they have persevered in forming systems by mixing up the most obvious phenomena of Scripture with their own imaginations!"

This is perfectly true; and he might have added, that not contented with forming systems, which set all Scripture at defiance, and are as destitute of reason as he can wish, they have tried to rivet them on the conscience of their brethren, and enforced *subscription* to them, in violation of Christian liberty and right. They have substituted the unhallowed reveries of ignorance and fanaticism in place of the Bible. They have stamped with the title of *orthodox*, such crude malevolent compilations as the "Westminster Confession," and imposed it on the world as the oracles of truth.

Mr. C. exposes the proficiency he has made in theological studies, when he objects to the practice of confronting one text of Scripture with another. He should know, that it is only by thus confronting them, that we can ascertain the meaning of the very terms in which doctrines are conveyed. He forgets, and his book evinces that he must be subject to frequent lapses of memory, that he had himself, but two pages before, said something approvingly about comparing "Scripture with Scripture, for the purpose of discovering what is the mind of the Spirit in *every sentence* of the sacred Volume." Now, we beg leave to ask, what difference is there between comparing Scripture with Scripture, and confronting text to text? "If one text," says he "intimates, that there are more persons than one in the Godhead, he (the Unitarian) finds another which declares, that there is but one God." Well—how many Gods are there?—what number, Mr. Carlile, would content you? We are contented with one. We take our stand on the authority of him who said *"there is none other God but one."* Confront this text if you can, by any text which says, there are three. Marshal all your tritheistic powers, and bring them up in line, column, or hollow square, and we will *confront* them with this single weapon of divine truth, and scatter them like smoke. Our author is under a mistake in saying, that if a passage be adduced, in which Jesus is expressly called God, we confront the declaration by showing, that he is called man. We cannot find any passage, in which Jesus is expressly called God, unless in a subordinate sense, and that in two or three instances; nor in which Jehovah is called a man, though we know well where it is expressly affirmed, that "God is not a man, neither the son of man;" and where it is as expressly affirmed, that Jesus was both. We can find no text which affirms, that there is more than one person in the Deity. We interpret what is obscure by the aid of what is clear; and do not, for the sake of supporting an hypothesis, admit one dark or doubtful text to overthrow the bright array of a whole phalanx of Scriptural authorities, by which it is opposed. Did Unitarians endeavour, by one or two garbled expressions, to establish their doctrine of the divine Unity, in contradiction to a multitude of passages, clearly teaching the doctrine of the Trinity, there might be some reason for complaining, that we endeavour to neutralize one text by another: but the reverse is notorious; and for one text, which the defenders of the Three-in-One adduce on their side, we can oppose, at least, a hundred: and we have this great advantage, that the texts in favour of the Divine Unity, cannot, by any possibility, be tortured to the side of Trinitarianism; whereas, there is not a text adduced by Trinitarians, which cannot be explained most satisfactorily to accord with the doctrine of the Divine Unity.

It is entertaining to hear our author say,

"We have no desire to believe in the existence of such a God, as he (the Unitarian) describes a *spirit*, simple, uncompounded, indivisible, because we do not find any such language in Scripture, in describing the nature of Deity."

And immediately subjoining :—

"We believe that the Father is God, and the Son is God, and the Holy Spirit is God, for the Scriptures say so."

Where ?—where ?—Good dear Mr. Carlile, tell us where, and where the three are declared to be in substance one, for verily we can find no such declaration in the sacred volume; and, in return, we shall inform you where God is denominated a spirit.—" a most pure spirit, without body, *parts*, or passions,"* and therefore, as we have stated, simple, uncompounded, indivisible.

We are accused of giving an erroneous and distorted statement of the sentiments of Trinitarians. Our author terms it preposterous and absurd, and asks, *Where did he find it?* We reply, in a well-known book called "The Westminster Confession of Faith." " *Can he point out any person, who has avowed such a scheme?*" Yes, Rev. James Carlile, thou art the man. " *I hope he will believe me when I assure him, I never heard of it, or met with it, except in the writings of Unitarians.*" Nay, Rev. Sir, be not so positive in assertion; you must have often seen it, and committed it to memory too, though not exactly in the mitigated language in which we have expressed it, but in the words of that unhallowed book, which you have subscribed, and which teaches, that "it was requisite that the Mediator should be God, that he might sustain and keep the human nature from sinking under *the infinite wrath* of God ;" i. e. according to your system, that God the Son—the merciful and the meek,—might be sustained under the infinite wrath of God the Father, the merciless and vindictive, The book of heaven teaches, that " God is good unto all, and that his tender mercies are over all his works." The book which you have learned teaches, that all mankind, except some predestinated

---

* Westminster Confession.

handful, are under God's "displeasure and curse; so as, we are by nature children of wrath, bond-slaves to Satan, and *justly* liable to all punishments in this world, and that which is to come;" which punishments are "everlasting separation from the comfortable presence of God, *and most grievous torments in soul and body, without intermission, in hell-fire for ever.*" We hope you will recognize these to be the *ipsissima verba* of your favourite repository of theological lore, and that you will do penance, by nine times repeating the ninth commandment, before you again affirm, that we take our statement from Channing, and that "Channing either invented, or got it from some other Unitarian." The book from which the above comfortable passages are extracted, and which you have subscribed, depicts the Father of mercies, by the everlasting decrees of election and reprobation, as acting a part more cruel and unjust, than aught that has ever been feigned of the spirit of evil himself. We have read of Satan being changed into an angel of light; but that unrighteous book, to which you have fixed your hand, would transform him, whose name is Love, into a sanguinary Moloch: it makes heaven perform the work of hell. No longer needs the devil go about like a roaring lion, seeking whom he may devour: he may retire to his fiery pavilion, and loll at ease on his brimstone couch, since the omnipotent and eternal God himself, according to the doctrine of that impious book, has predestinated generation after generation—millions of millions of his intelligent creatures, to be born for no purpose, but after a few years' brief existence on the earth, to descend and people the infernal dominions. Nor is there left to them the slightest chance or possibility of escape; their day of judgment was past, ages before they were born. The devil is sure of his prey; for they are fast bound by the adamantine chain of an eternal decree, which the death of the Son of God himself had no efficacy to relax or dissolve. And all for what? For an offence committed some six thousand years ago, when there was but one man on the face of the earth. This the Calvinists call an act of justice for the glory of God! Horrible impiety! For any parallel to a doctrine that so atrociously outrages every feeling and every principle of justice, to say nothing of benevolence, the archives of history, and the fields of imagination, are explored in vain.

Shocked by the impiety and blasphemy of the system, which he has subscribed, our author says,

"We do not believe, that the Father is more rigorously or inflexibly just than the Son. We do not believe, that the Father was filled with ineffable fury or inexorable wrath against sinful man."

We rejoice to hear this; and hope that Mr. C. is in a fair way to give up all the other monstrosities of Calvin's theological code, and embrace the Gospel as the only sure guide to truth and salvation. But we are not sanguine, nor shall we be greatly disappointed if our hope be not fulfilled; for though he promised to give us " something like" reason and common sense principles, we have received from him as yet not even their shadowy resemblance.

As Mr. C. appears to have forgotten his catechism, *non mi ricordo!* perhaps he may be able to call to recollection the following sentiments, the recent and genuine offspring of the principles laid down in that work :—

" Not the most wretched criminal, chained in the condemned cell of a prison—not the most *debased grovelling miscreant*, dragged from the *impurest sty of profligacy*, bears so revolting an aspect in the eyes of the most virtuous member of exalted and polished society, as every child of Adam, till he be regenerated, renewed, purified by the Spirit of the Lord, bears in the eyes of Him, before whom the heavens are not clean." • • •

Again—" How utterly incongruous is it—how out of place—how unseemly for persons in this humiliating condition, who have no means of avoiding a public degrading execution, but putting, as it were, *the halter round their necks*, and availing themselves of an intercessor with their sovereign, to confess their guilt, and to implore his forgiveness; how incongruous, I say, is it for such persons to feel or to manifest pride !"—(*heu quale bathos!*)

Again—"The Lord views the whole race, as a king does a rebel army. He takes no cognizance of the diversities of character that may be in such an army."

Such are the doctrines of Calvinistic orthodoxy, as taught by the Rev. James Carlile, in a *Charity Sermon*, delivered in Mary's Abbey Meeting-house, on the 4th of March, 1827, and since published ; doctrines so utterly at variance with all that the Scriptures reveal of the paternal character of the Deity, and his merciful dealings with the children of men—nay, so utterly repugnant to every principle of justice and benevolence, implanted by God himself in the heart of man, that even they who have adopted them can scarcely be persuaded that they are their own, and not Unitarian forgeries constructed to misrepresent them. " In them is fulfilled the prophecy of Esaias, which saith, This people's heart is waxed gross, and their ears are dull of hearing, and their eyes they have closed, lest at any time they should see with their eyes, and hear with their ears, and should understand with their heart, and should be converted, and I should heal them." ·

Justice, with Calvin and his disciples, is not a principle of righteousness in the bosom of the Eternal Sire, but a power similar to the *fate* of pagan antiquity, stern and inflexible, standing behind the throne of God, greater than he who sitteth thereon, and overruling all his beneficent purposes, to serve the cause of the spirit of evil. But we turn with disgust from the mind-debasing system ; we rush from it as from the dark den of falsehood and cruelty, and turning our eyes to the glorious light of nature and revelation, we read in the volume of each, that the " Lord is good to all." We hear the voice of wisdom proclaim, as the sound of celestial music pealing from heaven, and re-echoing round the earth, " The Lord—the Lord God, merciful and gracious, longsuffering, and abundant in goodness and truth." Again, it speaks

with trumpet-tongue, "Hearken unto me, YE MEN OF UNDER-
STANDING: far be it from God that he should do wickedness;
and from the Almighty, that he should commit iniquity. For the
work of a man shall he render unto him, and cause every man to
find according to his ways. Yea, surely God will not do wickedly,
neither will the Almighty pervert judgment."

Mr. Carlile having charged us, on the one hand, with fabricating
his own horrible creed, so does he, on the other, impute to us
certain opinions which we do not hold. We have no where said,
as he alleges, that a manifestation of God in human nature is gross
and heathenish; on the contrary, we believe that there is not an
atom of the human frame, from the machinery of the heart and
brain, to the composition of a hair, that does not manifest the
matchless power and wisdom of the Creator. The incarnation of
God in the form of a man, is what we believe to be a gross and
heathenish notion. Neither is it true, that any Unitarians, so far
as we know, maintaining Christ to be a man, worship him as God:
Unitarians own no object of worship but the Father. As to those
discrepancies of opinion on speculative points, which exist among
us, as among all other denominations, they only shew with what
beauty and harmony our Christian liberty is enjoyed; and that we
do not make slaves and hypocrites by aiming at a uniformity,
which the Papal hierarchy, in all the plenitude of its power,
could never effect.

Our author, in conformity, we presume, to the example of the
heart-probers of his Synod, becomes inquisitorial and asks, "Who
is Jesus Christ?—whence came he?—was he a created angel?—
or was he God manifest in human nature?" To these questions
we could give a clear and definite answer in the ipsissima verba
of Holy Writ; but it will be time enough for him to receive it,
when his own opinion on those points has been fixed. His declarations concerning both the Father and the Son, are so irra-
tional, so unscriptural, and so full of contradiction, that we find it
impossible to determine what may be his belief, either as to the
one or the other. Notwithstanding, he is well-pleased with himself—and in a style of sweet and dignified complacency says,

"Nor do I think that any man should be greatly offended, if we should
refuse to him the appellation of a Christian, till he declared his belief on those
elementary points on which the whole nature of the Gospel depends. How
can a minister feed his flock with a mere negative on such a subject?

"The hungry sheep look up, and are not fed."

Thank you, Mr. Carlile; that is a line from Milton's Lycidas—
and Milton is a favourite of ours, not less because he was a good
Unitarian, than because he was a good poet. He is describing
ignorant pastors—

> " Blind mouths ! that scarce themselves know how to hold
> A sheep hook, or have learned ought else the least
> That to the faithful herdman's art belongs !
> What recks it them ? What need they ? They are sped :

they have got their lesson in orthodoxy, and have only to chant
out the same eternal *sing-song* of election, reprobation, satisfaction, and the *Three-in-one ;*

> " And when they list their lean and flashy songs,
> Grate on their scrannel pipes of wretched straw.

We can fancy that we see the great poet sitting in a certain meeting-house, listening to one of those jejune and windy declamations,
with which orthodox congregations are so often ventilated, and
which in his poetical language he calls *lean and flashy songs*, till
at last he rises through impatience and indignation, and accosting the orator, exclaims,

> " Thy hungry sheep look up and are not fed,
> But swoll'n with *wind* and the *rank mist* they draw,
> *Rot inwardly, and foul contagion spread !* "

As to Unitarians being *greatly* offended by Mr. Carlile's re-
fusal to give them the name of Christians, we believe he may set
his mind at ease. Though not without sensibility, they have philosophy enough to possess their souls in patience, and will be able
to support this calamity without any *great* feeling of mortification.
    The next position on which we are obliged to animadvert,
sounds to our Unitarian ears somewhat paradoxical. The Old
Testament, he affirms, is to be explained by the New, and not
the New Testament by the Old. He illustrates this novel rule
of Scriptural interpretation by two acts of parliament, of which
" the former is always explained by the latter ;" i. e. the more recent one gives the proper meaning of whatever terms have become obsolete in its predecessor ! The language of the 19th
century is to reflect light back on that of the 13th !—and the old
Irish Brehon laws, which have so long puzzled our most learned
antiquaries, by the proper application of this new canon in law
and in criticism, will soon become intelligible to every school-boy !
Hitherto we were of the Apostle's opinion, that " the law is our
school-master to bring us unto Christ ;" but now we are taught
that the Gospel is our school-master to bring us unto Moses !
Our author illustrates his rule, by a quotation from the 45th Psalm,
" Thy throne, O God, is for ever and ever ;" which words, he alleges,
would be quite incomprehensible if their explanation had not
been given in Hebrews i. 8. We refer the reader to what we
have said on that Psalm in the text and note, page 58; and in addition maintain here, that the words would have been as well understood, and in their genuine sense, if the epistle to the Hebrews
had never been written. They are borrowed by the author of the

epistle, and applied to Christ as an *accommodation*, but it was to
Solomon they were primarily addressed. The Psalm is our
school-master here, to teach us how they are to be understood;
but Mr. Carlile and the theologians of his school, by scorning such
tuition, deserting their " something like common sense principles,"
and applying it altogether to Christ and his Church, turn it into
sheer burlesque. What, will they have the kindness to inform
us, could the author of the epithalamium mean by apostrophizing
Christ a thousand years before he was born, and saying, " Gird
thy sword upon thy thigh '—and—" thine arrows are sharp in the
heart of the king's enemies," to him who not only never wore
any weapon of war, but forbad his disciples to carry even staves?
What was the meaning of saying to him, whose simple robe was
without seam—who was " a man of sorrows," and had not where
to lay his head, " All thy garments smell of myrrh, and aloes, and
cassia, out of the ivory palaces, whereby they have made thee
glad?" We doubt not, they can give some very mysterious,
unintelligible comments on these passages, and on all that the
divine poet has so beautifully written of the royal bride in her
clothing of needle-work and wrought gold, with the daughter of
Tyre, and the maids of honour ; and that they can mystify and
stultify to perfection the credulous dupes, who have patience to
read or listen to their homilies. Expounders, such as they, bring
ridicule and contempt on the inspired Volume ;—it is they, who
have furnished the model for such burlesque criticisms as that on
the tale of Bluebeard, written in the style of their Scriptural comments, in the works of the King of Prussia. Such commentators
could easily spiritualize the history of Tom Thumb, give a re-
condite meaning to Cinderella, and apply both to some of their
sublime mysteries.

A few instances will suffice to shew off Mr. C.'s qualifications
as an expounder of Scripture. He has the candour to acknowledge the difficulty, on his scheme, (Unitarians have none on theirs)
of Mark xiii. 30—" Of that day and that hour knoweth no man;
no, not the angels which are in heaven, neither the Son, but the
Father;" but thinks that he can yet over it, by adopting the
Unitarian latitude of interpretation, and *confronting* it by a parallel
text. Accordingly he says, he might bring forward Hosea viii. 4,
" They have made princes, and I (Jehovah) *knew it not.*" On
what principle he would bring forward this text, we cannot tell,
persuaded, as we are, that no Unitarian writer could be so profoundly ignorant of the Prophet's meaning, or so absurd as to institute a comparison between two texts, so totally irrelevant. His
comment on the words of Hosea is truly admirable :—

" Although God knew well that the Israelites had set up princes, yet he
did not know it *officially* (*officially*, proh ! *pudor.*) He was not informed, or
made acquainted with it, and therefore speaks of himself as *ignorant* of it."
Nefas infandum !—See pp. 20, 21, *note.*

After speaking in such language of the omniscient Jehovah, we cannot be surprised to find him speaking of the Saviour in a style equally repugnant to good sense and good feeling. He says of that passage in John x. 33—36, where our Lord disclaims the appellation of God (*Elohim*) and styles himself the Son of God, that at one time it was to him the most difficult of any in the Scriptures. Where was the difficulty? To those who suffer themselves to be led solely by the Word of God, it presents none; to those who support the doctrine of the *Three-in-one*, it is insurmountable. But attend to our author:

"It appears to me," says he, "that this explanation given by our Lord would have been uncandid, if he at the same time claimed the title of God in a superior sense."

But having a system to support, to that system the Scripture must be forced to bend. Accordingly he cheats his better judgment, and has recourse to a legal artifice.

"My error was in viewing the text as an explanation, whereas it was a *mere legal defence*, used with *perfect fairness* by our Lord, to arrest the Jews in their purpose of stoning him."

A legal defence!—perfect fairness!—miserable subterfuge! To make him, that feared not man, neither regarded the person of men, as his very enemies testified, condescend to the mean arts of a petty-fogging village lawyer—to practise a contemptible evasion, and all through fear of letting the people know who he really was, lest he, the omnipotent and immortal God, should be stoned to death!

We do not recollect to have ever seen any work, that contains such frequent and such positive contradictions of its own statements, as that of Mr. Carlile. It refutes in one page the very propositions, which it had endeavoured to demonstrate in another; and leaves the reader utterly at a loss to know what are the real sentiments of its author, or whether he has any that can be justly called his own.

Of the manifestation of God to his creatures he affirms, that "the book of nature says absolutely nothing." Presently, however, he refutes himself by saying,

"When a man leaves his country, and passes to the most distant regions of the earth, he finds himself surrounded with the *manifestations* of the presence of the same God, to whose presence he was accustomed in his native climate—the same wisdom, and power, and goodness—the same attention given to every, even the minutest creature; and wherever he goes, he may say with Jacob, "Surely God is in this place.""

Magna est veritas, et prævalebit!

It has been stated in our Essay, that "If such a doctrine as the Trinity constituted any part of the Christian religion, we must believe, on every principle of reason and common sense, that it

152

would have been revealed as clearly, and as much to the satisfaction of every inquirer, as the being of God himself." Our author devotes a whole section of his first chapter to expose the folly and absurdity of such a position; but presently forgetting what he has written, he adopts our very sentiments and chants another palinode, (*non mi ricordo!*) and expresses himself like a heretical Unitarian thus:

"If it be true that the Lord Jesus was indeed God manifest in the flesh, it may be expected that so wonderful an event as the manifestation of God in human nature—nay, as a poor despised man, will be *more fully developed than by a bare intimation of it.*"

Magna est veritas et prævalebit!

Sometimes forgetting that he is a Tritheist, *non mi ricordo!* he becomes a Unitarian; and then he unconsciously begins to fulfil his promise of giving us something like reason and common sense. He is shocked, with ourselves, at some Trinitarian opinions, and asks, if Unitarians really imagine that any man ever maintained so preposterous a notion, as the death and burial of God? If none hold such a notion, we again request to be informed, what is the meaning of invoking God the Son, in a solemn act of adoration, by his agony and bloody sweat—his precious death and burial?

He censures us for affirming, that because Christ is called *the image of God* he could not be the omnipotent Being himself; yet does he, in the very same paragraph, make an equivalent declaration, viz.

"His being the image of God signifies, that he is to us the manifestation, or representative of God!"

Magna est veritas et prævalebit!

"I infer," says he, "that the Apostle Paul most explicitly taught the Hebrews, that the Son of God, the Lord Jesus, was that everlasting Father manifesting himself to the world in human nature."

But when he wrote this he had fallen into one of his fits of forgetfulness a *non mi ricordo*, for a few pages before he says,

"If by God we are to understand the Father, the King, eternal, immortal, and invisible, it would contain an intimation of the appearing of God the Father, which is no where intimated in Scripture, but on the contrary, seems to be inconsistent with some of its declarations."

Magna est veritas et prævalebit!

Our author, though eagerly bent on disputing every inch of ground, becomes, notwithstanding, so retrograde in his movements, and makes such numerous concessions, that we begin to feel that we owe him a large debt of gratitude. We have alleged, that the words (Heb. i. 10,) *Thou, Lord, in the beginning,* are addressed to Jehovah; and he concurs with us so far as to say, " No Israelite could conceive of any other being described in these words, than his own Jehovah." And we are prompted to exclaim—A Daniel!—A Daniel !

Magna est veritas et prævalebit !

We cannot, however, follow our author in his *inference*, that the words are here " employed to describe the glory of the Son, who is, therefore, the Jehovah of the Israelites." In trying to prove this position, he falls into a train of reasoning, if reasoning it may be called, which reasoning is none distinguishable in form, figure, or mode, and which is paralleled only by the same syllogistic process, by which our unknown friend, "The Barrister," shews that the earth can be proved to be the sun, (see p. 106.) After affirming that " the mighty God, even Jehovah, will come in great glory to judge his people, for that he is judge himself," in the very next sentence but one he says, " Nor is there any intimation of God the Father coming or appearing for that purpose :" but here he seems to have fallen into a *non mi ricordo*, for he had assured us only ten pages before, that " The name Jehovah is never given to any but the living and true God ;" and that " this name is claimed by God as his own peculiar name." Whence it inevitably follows, that if the Son be Jehovah, God the Father is not the living and true God; but if God the Father be the living and true God, the Son cannot be Jehovah. *Utrum horum mavis?* But why should our author speak of either Father or Son coming to judgment, since, according to the book which he has subscribed, the day of judgment was past 6000 years ago; and, surely, he is too good a Protestant to attribute to heaven a work of supererogation ?

Our author, notwithstanding the Athanasian prohibition, accounts it a mere trifle to " confound the persons;" and also deems it

" Very singular, that some who believe there are three persons in the Godhead, feel difficulty in conceiving that the title of Father should be given to Christ, who is called the Son of God ; * * but there is no inconsistency in a person bearing the relation of son to one, and of a father to another. Jesus *might* stand in the relation of Son to God, and in that of Father to the whole human race."

Where, or in what sense, is Christ denominated a *father* in the whole Bible? Our author affirms, that the epithets given to Hezekiah (Is, ix. 6,) belong to Christ; but we defy him to point out the chapter and verse in the N. T. in which any one of those epithets, (and in the Septuagint they are seven in number) is, in any one instance, applied to him. He further says, that to denominate Christ the Saviour and not believe him to be the supreme Deity, is idolatry; for " the Lord Jehovah proclaims himself in the O. T. the only Saviour, and Jesus in the N. T. is emphatically and exclusively called the Saviour." But he evidently falls into a *non mi ricordo,*

U

The Saviour, κατ' ἐοχην, is the Father, and beside him there is, in the superlative sense, no Saviour. But the term, like *God*, is appellative, or applied, to many. Thus, in 2 Kings xiii. 5, it is stated that, " The Lord saw the oppression of Israel, because the King of Syria oppressed them, and the Lord gave Israel a Saviour, (probably the son of Jehoahaz,) so that they went out from under the hand of the Syrians." See also Is. xix. 20. Both Jeremiah and Obadiah use it in the plural. Jonathan " wrought a great Salvation" for the people; and therefore he might have been properly denominated a saviour by the most conscientious Israelite. Christ is termed a Saviour, the Saviour of the world, and our Saviour, but all in subordination to Him who, as the Apostle informs us, "*exalted* him, with his right-hand, to be a Prince and a Saviour." The distinction between God our Saviour, in the highest sense, and Christ our Saviour, in an inferior sense, is most clearly marked in Titus iii. 4—6 : " After that the kindness and love of *God our Saviour* toward man appeared— not by works of righteousness which we have done, but according to his mercy *he saved* us, by the washing of regeneration, and renewing of the Holy Spirit, which *he shed* on us abundantly *through* Jesus Christ our Saviour." Here it is evident to the understanding even of a child, that God the Father is the prime mover, the great bestower—and that Christ is the agent by whom he communicates his blessings. The title of *Redeemer* is equivalent to that of Saviour. Now, we beg to ask Mr. C. to whom is that title given in the N. T.? He will guess, we suppose, to Christ? No. To the Father? Wrong again. To whom then? To Moses? He is the only one in the N. T. who is denominated a *Redeemer*, λυτρωτην, Acts vii. 35. But Jehovah is thus denominated in the O. T. and, therefore, according to Mr. C's logic, Moses is Jehovah ; and if Stephen did not believe him to be so, he was guilty of idolatry in giving him that appellation !

Our author comments at great length on Christ's being the image of God, and observes,

" The substance of the Deity is invisible and incomprehensible ; we could no more form a conception of it, than we could of the m'nd of man *without the aid of his bodily form. features, gestures, &c , which are to us the image of his soul.* So the Lord Jesus, being the brightness of the glory of God, is to us the outward visible image, or manifestation, of his inward invisible nature."

Gentle reader, is not this entertaining? We hope it will repay you for the honour you have done our pages, in perusing them thus far. And since our learned metaphysical divine, who understands and explains the phenomena of mind so lucidly, assures us that bodily form, features, gestures, &c. are to us the image of the soul, we hope, with all due benevolence for your courtesy, that you are, in form, of faultless symmetry—in features beautiful as an angel, and in gestures adorned with matchless grace, for then must your soul be graceful, beautiful, symmetrical. But, alas! for the ugly, the awkward, the deformed, the lame, and the blind; for their souls must be blind, lame, awkward, deformed, and ugly!—Poor Æsop! we were under an error, it seems, in having supposed that the excellency of thy mind compensated for that deformity of face and of person, ascribed to thee by thy biographer. What idea are we to form of the mental qualifications of one who was "flat-nosed, hunch-backed, blobber-lipped, a long mishapen head, his body crooked all over, big-bellyed, badger-legged, and his complexion so swarthy that he took his name from it, for *Æsop* is the same with *Æthiop*?" Our quondam acquaintance too, he who sacrificed Chanticleer, though pronounced by the oracle to be the wisest of men, is now demonstrated, by the deformity of his features, to have been no better than a fool! Hitherto we had supposed, though not unfriendly to phrenological studies, that the connexion of mind with matter was not of so very intimate a nature that the one must necessarily express the character of the other, but that a little body might lodge a mighty mind; and a soul of incomparable beauty, be the tenant of a decrepid habitation of clay. We had supposed that the similitude of Christ to God lay not in bodily form, gesture, and feature, but in rectitude, goodness, and truth; that the similitude was moral, of which we can have an idea, and not physical, of which we can have none. Of what is called the substance of our minds, there can be no image—how much less of the substance of God?

Of our author's powers, as a logician, a critic, and expounder of the Scripture, the reader may form his own estimate from the specimens given. We are next to consider his pretensions to scholarship, of which he gives us a proof in his censure of Dr. Young, who, in his translation of the 45th Psalm, renders the Hebrew *Elohim* by *Prince*, (see Essay, p. 58,) in which he was perfectly justifiable, as every one must know, who has the slightest pretensions to a knowledge of the original. Parkhurst says, the word signifies princes, rulers, judges. " I have appointed thee a God (Elohim) to Pharaoh.' Exod. viii. 1. The Latin translation of the Chaldee is *principem*—of the Arabic, *dominum*. Simp. 2 vol. p. 13.

" *Elohim* tribuitur non tantum Deo vero, ut Gen 1, 2. et ii, 4, et sæpe alibi, sed etiam ;—1 Idolis, Exod. xxii. 20—Jos. xxiii. 16, et passim alibi ; 2 Angelis bonis, Ps. lxxxvi. 8—Ps. xcvii. 7 ;—3 Hominibus magnis et divinis, *ut* judicibus, magistratibus et prophetis, Exod. xxi. 6 ; et xxii. 8, 9, 28 ; I Sam. ii. 25. *Castelli Lexicon.*

The XXIVth Canon of GLASSIUS *de Philologia sacræ*, informs us, that the plural number is used by the Hebrews to denote magnitude and excellence. *Pluralis numerus pro singulari quandoque ponitur, ad denotandam magnitudinem et excellentiam.*

Thus the largest of quadrupeds is termed *behemoth*, a word with a plural termination. Thus, *wisdom*, in Prov. i. 20, is named *hocmoth*, also a plural. Bellarmine, one of the brightest luminaries of the Roman Catholic Church, as quoted by Drusius, concurs in this opinion of the use of the Hebrew plural, and says, they have the same practice in Italy. " *Quam consuetudinem nos Itali ex parte imitamur, dum viris gravibus non dicimus, tu sed vos; licet unum non multos alloquamur.* Cajetanus agrees with Bellarmine, and thinks the connexion of the Hebrew plural with a verb singular, an idiom, and not a grammatical incongruity : *nulla interveniente grammaticæ incongruitate.* The application of the plural form to single objects, is by no means peculiar to the Hebrew. The names of ancient cities are often in the plural, as *Athenæ, Thebæ, Salonæ.* The Latins express *darkness* by the plural *tenebræ.* The Hebrew of *life* is a plural noun, and the reader can easily find in his vernacular tongue, plurals which have no singular.

The XXVth Canon of Glassius informs us, that appellative nouns, signifying dominion or authority, are used in the plural for the singular. We have quoted R. Roy, as illustrating this canon by two examples, in which the plural *masters* and *owners* are used for the singular *master* and *owner*, Exod, xxi. 4—6—19. Mr. Carlile, who, it seems, understands Hebrew better than Drusius, Bellarmine, Cajetanus, and Glassius, assumes the professor's chair, and with magisterial authority exclaims,

" Surely R. Roy does not *pretend* that the plural word *masters* is here used as an expression of respect, when no particular master is meant. *Had he been acquainted with Hebrew idiom,* he would have known that a plural word thus used, where a singular might be expected, indicates a distributive meaning."

We hope the unlearned Orientalist will profit by this lesson of his erudite Occidental instructor. Were he at hand, he would, no doubt, make due acknowledgments for this lesson, but as it may be long before it travels to Aurora and the Ganges, we return thanks in his name ; and with deference to the authority of such a *magister linguarum* as Mr. C. humbly submit, that the word *master* is in itself a word of respect, independently of its individual application. In some instances it might lose respectability by its connexion with individuals. *Owners* too, we think, still with due submission, is a word indicative of respect, his possessions being often the only claim to regard, which a man enjoys.

" Let R. Roy," again vociferates our *Orbilius plagosus,* " find any individual man or master, called men or masters, and he will at least hit his mark."

Dear Sir, "let not the sun go down upon your wrath." We shall endeavour to find an example for your satisfaction. Open

your Bible; turn to Gen. xxiv. 9—there you may read, " The
servant placed his hand under the thigh of his *master*, viz. Abraham;" in the original אדני *Adonaiv, his masters.* Does this hit
the mark? Again, turn to chapter xl. and there you may find,
more than once, Joseph denominated ארני הארץ *lords of the
earth.* Does this hit the mark? Gird up thy loins and answer
like a man. If *Elohim* intimates a *triad*, why should not *Adonim*
and *Baalim* be equally significative? But Elohim is repeatedly
applied to objects which are strictly singular. To one angel,
Jud. xiii. 22; was the angel, like Geryon, tricorporate? To one
golden calf, Exod. xxxii. 31; was the calf three-headed like
Cerberus? To Dagon, Jud. xvi. 23; was this beautiful *Elohim*,
with the fish's tail, a triplicity? To Ashtaroth (a plural noun,)
the goddess of the Zidonians, who, by the charms of her ox-head
and horns, wooed men to idolatry—to Chemosh, the god of the
Moabites, and to Milcom, the god of the children of Ammon, that
cannibal divinity, who delighted in the odour of roast infants,
1 Kings xi. 33; to one legislator, Moses, Exod. vii. 1 ; to one
Prince, Solomon, Ps. xlv. 6; to one ark, that of the covenant of
Jehovah, 1 Sam. iv. 7.

Instances of the plural being used for the singular, both
in the Old and the New Testament, are innumerable. Thus,
the ark rested on " the mountains," i. e. on one of the mountains
of Ararat. " He was buried in the cities;" i. e. one of the cities,
of Gilead. " Hananiah, the son of the apothecaries;" i. e. of one
of the apothecaries. " A foal, the son of she asses;" i. e. of a she
ass. " When the disciples saw it, they had indignation;" i. e.
when one of the disciples, viz. Judas, saw it. " The thieves
also;" i. e. one of the thieves, " cast the same in his teeth."
Again, we find the singular sometimes used for the plural:—
" The children of Israel went up and asked counsel of the Lord,
saying, Shall *I* (not *we*) go up again to battle, against the children
of Benjamin, *my* (not *our*) brother?" Sometimes the singular and
plural are used indiscriminately by the same person in the same
sentence. Thus, David said unto Gad, " *I* am in a great strait; let
us fall now into the hand of the Lord, for his mercies are great;
and let *me* not fall into the hand of man," Here is a fine foundation for maintaining, that King David was a *triad*; for does he
not use the personal pronoun thrice, twice in the singular, and
once in the plural, in the same sentence? Is not the *I* one?—and
is not the *me* another?—and is not *us* a third? Here, then, we
have the three—singular and plural, plural and singular—*three-in-
one*, and *one-in-three !* Q. E. D.

What weight should be laid on the grammatical anomalies of
the Hebrew language, in founding doctrines upon them, the reader
may form a tolerably accurate judgment, from what has been offered to his consideration; and still more, from the following observations of Boothroyd, in the preface to his " Biblia Hebraica."
In the Hebrew-language,—

" The most obvious rules of syntax are often disregarded. A noun of multitude in most languages admits either a singular or plural verb; but surely no correct writer would, in the same sentence, first use one verb in the singular, and then another in the plural, or vice versa; yet this occurs in the Pentateuch and Historical books. False concord is also frequent. We have plural verbs in construction with nouns singular, and plural nouns with singular adjectives and verbs; also the masculine pronominal affixes occur often instead of the feminine, and nouns feminine are frequently found in construction with verbs of the third person masculine."

Even Calvin thinks, that the plural *Elohim* (see Gen. 1) affords no foundation for the argument of three persons in the Godhead, and cautions his readers against such *violent glosses*.

" Habetur apud Mosen *Elohim*, nomen pluralis numeri. Unde colligere solent, hic in Deo notari tres personas; sed quia parum solida mihi videtur tantæ rei probatio, ego in voce non insistam. Quin potius monendi sunt lectores ut sibi a *violentis* ejusmodi *glossis* caveant."—CALVINI *Opp.* vol. 1, p. 2, Amstel. M.DC.LXXI.

Mr. C. has such an extensive knowledge of the Hebrew and Greek language, that he lays down certain principles concerning them, which no Hebrew or Greek ever heard of before. He informs us that when the former had only one word to express two ideas, the latter had a word for each of those ideas. We wish he had illustrated his assertion by a few examples, and told us the precise Greek words for the Hebrew, *Ieue*, or *Jehovah, Jah, El, Eloah, Elohim, Ee-shaddai, El-geber, Adonai, Ejeh-asher-ejeh*, &c. in all their acceptations. The word God (Θεος) he affirms, " has but one sense in the whole N. T. viz. the one living and true God, except when some word is added to alter the meaning as " your God Remphan." But he makes a rash assertion, which every novice in Scriptural criticism can shew in an instant to have no foundation. When the people of Melita, seeing Paul unhurt by the viper, which he cast into the fire, said Θεον αυτον ειναι, that he was a God; did they mean the living and true God, or, as it is properly rendered in our translation, a God? When the flatterers of Herod shouted Θεου φωνη, " it is the voice of (a) God, and not of (a) man," did they mean the living and true God? No. The word God is used both in the singular and plural, with the same latitude of meaning in the N. T. as in our own, or any other language; and we must be led by the general scope or tenor of the passages where it occurs, to mark its true meaning. But we find we might have spared ourselves the trouble of this criticism, since our author, as is his wont, having forgotten, *non mi ricordo*, what he had so recently affirmed, informs us, and more than once, for he abounds in tautologies, that " the word God is an appellative, * * * * and that it may be compared to the word *king*, a title descriptive of the rank, power, office, &c. of the person who bears it!"

With respect to the divine name, the Hebrew is more precise

and definite than the Greek. The latter had no incommunicable *tetragrammaton* like the former, for the supreme object of adoration; if they had, Mr. C. will have the goodness to favour the learned world by revealing it. But after all his criticism about the extreme precision of the Greek language, and its power of expressing, by two different words, the two ideas which the Hebrew language, from its poverty, is obliged to express in one, he can find no equivalent for *Jehorah*, but κυριος, *Lord*, a word of various meaning and application, and which he admits has the same variety and ambiguity as in English. As for the jargon he has uttered about the article ὁ, ἡ, το, from which he would deduce a proof of the Trinity, we deem our time and paper too precious to be wasted in its exposure.

Will it be credited that the scholar and critic, who has given us such astounding proofs of his skill in the learned languages, has the modesty to say of that excellent oriental linguist R. Roy, that "he is *extremely ignorant* of the Hebrew idiom!!!"

In the adoption and handling of general arguments, Mr. C. is even more unfortunate, if possible, than in his expositions of Scripture. He acknowledges himself under particular obligations to Dr. Wardlaw for an argument about "delegated authority," which, he contends, does not *confer qualifications;* though Almighty God might delegate his minister to the performance of a task, the delegation cannot give power adequate to its execution. Let us examine this:—in the first place, delegation implies a superior and an inferior: he who delegates must be greater than he who is delegated—the sender than the sent; this might be enough to settle the main point in question. This, however, Mr. C. always willing to avail himself of a sophism, will not admit, because a case may occur in which the sent is greater than the sender; and on this principle the Son might have sent the Father, as well as the Father the Son! But in the case which he supposes, the inferior is found incompetent to the task; and when he is said to send his master, he does not act by virtue of any independent authority; on the contrary, the very act of sending his master in the place of himself, is an acknowledgment of his own inferiority; and when the master goes, it is not as a missionary, but of his own proper and voluntary motion, to execute, by his superior power and personal influence, that which his minister was unable to accomplish. Delegation, says our author, does not confer power. That depends on circumstances. But why not? May not the deputer not only give the deputy instructions, but furnish the means of carrying them into effect? Not in the present case, you reply, for omnipotence is the attribute that should be conferred, and this is incommunicable. Incommunicable, say you?—thank you, my good Sir—and therefore it could never be communicated. You admit the truth of our argument in the 14th Section of our Essay, that there can be only one Omnipotent. But you affirm that Christ created the world, that creation is the work of almighty power, and therefore Christ is almighty. We deny the premises; and even if we did grant them, we should deny the conclusion, until it was proved that no power short of omnipotence can create. Though we believe creation to be the peculiar act of the Father Almighty, and that he alone " in the beginning created the heavens and the earth," we see no reason for supposing that he might not confer a limited power of creating on his creature;—he who gave power to raise the dead, might also give power to create a planet, for a living soul is of more value than a world of inert matter. A power less than omnipotent might create a system, and until the negative of this be proved, which is impossible, this argument, for which our author is so much obliged to Wardlaw, is not worth a rush. But it betrays an irreverence for the Scriptures, as heinous as the endeavour is impotent, to conjure up such arguments from the father of lies, in opposition to the numerous declarations of Christ himself, that his power was both limited and derived. A single text tears the whole web of such sophistry into tatters: but we need not quote Scripture, for our author virtually gives up his position, and concedes all for which we contended, when he says, " That the power by which the man Christ Jesus wrought his miracles, and by which miracles were wrought in his name, was from God, is, doubtless, true."

Magna est veritas et prævalebit !

The Rev. W. Bruce, in his observations on Mr. C.'s book, says, that " The most important chapter in it, is the 12th, on Christ's mediatorial kingdom ; it is pure Arianism from beginning to end." What will the orthodox say to this ? Up, ye drowsy inquisitors!— *heart-probers*, do your duty !—there is an enemy in the camp—a traitor in the citadel !—your champion of the Trinity rebels against your sovereign oligarchy, and joins the standard of the heretical Arian ! Listen to his own confession, and haste to guard your immaculate body from the contagion of his heresy :—he has the traitorous audacity to affirm of the *second person*, whom he denominates Jehovah, the Great God our Saviour, that

" As mediator, he is *inferior* to the Sovereign of the universe." " He is a servant, having taken on him the form and condition of a servant ; * * in *his person he was inferior to God ; he descended to the condition of a created being ;* he was a person *formed* by the will and wisdom of God for a particular end ; *he had therefore a beginning ;* the Lord Jesus, thus constituted, was inferior to the Father of all, *not only as to his person, but as to his offices.*"

Thus, we are taught by an orthodox divine, that the immutable God *changed* his nature—the self-existent, uncreated One, the second of the three co-equals, became *a creature* and an *inferior !* and being joined to a human soul and a human body, he is to continue in that inferior condition, constituting, we suppose, a Trinity in himself, for ever and ever! But, notwithstanding this everlasting change in the condition of the unchangeable Jehovah, from a higher to a lower sphere, our author has a whole chapter, in which he endeavours to shew that, "the exaltation of Christ is inconsistent with his being a mere creature." He seems to consider exaltation not by a "something like common-sense principle," as advancement from a lower to a higher grade, but by a contrary rule of descent from the higher to a lower; and thus "Christ, the great God our Saviour," was exalted *more nostratum*, or *Hibernicorum*, might our author say, did he not happen to be of Paisley, by becoming an inferior. The unchangeable was exalted by being changed—the Almighty, by rendering himself powerless—the Immortal, by being crucified as a slave—and after his resurrection, by being appointed to a station far below his original state, when he reigned as Jehovah God, the Supreme Ruler of the universe! The kingdom to which he is exalted, our author informs us, is *inferior* in duration and in extent, to the dominion which he possessed before, and is subordinate to the universal kingdom and sovereignty of the Deity; and after all, it is to be

"*Delivered* up to the Sovereign of the universe, and shall, as it were, merge into the general government of the universe, that God, the one invisible, eternal God, may be all in all, and his universal empire all in all." Again he says, "Jesus will still continue to dwell in his human nature among his redeemed people * * and in that condescending station, as the man Christ Jesus, he *shall be subject* to the Sovereign of all, his whole conduct regulated by the same law with that of the people; and he and they, as one living temple, subservient to the well-being of the universal dominion of the Father of all."

This is almost as pure Unitarianism as we could write ourselves. It is one of the few passages, in which our author gives us "something like" common sense. But we are sorry that his unfortunate *non mi ricordo* assails him so frequently, and that he should presently endeavour to confute all his own statements, convert what is intelligible into sheer nonsense, and confound him, who exalts, with him who is exalted, but who, by his own representation, is not exalted, but degraded.

In the "Recapitulation" of his work, our author has a large piece of mockery, founded on his ignorance of prophetic language. His readers should feel obliged to him for the benevolent attempt to enliven the somnolescence of his pages with a little sprinkling of wit. But it is a miserable failure; yet it is entertaining by the very awkwardness of its attempts to succeed;—the intended smile wriggles into a contortion, and the incipient laugh expires in a sardonic whimper.

Our author has great difficulty in suppressing his wrath at our having stated in our first Edition, that we should deem a positive declaration from the mouth of Christ, more worthy of credit than any contradictory declaration of Jeremiah or of John. This he calls a "daring insinuation;" and lest his readers should forget it, he refreshes their memory by its repetition. Now, what does it insinuate? That we hold one part of Scripture in higher estimation than another. Verily, this is no insinuation, but a clear and avowed truth. We do prefer some parts of Scripture to others—Genesis, in some respects, to Leviticus, the Gospels to the Epistles, Matthew to Mark; nay, we prefer some of our Saviour's discourses to others—one doctrine to another doctrine, one virtue to another virtue, one truth to another truth, and the *ipsississima verba* of him who had the word of eternal life, to those of Moses and all the other inspired writers put together. Now, if it should happen, we do not affirm that it does, for our proposition is altogether hypothetical, that Jeremiah or John should, or should seem to teach, or intimate that there are three Gods, in contradiction to our Lord's declaration that there is but one, we should, most assuredly, deem our Lord's declaration more worthy than theirs of all acceptation. When one authority must bend to another, it should be the less to the greater—Paul to Christ—he who had the spirit in measure, to him who had it without measure. Should there arise " a prophet, or dreamer of dreams," and teach that there is a triplicity, or three persons in the Godhead, and though he should support his doctrine by signs and wonders, we should " not hearken unto the words of that prophet, or that dreamer of dreams: for the Lord your God proveth you to know, whether ye love the Lord your God, with all your heart, and with all your soul. Ye shall walk after the Lord your God, and fear him, and keep his commandments, and obey his voice; and ye shall serve him, and cleave unto him." Deut. xiii. 3, 4. Christ himself ratified this doctrine by his divine sanction and authority: but had he, in opposition to this doctrine, taught *tritheism*, no Jew *could*, and no Jew *ought* to have ever believed in him; and we ourselves should join issue with the Jew, in saying, that in such a case we should reject him as a false prophet, and consider his doctrine just as contradictory to the grand fundamental principles, both of natural religion and of that which was revealed by Moses and the prophets, as if he had reversed all the commandments, and said, Thou shalt kill—thou shalt commit adultery; for a true prophet could no more reverse or subvert the first commandment, than the sixth or the seventh. But we rejoice that our Lord came not to destroy, but to fulfil; that he spake with more power and authority than Moses, and that we are emphatically enjoined to *hear him*; therefore, we place the highest value on all his divine communications, and believe he uttered an incontrovertible truth when he said, "My Father is greater than I"—in every sense greater. We believe that he uttered another truth, which no disciple of his will dispute, when he said, " I and my Father are one"—one in the sense which he himself so clearly explains when he prays, that the disciples may be *one* with him, as he is *one* with the Father. These are truths which no ecclesiastical authority can

ever invalidate.—Should any expressions, even of the Apostle Paul
seem to controvert them, we should suppose, either that those
expressions did not clearly convey the Apostle's meaning, or that
he wrote from himself, as he informs us, and we believe him, that
he sometimes did, and not from the dictation of the Holy Spirit:
"*I* speak," says he, "and not the Lord ;" and again, "that
which I speak is not after the Lord, but, as it were, foolishly."
Yea, though an angel from heaven should preach any other Gospel
unto us than that which the Saviour preached, we should justify
its rejection by Apostolical authority. We could not, with
Mr. C. believe two contradictory propositions to be equally true.
Though thrice twelve Apostles should aver that there are three
Gods supreme, and yet only one God supreme, we should not
trust them ;—we should dishonour the God of truth by supposing
that he required us to believe, or profess belief in an absurdity.
We regard with scorn the Pharisaical pretences of those who
affect to hold in equal estimation, every part of the Sacred Volume, no matter through what channel it may be conveyed,
while they contemn and endeavour to set aside its clearest—its
most important, and most frequently repeated truths ; who call
out " to the law and to the testimony !" while they stretch every
nerve and sinew in working the machinery of false readings, false
translation, false punctuation, glosses, interpolations, Hebrew
plurals, Greek singulars, and *ho, he, to ;* and in twisting and torturing the plain language of Scripture into conformity with their
creeds—who strain out gnats while they swallow camels, and
trample down the simple majesty of the divine Word, to enthrone
and deify their own carnal *inferences.* With some the Song of Solomon is the choicest morsel of Scripture ; others prefer the
Book of Revelations ; and a third class gratify their appetite for
spiritual food by studying the Book of Leviticus. We have been
informed of a fair " Evangelical," who has discovered in it all
the sublime mysteries of the Athanasian creed ! This is not our
taste. We think that, by every Christian, Christ's Sermon on the
Mount is more to be prized. Mr. C. himself, we presume, has
his favourite passages ; and he may know, at least he may have
read of some orthodox believers, who consider the Epistle of
James as an Epistle of straw, *straminea,* because it so strongly
advocates the heretical, though Christian, doctrine of good works.
There are certain texts which, with them, are no favourites ; and
which they would willingly exclude from the sacred canon, on
the authority of " Ambrose," or of Mr. C.'s new detector of interpolations, " Dobrowski at Prague," or ".Doustersnivel," at
the Hartz mountains ! We cannot boast of what Professor
Bruce calls Mr. Carlile's " enviable faculty," of believing contradictions. We are not gifted with a deglutition wide enough to
gulp down dogmas bristled all over with the spinosities of Calvinism ;—we cannot *bolt* hedge-hogs ; they require time for
mastication. Even some of the Rev. worthies of Mr. C.'s synod

have experienced difficulty in swallowing such morsels, and would have found it impossible to get them down, had they not been well lubricated with the essential oil of *regium donum.* We have been informed of one Gentleman, a Reverend, who has been able to *bolt* Mr. C.'s Book with all its *chevaux-de-frise* of antilogies :—whether his mind and conscience have been lacerated or excoriated by the effort, we know not; but there are spiritual empirics at hand who can assure him, that

> " The sovereignest thing *on earth,*
> Is *kirk* with *donum,* for an *inward bruise.*"

Mr. C's mode of exercising his " enviable faculty," is ingenious, though not altogether original. The doctrine of the *two natures* is of infinite use in the great question. When a difficulty cannot be explained by the one nature, it may by the other; and when both are insufficient, a new character is introduced to cut asunder the Gordian knot. Our author, like the manager of a drama, has an appropriate mask and costume for the Saviour in every emergency, and represents him in as many forms as were assumed by Proteus of old :—at one time he is Jehovah, God supreme over all ; at another, he becomes inferior and subordinate ; now he is the Father everlasting ; anon, the begotten Son; then a " poor despised man," acting withal the part of a cunning man of law, and defeating his enemies by a legal stratagem ! At one time he acts in a public, and at another in a private capacity ; this hour *ex officio,* and the next *in officio;* and this is the mode in which orthodoxy " honours the Son even as it honours the Father."

" We have now come," says our author, " to the limits of explicit revelation, and are entering upon the region of reasoning and inference,"

He honestly admits that,

" A doctrine of inference ought never to be placed on a footing of equality with a doctrine of direct and explicit revelation; * * and that so far as out belief of any doctrine is the result of inference, it is not an exercise of faith in the testimony of God, but in the accuracy of our own reasoning !"

We are rejoiced to find Mr. C. paying such homage to truth, and at last fulfilling his promise to give us *something like* reason and common sense. He admits, " that the Holy Spirit is a distinct person from the Father and the Son, seems to be removed one step from a direct explicit revelation, * * and that there are three persons in the Godhead, is a second remove from explicit direct revelation ;"—and so after all our " bubble, bubble, toil, and trouble," we have nothing to depend on for the doctrine of the Trinity, but Mr. C.'s *inferences,* and how logically he can *infer,* let the reader judge. He honestly acknowledges that before he arrives at the doctrine of the Trinity, he has passed " the last lamp" of revelation. When he came to the last lamp he should have stopped ; for, as he truly observes, he has thenceforward no light but what shines behind, and that he cannot proceed far without being lost in the thick darkness. "He might have added," says Professor Bruce, "that at every step he is *in danger* of tripping and stumbling in the darkness caused by his own shadow." *In danger*, quotha? In sooth, at the very first step he tumbles down headlong, and we shall find him presently floundering in the Serbonian bog of infidelity and atheism.

We have asserted, on the highest authority, that it is contrary to sound philosophy to ascribe any effect to more causes than are necessary to produce it, and on this principle proceeded to affirm that there is but one efficient cause of all. Our author is in wrath at this declaration—looks big—again assumes the inquisitorial chair—brings our unhappy selves to the question, and demands imperatively to know whose philosophy we mean. When his interrogatory is answered, then he says, " we may find that it is contrary to the opinion of Hartley, or Malebranche, or Priestley, or Hume, or Reid, or Stewart, or Brown." He might have shewn a still further acquaintance with philosophy by adding the names of Sanconiathon, Berosus, Ocellus Lucanus, Yao, Chun, Li-Lao-Kiun, Mango Capac, Kong-Fu-Tse, Ferdinando Mendez Pinto, and all the great philosophers both of ancient and modern times, except the cosmogonists of the "enormous crab;" and how the good folks of Mary's Abbey would have been amazed at their pastor's tremendous knowledge of philosophers and their systems! But "let him not," he continues, "attempt to *frighten* us with the terrors of an abstract word."

Courteous reader, give us leave to assure you, that we were not aware of the "abstract word," philosophy, we presume, having any terrors—we hope it has had none for you ; and we positively disclaim all intention of *frightening* our Rev. interrogator ; while we lament that our use of that "abstract word" has thrown him into such a fit of apprehension as to cause him to write a whole paragraph, which, by its complete unintelligibility, shews but too truly the distraction of his mind. Having affirmed, that " it is *inconsistent* with the simplest axioms of arithmetic, that *three is not* one, and one is not three;" and demonstrated that one king is two kings, his body being one, and his soul another—he should have added, his mind a third,—the paroxysm subsides, he recovers his tranquillity, and proceeds to argue against the philosophical principle laid down in the Essay, viz. that "the unity of design apparent in the creation, argues unity of cause." He says we have forgotten to prove that unity of design; but this is a mistake ; we did not forget ; we intentionally omitted it, deeming it unnecessary, according to an example approved of by great critics, to begin *ab ovo*, or to prove what we did not contemplate the possiblility of any one disputing; neither did we imagine that there could be found in this age of scientific improvement, any one who would manifest a disposition to lead us back to the dark ages, and treat with contempt the sublime principles of Newton's philosophy, by placing them on a level with the *occult qualities* by which the philosophers of old explained every phenomenon, for which they could assign no cause. But it is perfectly consistent, that he who is fond of mystery in religion, should be fond of occult qualities in the study of nature, and that he should consider as "palpable nonsense,"* every attempt to expose the folly of the one and the other. The philosophic poet thought he was a happy man, who could ascertain the causes of things :—

Felix, qui potuit rerum cognoscere causas.

More happy he, thinks our sage divine, who wraps himself up contentedly in his ignorance, and accounts for every phenomenon more simply by an occult quality. "Of causes," says he, "we are now as ignorant as the Academics, the Peripatetics, or the Stoics." Their occult quality† was just as good as our gravitation, and explained the grand phenomena of nature, as well as Kepler's laws of motion, and Newton's Principia ! One of those old gentlemen, who said that water rose in a pump, because nature abhors a vacuum, knew as much as he who thinks he knows more, because he ascribes it to the pressure of the atmosphere. The clown can see through the optic glass as clearly as he who makes it, and satisfy his curiosity by attributing its powers to some magical property, as well as he who, by principles of optical science, leads to such telescopic and microscopic discoveries, as enlarge our views of nature and open a wide field of entertaining and instructive investigation in the lower departments of creation. Franklin, he of whom it has been said, in the true spirit of philosophic poetry, that he disarmed Jove of his thunderbolt, and tyrants of their sceptre—

Jovi eripuit fulmen, sceptrumque tyrannis,

needed not to have been at such pains with his vitreous and resinous machinery to delight the world with a new influx of knowledge, and shew the causes of thunder and lightning, and all the magnificent phenomena of electricity, since our author's "occult quality" might have been deemed sufficient cause, and equally satisfactory to every one who, like him, is so greatly superior to the dictates of reason and common sense. Priestley and Lavoisier too, might have spared themselves the trouble of their experiments in chemistry, which have led to so many important discoveries, and such innumerable benefits to the merchant, the traveller, the mechanic, and the whole race of man. After all,

* This is what our author terms that strikingly sensible passage, which we have quoted in a note, p. 98, from a work of Dr. W. Robertson.
† " It was usual with the Peripatetics, when the cause of any phenomenon was demanded, to have recourse to their *faculties,* or *occult qualities,* and to say, for instance, that bread, nourished by its nutritive, and senna purged by its purgative ; but it has been discovered, that this subterfuge was nothing but the disguise of ignorance."—HUME's *Dialogues,* p. 62.

is it not an occult quality which has constructed the steam-engine, the rail-way, the diving-bell, the forcing-pump, the safety-lamp, and lighted our streets with gas? Happy occult quality! it satisfies all doubts—solves all difficulties—makes all improvements—explains all phenomena. Happy mystery! that performs in religion, what occult quality performs in philosophy,—it swallows all absurdities—believes all contradictions—extinguishes all reason—perverts all truth—and perpetuates the golden age of ignorance, fanaticism and priest-craft. Twin sisters! exclaim the friends of mental darkness and religious slavery, wide be the spread of your dominion!—together may ye reign for ever!

Our author, reluctant to admit any single position which we lay down, though eventually he concedes every thing, disputes the justice of our assumption, that there is unity of design in the universe, and says,

"We can ascertain unity of design only in *that portion* of the universe that falls under our observation. Of those remote portions of the universe which lie beyond the sphere of our research we are totally ignorant, and cannot therefore argue upon them."

We think we have seen this and similar objections stated with superior force and eloquence elsewhere. It is contended by some sceptics, that the universe being a singular phenomenon, there is nothing with which it can be compared :—there are no analogies to lead us to any conclusion respecting its origin ; it may have sprung from chance ; it may have existed from eternity; it may have been the workmanship of a number of bungling artificers ; our earth may be an animal, or the egg of some superior planet ! Unity of design ! Fiddle-faddle ! exclaims a cosmogonist of the "crab"—"Of those remote portions of the universe which lie beyond the sphere of our research, we are totally ignorant, and cannot therefore argue upon them." We have no right even to assume that they sprang from any cause either intelligent or fortuitous! The orthodox divine accords with the sceptical philosopher, and adopts a principle which precipitates him into atheism; he tries, however, to escape from the consequences of his temerity by having recourse to Scripture :—

"I believe," says he, "on the *testimony of Scripture*, that the same unity of design must extend over the universe; but without the Scripture (and he might have added, with it) I am no more capable of arguing upon universal unity of design, than an animalcule shut up in one of the books of the library of St. Paul's Cathedral, in London, is capable of reasoning upon the unity of design discernible in the whole of that edifice."

We give Mr. C. all the credit he can wish for the modesty of this declaration ; but we wish to learn from him, what part of Scripture inculcates that doctrine, which, he says, he believes on *its testimony*. To us it appears, that unity of design is a philosophic idea, attained by observation and the exercise of reason on the phenomena of nature ;—of that idea the Scriptures say " absolutely nothing ;" and we cannot but marvel that any one, whose religious system teaches that the world is under the curse of God, that, as the Rev. Edw. Irving states, " he made a present of it to the devil," and that it is a chaos of deformed ruins, should be so grossly inconsistent as to maintain, that the Scriptures say any thing about unity of design. The Unitarian can *infer* it fairly and legitimately from his views of Scripture doctrine. Revelation in teaching him that God is one, teaches also, that God's works must be characterised by their conformity, not only to his attributes of power and wisdom, but also to his individuality of purpose. From the cause he descends to the effect; but philosophy mounts from the effect to the cause; and seeing an individuality of purpose and contrivance in the works of creation, concludes that their author must be ONE. Thus, does true philosophy harmonize with revelation, and the one corroborates the conclusions of the other.

Since, as Mr. C. affirms, we are so totally ignorant of things which lie beyond the sphere of our research, that we cannot form an argument upon them, we ask, on what principle does he argue when he compares his knowledge of design to that of an animalcule shut up in a book in the library of St. Paul's Cathedral? Are all the appurtenances of that edifice so perfectly within the sphere of his research that he is justifiable, according to his own doctrine, for reasoning upon them? Has he ascertained that unity of design is " discernible in the whole of that edifice ?" Has it a library? Is there an animalcule shut up in one of the books? Has he subjected that animalcule to the test of microscopic examination? Has he anatomized it, as we have anatomized his book, to discover whether it has a cerebellum, or is altogether brainless? Has he examined it in logic; or discovered whether it has any knowledge of the various styles of architecture, and whether it prefers the Gothic to the Greek; and above all, whether it has such just notions of art and unity of design, as would merit the approbation of Palladio, Michel Agnolo, and Sir Christopher Wren himself, the architect of the Cathedral? If Mr. C. says that these subjects are "out of the sphere of his research," we again ask him, wherefore, then, does he presume to institute a comparison which may be degrading to the animalcule, and bring its knowledge of *design* into disrepute? It is a subject, of which he is so totally ignorant, that, by his own rule, he cannot draw from it any argument. Let him not judge of animalcules by himself; some of them, for aught that he knows to the contrary, might be as capable of teaching a lesson as Solomon's ant ; some of them may reason as well as certain divines—to reason worse is impossible. If Mr. C.'s animalcule had a particle of intellect it *could not* misunderstand, and if it had a particle of honesty, it *would not* misrepresent, as Mr. C. has done, the question between Mr. Pope and ourselves respecting *a fact* and its *explanation*. We have said, in reference to the Trinity, "*prove the fact* and it will not be disputed." Notwithstanding this, and his quotation of our very words, he has the matchless effrontery to affirm that we say, "its being *incomprehensible* is a sufficient reason for rejecting it!" He farther asserts, after having distinctly stated that the doctrine of the Trinity is a doctrine of *inference*—that he "has proved the fact from the Scriptures, and that we will not believe it, *because it is incomprehensible*." On the contrary, it is stated in the Essay, (p. 101, and of the second edition, p. 64,) that the Unitarian admits "that the incomprehensibility of a doctrine may be no just ground of objection." But Mr. C. contends, that he "has proved the fact!" *Risum teneatis, amici?* We should as soon believe that he has unsphered a fixed star. And how has he proved it? By telling us, that the doctrine of the Trinity is "a doctrine of *inference*, and of *indirect* intimation * * * rather than a doctrine directly and explicitly declared." Proved the fact! What pity that he had not been born fifteen centuries ago, that his proof might have preserved the Christian world from the controversy, in which it has ever since been so unprofitably engaged? But his proof is of such a subtle and intangible consistence, as not to be seen, felt, or understood by any minds, which are not gifted with his own "enviable faculty." That which the most eminent divines of the Roman Catholic Church have acknowledged to be incapable of any proof by Scripture, or by any thing but tradition and church authority, is now made plain by a disciple of Calvin! That which the most erudite Protestants have been obliged to abandon to mystery, as impenetrable and inexplicable, is now demonstrated by the Rev. James Carlile, Minister of the Scots Church, Mary's Abbey, Dublin!—*Io, triumphe!* We shall expect soon to hear that, by means of his *occult quality*, he has discovered the perpetual motion, the philosopher's stone, and the elixir of life. Proved the fact! He has betrayed the cause which, in a foolish spirit of knight errantry, he came forth to defend. The deepest degradation and hopelessness, in which any cause could be plunged, would be condemnation to such advocacy as that by which the doctrine of the Trinity has been exposed to scorn and ridicule in the pages of the Rev. James Carlile.

To accompany our author farther would be superfluous. We have cited enough of his book to enable the reader to form a tolerably just opinion of its merits. Some of our fair and sensitive Unitarian friends will think, perhaps, that we have expressed ourselves strongly on this subject; we admit it, but not more strongly than the subject required. In the cause of great and important truths, we can yield nothing to complaisance; we make no compromise with error, especially when it is defended by disingenuous arts, and an ostentatious parade of learning without the reality; least of all should we feel disposed to be lenient to any antagonist who evinces a reckless disregard for the name and character of individuals infinitely his superiors. What must we think, and what should we say of the writer who, without any just pretensions to the critic's chair, says of R. Roy that he is *extremely*

Y

ignorant of the Hebrew language ?—who, with lordly disdain, speaks of *a* Dr. Young—(did he ever hear of *one* John Milton?)—the learned Bishop of Clonfert, who, as a scholar, was an ornament to his university, and, as a divine, an honour to his church?—a writer, who defames Unitarians as capable of forging his own abominable creed, with a view to misrepresent Calvinism, forsooth, that dark anti-christian system, of which no portraiture has yet been presented to the world half so hideous as the original?*—and who himself commits, to a flagrant degree, the very offence which he condemns? For how does he treat Dr. Priestley, that truly Christian divine and excellent philosopher, whose name is embalmed in the history of science, and which will be remembered with gratitude for ages after his calumniators and persecutors have sunk into oblivion—Priestley, who stood boldly forward as the champion of Christianity, and in its defence threw down the gauntlet of defiance to the celebrated author of " The Decline and Fall of the Roman Empire"—Priestley, of whom it might be truly asserted, that he had his whole conversation in this world,

---

* As Dr. Wardlaw is the *Magnus Apollo* of Mr. C. we recommend to his consideration the following extract from the Christian Pioneer, for December, 1830. It occurs in an article entitled *Orthodoxy, and its advocate Dr. Wardlaw, in conflict with the New Testament* :—
" One of the most revolting principles of Calvinism, is fully set forth in the discourse of which we are speaking : ' The delight of God in Christ is manifested *in the perdition of those that perish, as well as* in the salvation of those that are saved,' is a proposition which this Divine lays down, and labours to establish. There is, in these few words, enough to sink any system whatever. If proved from Scripture, Scripture is thereby disproved ; if a part of Christianity, Christianity is not of God :—but they are, thank God ! Calvinism, not the Gospel. The benevolent Jesus is not answerable for so foul a libel on the Creator. Man's damnation God's delight ! Horrible idea ! The God of Jesus delighting in the eternal torments of the vast majority of his creatures ! If this be not blasphemy, it is something worse.—' Hell shall bear testimony to this,' viz. God's delight in Christ, ' as well as heaven The lesson shall be read for ever by the fires of Tophet, as well as by the light of Paradise.' And this is said of God, who ' is love,' and Christ who was tenderness itself ! This said in the 19th century, and men expected to believe it ! Surely, this is, now-a-days, *un peu de trop.* We would advise Dr. Wardlaw (and Mr. C.) to abandon Calvinism, and preach the Gospel, which they would do well to remember, whenever their Calvinistic impressions are too strong for their good sense and humanity, means ' good news'—' glad tidings'—' peace on earth'—good will to man'"
Let us hear no more of Unitarians misrepresenting Calvinism. We cannot describe it in any colours more dark, nor in any forms more hideously revolting, than those in which it is pourtrayed by its own advocates. The style employed by Mr. C. in describing the God of the Calvinists, forms an exact parallel to that employed by the Rev. Dr. Buchanan in describing Juggernaut, the Moloch of Hindostan. The former says " The Lord (*i. e. his Lord*) views the whole race (of mankind) as a king does a rebel army. He *takes no cognizance of the diversities of character* that may be in such an army," (see p. 147.) Dr. B. says, " So great a God is this. (Juggernaut) that (on the day of his great feast) the dignity of high cast disappears before him. The great king *recognizes no distinction of rank* among his subjects ; all men are equal in his presence."—(Ind. Researches, 3rd Ed. p. 27.) But it is only *distinction of rank* that Juggernaut does not recognize, and in this there is some justice. The God of Mr. C. takes *no cognizance of diversities of*

"in simplicity and godly sincerity?" After affirming of this great philosopher and admirable Christian, that he had exposed his learning to utter contempt, and forfeited all claims to the character of an honest man, he endeavours to fix upon him the foul imputation of having declared of Christ that he was "a *sinful* man."* Now, if Mr. C. has any regard for his own character, he will either prove, or retract this charge. He will prove it, not by *inference*, as he says he has proved the Trinity, but by referring us to the book, chapter, page, and the *ipsissima verba* in which Dr. Priestley has made that declaration, or else he will avow that it is a slander, fabricated to injure the reputation, and destroy the influence of a great and a good man's name. Perhaps, on consideration, he may find that he made a slight mistake in attributing to Dr. Priestley what, some may think, more properly belongs to his own orthodox friend, the celebrated Rev. E. Irving, who describes the human nature, "*which the Son of Man was clothed upon withal, (as) bristling thick and strong with sin, like the hairs upon the porcupine!*"

We now take leave of Mr. C. without any personal feeling of unkindness. We have spoken of him freely as an author, and as we thought the interests of truth exacted. We have pronounced

---

character, and in this there is such a flagrant disregard to morality and right, as would put the priests of Juggernaut to shame if imputed to their God, and make them rise indignantly to repel the imputation as a slander. The barbarous superstition of Hindostan, sacrifices children "by drowning them or exposing them to sharks and crocodiles." The more barbarous superstition of Calvinism, condemns unregenerate children with their parents to "*the most grievous torments in soul and body, without intermission, in hell-fire, for ever!*" and tells us, that "there are thousands of them, not a span long, frying in hell, being appointed as vessels of wrath"—and all for the glory of God! We ourselves, though holding the Gospel of peace and salvation in our hands and to our hearts, are denied the name of Christian, sentenced to the same hard fate, and damned "*soul and body in hell-fire for ever,*" as heretics and soul destroyers, because we cannot believe such blasphemous abominations. How long will men, who have the least claim to sense and reason, suffer themselves to be "*mocked, insulted, and abused!*"

* When Dr. Priestley revolted from the principles of Calvinism, in which he had been educated, it is surprising, that in his recoil from its impious dogmas, he was not hurried into infidelity. But determined to follow the Apostle's advice to "prove all things," he informs us, that he "became a High Arian, next a Low Arian, and in a little time a Socinian of the lowest kind, in which Christ is considered as a mere man, the son of Joseph and Mary, and *naturally* as *fallible* and *peccable.*" This, as quoted from that chaotic mass of theological trash, called "Magee on the Atonement," is the passage, we presume, which has furnished such authors as Mr. Carlile, who *do not*, or *will not* understand it, with a pretence for imputing to Dr. Priestley opinions which he never held nor expressed. We believe that no divine in existence would have more cheerfully subscribed to the Apostle's declarations, that Christ was "declared to be the Son of God with power, according to the Spirit of Holiness, by the resurrection from the dead;" and that though he was "*in all points* tempted like as we are, yet (was he) without sin." Do not the most orthodox writers admit, that Christ had a human nature, and was tempted? What constitutes human nature? Is it infallibility or impeccability? A being who, by virtue of his physical constitution, is infallible and impeccable, partakes not of the constitution of

upon his book a sentence not more severe than merited and just. If he act wisely he will in future confine his lucubrations to his own pulpit and to his own people, who can understand them, and ask no more questions about the "accredited pastors" of other congregations feeding their flock with negatives. But should he have the temerity to come again before the public, he will do well to remember that those principles of reason and common sense, which he has laboured to explode, are likely to become the fashion. The reign of *occult qualities* is long since past, and that of *mystery* is hastening to a close. Unitarian Christianity, the simple and beautiful, the heart-dilating, the mind-expanding religion taught by Christ and his Apostles, is prevailing more and more; and all such efforts as his to throw obstacles in its way, and retard its progress, serve only to accumulate its volume, and roll it forward with accelerating speed.

----

humanity. We affirm, on the highest authority, that there is none good but God—none wise but God—therefore none infallible—none impeccable but God. A being who cannot be tempted, has no more virtue in resisting temptation, than Mount Atlas in withstanding the breath of a zephyr. The virtue of Christ lay in his *moral,* not in his *physical* superiority to temptation. How could he have been tempted *in all points,* or in *any point,* like as we are, if no part of his constitution was liable to assault? Can the blind be tempted by beauty, or the deaf by a Siren's song? Where was the merit of his triumph over the tempter, if he was incapable of feeling the charms of ambition and glory? If he had not hungered, would the devil, with all his subtlety, have acted so like a simpleton, as to desire him to convert the stones into bread? The gentlemen, who are in such wrath at Priestley for openly expressing what they virtually admit, inform us, on their own authority, that Adam was created *perfect.* How, then, we ask, did he fall before the very first temptation that assailed him? Oh! he was fallible.— Admirable consistency! And also peccable?—It must be granted. And consequently, that a being may be perfect, and, at the same time, liable to be deceived, and to be tempted to sin. Adam was not only fallible and peccable, but he was actually deceived, and he actually sinned. This cannot be predicated of Christ, the second Adam. He also was tempted. But he did not yield to temptation; and herein lay one part of his superiority to the first Adam. He was " without sin :"—this Dr. Priestley would not only admit, but maintain; and so far from alleging, as Mr. C. says he does, that Christ was " a sinful man," he would have been among the most strenuous in maintaining that he was altogether *sinless,* " holy, harmless, undefiled, separate from sinners." A well-known author, whom the orthodox would fondly claim as their own, while he yet stood on the high pinnacle of orthodoxy, eloquently said, " As the Son of God put on our flesh and blood, so he assumed the various powers and properties of human nature—the appetites and passions of mankind; he endured hunger and thirst; he had fear and love, hope, and joy; nor were the more troublesome affections of anger and sorrow left out of his constitution; but they were all innocent and holy— (*Priestley would have said the same ;*) they were never tainted with sin as ours are; they had no corrupt mixtures to defile his soul—(*Priestley would have said the same ;*)—our passions are like water with mud at the bottom; when they are moved, they too frequently raise the mud and betray their impurity. But the passions of Christ were ever pure; like water from the clearest fountain in a glass of crystal, which, though it be never so much agitated, is still unpolluted." *Priestley would have said the same.*

END OF THE REVIEW.

CPSIA information can be obtained at www.ICGtesting.com
Printed in the USA
237602LV00003B/15/A

9 780548 176337